JUGGERNAUT

WASHINGTON DC ▪ MOSCOW ▪ BEIJING ▪ BEIRUT ▪ BRUSSELS

URI DADUSH **&** WILLIAM SHAW

JUGGERNAUT

HOW EMERGING MARKETS ARE RESHAPING GLOBALIZATION

CARNEGIE ENDOWMENT

FOR INTERNATIONAL PEACE

Carnegie Endowment for International Peace
1779 Massachusetts Avenue, N.W., Washington, DC 20036
Phone: + 202 483 7600   Fax: + 202 483 1840
CarnegieEndowment.org

The Carnegie Endowment does not take institutional positions on public policy issues; the views represented here are the authors' own and do not necessarily reflect the views of the Endowment, its staff, or its trustees.

To order, contact Carnegie's distributor:
Hopkins Fulfillment Service
PO Box 50370, Baltimore, MD 21211-4370
Phone: + 1 800 537 5487 or + 410 516 6956   Fax: + 410 516 6998

Library of Congress Cataloging-in-Publication Data

Dadush, Uri B.
   Juggernaut : how emerging markets are reshaping globalization / Uri Dadush and William Shaw.
      p.   cm.
   Includes bibliographical references and index.
   ISBN 978-0-87003-262-2 (cloth) — ISBN 978-0-87003-261-5 (pbk.)
   1. International economic relations. 2. Developing countries—Economic conditions—21st century. 3. Globalization—Economic aspects. 4. Globalization—Political aspects. 5. International trade—History—21st century. 6. International finance—History—21st century. 7. Economic history—21st century. 8. Economic forecasting.
   I. Shaw, William, 1953-. II. Title.

HF1359.D33 2011
337.09172'4—dc22

2011011643

Cover Design by Jocelyn Soly
Composition by Communications Development Incorporated
Printed by United Book Press

MIX
Paper from
responsible sources
FSC® C010236
www.fsc.org

CONTENTS

FOREWORD

The rapid rise of what we used to call the developing world is a defining trend of our time. In this book, Uri Dadush and William Shaw provide the first systematic examination of the long-term implications of this tectonic shift for the international economy and global governance, covering both domestic and international economic policies.

Two centuries of history show that there is nothing automatic about economic development and catch-up. In recent years, however, an extraordinary confluence of factors has allowed an unprecedented number of countries—and people—to achieve rapid income growth. These factors include access to technology, the opening up of markets, stabilized macroeconomic conditions, higher savings and investment rates, and effective government interventions to support private-sector development.

A realistic assessment suggests that this combination may persist in coming decades, but only if the global community mitigates a number of significant risks—climate change, geopolitical breakdown, financial crisis, and protectionism chief among them. If these risks are contained, the next forty years are likely to see extraordinary changes. By 2050, China's economy will be almost twice the size of the U.S. economy (in PPP terms), India will be the world's third largest economy, and no European country will be among the top eight largest economies.

Dadush and Shaw assess the impact of this shift along the four main lines of international economic interaction: trade, finance, migration, and the global commons. They ask: How will the rise of developing countries transform these four arenas? How should domestic policies adapt? How should international diplomacy respond to the changes? What role will be played by international coordination mechanisms, including international organizations and bilateral and multilateral treaties?

Despite rapid growth in the emerging powerhouses, their populations will remain significantly poorer than those of the advanced countries. By 2050, 6 of the 10 largest global economies will have per capita incomes far below Japan, the United States, and developed Europe. The dramatic differences in living standards—as well as in social values and political systems—among the major economies will greatly complicate reaching global agreements.

For better or for worse, the management of these historic forces will remain in the hands of sovereign nations—particularly the largest economies. Thus, global agreements—to mitigate climate change, expand the gains from migration, and avert financial crises, for example—will require increased awareness and appreciation within these countries and their polities of how their fate is inextricably linked to global developments.

International organizations and negotiations will play a large role, but the authors caution against excessive dependence on global agreements. The issues are far too complex and the potential divergences far too large for 200-odd countries to be able to agree on everything. Instead, the authors propose that countries rely increasingly on agreements among a critical mass of players on specific issues, with provisions to later include a broader group.

The rise of developing countries is an enormous opportunity to bring hundreds of millions of people out of poverty and dramatically increase the prosperity of rich countries as well. But as with any political-economic shift of this magnitude, there will be deep uncertainties, frictions, and the need for far-reaching policy changes. Individual countries as well as the global polity will have to develop the capacity to understand how things are changing and how fast, to adapt and to mediate the substantial conflicts that will arise. The first step is understanding, and for that Dadush and Shaw have provided an invaluable guide.

Jessica Tuchman Mathews
President, Carnegie Endowment for International Peace

ACKNOWLEDGMENTS

The authors are indebted to numerous people for their help over the past two years. Most important, this book would never have seen the light of day without the dedication of Shimelse M. Ali, Vera Eidelman, and Bennett Stancil from the Carnegie Endowment for International Peace. Their persistence in ferreting out data, improving our written style, and contributing numerous pieces of analysis greatly enriched the final product, and their good humor in performing all of these tasks eased the process considerably.

We are grateful to Jessica Mathews and Carnegie management for their understanding and support, and for furnishing the resources required to complete this work. We received extremely useful comments on earlier drafts from several astute observers of the international economic scene, including Kemal Dervis, Alejandro Foxley, George Kalan, Andrew Mold, and Moisés Naím. Nida Jafrani and Evelina Yeghiyan kept the office running smoothly. Ilonka Oszvald ably took care of production, making it all seem easy though we're sure it wasn't. And Bruce Ross-Larson helped enormously to improve the clarity and logical structure of the finished manuscript. Finally, this would have been an immeasurably more difficult, and much drearier, experience without the help and support of our wives, Gilda Dadush and Anne Vorce, and families.

ABBREVIATIONS

ASEAN	ASSOCIATION OF SOUTHEAST ASIAN NATIONS
CBO	CONGRESSIONAL BUDGET OFFICE
CFC	CHLOROFLUOROCARBONS
CCI	CONVERGENCE CONDITIONS INDEX
CO_2E	CARBON EQUIVALENT
ECOWAS	ECONOMIC COMMUNITY OF WEST AFRICAN STATES
FDI	FOREIGN DIRECT INVESTMENT
FAO	FOOD AND AGRICULTURE ORGANIZATION
FBI	FEDERAL BUREAU OF INVESTIGATION
GMR	GLOBAL MIDDLE AND RICH CLASS
G20	THE GROUP OF 20
G8	THE GROUP OF EIGHT
GEP	GLOBAL ECONOMIC PROSPECTS
GDP	GROSS DOMESTIC PRODUCT
GAO	U.S. GOVERNMENT ACCOUNTABILITY OFFICE
IMF	INTERNATIONAL MONETARY FUND
ICT	INFORMATION AND COMMUNICATION TECHNOLOGY
ICSG	INTERNATIONAL COPPER STUDY GROUP
ICRG	INTERNATIONAL COUNTRY RISK GUIDE
IPCC	INTERGOVERNMENTAL PANEL ON CLIMATE CHANGE
NAFTA	NORTH AMERICAN FREE TRADE AGREEMENT
OECD	ORGANISATION FOR ECONOMIC CO-OPERATION AND DEVELOPMENT
PPP	PURCHASING POWER PARITY
RTA	REGIONAL TRADE AGREEMENT

RF	RADIO FREQUENCY
SWF	SOVEREIGN WEALTH FUND
SADC	SOUTHERN AFRICAN DEVELOPMENT COMMUNITY
TFP	TOTAL FACTOR PRODUCTIVITY
UNCTAD	UNITED NATIONS CONFERENCE ON TRADE AND DEVELOPMENT
UNDP	UNITED NATIONS DEVELOPMENT PROGRAMME
UNEP	UNITED NATIONS ENVIRONMENT PROGRAMME
WTO	WORLD TRADE ORGANIZATION

CHAPTER 1

INTRODUCTION

THE POOR SHALL INHERIT THE EARTH

Against the long sweep of economic history, the current moment is special. The world has made extraordinary progress in income, education, and health over the past few decades—across all regions and almost all countries. Average life expectancy in developing economies rose to 68 years in 2010, up from 56 in 1970, and average per capita income nearly tripled to $5,873. There are no historical parallels to such rapid and broad-based improvements, and even the deepest recession since the Great Depression did not halt the progress.

Under plausible assumptions the world economy is set to more than triple over the next 40 years. The advance of several, though by no means all, developing countries—home to most of the world's population but dismissed as supplicants, rather than trend-setters, a generation ago—will drive this improvement.

However, in the years to come, the rise of these emerging economic powers will present risks as well as opportunities. Unless managed, these risks could abort or severely slow the process.

This is not the first book to treat the subject of the rising economic powers. Indeed, even a partial bibliography of recent works would include at least four excellent treatments—some originating in the policy community, such as the Organisation for Economic Co-operation and Development's *Perspectives on Global Development: Shifting Wealth* (2010) and the World Bank's *Global Economic Prospects: Managing the Next Wave of Globalization* (2007) (which we contributed to), and some appealing to a general audience such as Fareed Zakaria's *The Post-American World* and George Magnus's *Uprising*. But this is the first to systematically explore how the world economy might be reshaped by the rise of the emerging economic powers and to then analyze their effects through each of the four main channels of globalization—trade, finance, migration, and the global commons. The first three connect economies and political systems around the world and will catalyze the changes to come. The fourth requires international coordination for human survival.

A central conclusion is that the challenges posed by the rise of developing countries are such that continuing rapid economic progress is far from assured. Four risks—either alone or, more likely, in combination—could slow the process or stop it in its tracks. The emerging and established economic powers could fail to adjust to a new world order, leading to significant geopolitical strife. A financial crisis could erupt again, but this time it could originate in, or at the least engulf, the South as well as the North. Trade relations could break down as countries fail to adjust to an onslaught of competition from all sides. And perhaps most dangerous and urgent, failing to reach agreement on the right to emit greenhouse gases could lead to catastrophic climate change.

These risks are unavoidable because they are intrinsic to the economic advance of so much of the world's population. They can, however, be managed and mitigated with the right domestic policies and with stronger frameworks for international coordination in trade, finance, migration, and the global commons.

Since the end of World War II, advanced countries have dominated global economic decisionmaking through the G7, the International Monetary Fund (IMF), the General Agreement on Tariffs and Trade (GATT), and other institutions. Even more important, they have established the dominant paradigm in domestic policy, loosely characterized as the Washington Consensus.[1] These domestic and international policy frameworks have many shortcomings. They fail to deal adequately with the plight of the poorest and most fragile economies. And they fail to reflect the interests of developing countries more generally in agricultural trade and the governance of the Bretton Woods institutions.[2] Even so, the leadership by the established economic powers has coincided with great increases in both living standards and international economic integration.

These domestic and international policy frameworks helped get us to this historic moment. But they cannot, in their current configurations, manage the change to come. Resistance to globalization and its multifaceted manifestations, such as migration and increased international competition from low-wage economies, is widespread among the general public, increasingly finding a voice in the legislatures of nearly all the advanced economies. Geopolitical divergences are emerging in every international institution as the current set-up—which the rich countries lead—clashes with the reality that poor countries are becoming the biggest economies. Indeed, the poor are inheriting the earth. Three developing countries—China, India, and Brazil—are now among the world's 10 largest economies, and, though many developing countries are seeing little advance, 6 of the 10 largest economies are projected to be developing countries in 2050 (table 1.1). Their economic interests, social structures, and, in some cases, political systems differ greatly from those of the advanced countries.

The Group of 20 (G20)—which includes advanced and developing economies that together account for more than 80 percent of world GDP and global trade—recently replaced the anachronistic Group of 8 (G8)—Canada, France, Germany, Italy, Japan, the United Kingdom, the United States, and Russia—as the preeminent economic forum. Although this promises to be an important step forward, and may set the stage for a gradual overhaul of all the major international economic coordination mechanisms, the new structure remains unproven.

This book does not prescribe the precise ways the domestic and international policy frameworks must be reformed—that would be impossible. Instead, it explores the major trends associated with the rise of a large number of developing countries, and the broad challenges they pose for policy. Where possible, it identifies principles and approaches that appear most likely to work.

TABLE 1.1 THE WORLD'S 10 LARGEST ECONOMIES
(PERCENT OF G20 GDP, IN PPP)

2010		2050	
UNITED STATES	26.4	CHINA	33.2
CHINA	18.2	UNITED STATES	17.5
JAPAN	7.8	INDIA	15.4
INDIA	7.2	BRAZIL	4.3
GERMANY	5.3	MEXICO	3.4
RUSSIAN FEDERATION	4.0	RUSSIAN FEDERATION	3.3
BRAZIL	3.9	INDONESIA	2.7
UNITED KINGDOM	3.9	JAPAN	2.7
FRANCE	3.9	UNITED KINGDOM	2.1
ITALY	3.2	GERMANY	2.1

Source: IMF data; authors' projections.

How we got here

Stagnation has been the norm for most of human history, and most advances in economic growth have been short-lived. From the beginning of the first century to 1820, the average person's income grew imperceptibly, rising by less than one-fiftieth of 1 percent a year, compounding to a 50 percent increase over 18 centuries. While some groups saw rapidly improved living standards for a while, these improvements generally failed to spread to other societies and were lost over time. This prolonged stagnation was directly associated with a lack of significant technological progress.

The Industrial Revolution in the middle of the eighteenth century broke this long-term stagnation, but also divided the world in two. One group advanced, as the rapid technological progress of the Industrial Revolution, which originated in England, spread to Western Europe and to the less populated European outposts in the New World—which, in many ways, had reproduced European societies, with the added ingredient of abundant natural resources. The rest of the world, by contrast, was left behind because it was geographically isolated, closed to trade and foreign ideas, or hobbled by customs and institutions (including those imposed by European colonizers) that were not conducive to the technologies and approaches boosting living standards for the first group.

Japan was the first country to break out of the lagging group as the state opened and industrialized the economy during the Meiji restoration in the second half of the nineteenth century. A second notable advance began in Russia at about the same time, reinforced by industrialization under the Soviets, but the model eventually collapsed.

It was only after World War II ended and the institutional vacuum created by decolonization began to be filled, however, that growth accelerated in a large number of developing countries, beginning with the economic miracle in Asia. And it is only in the last 20 or so years that economies with giant populations —notably China, India, and Brazil—have seen growth race ahead, as they centered their development strategies around market-friendly institutions and international economic integration. Today, of the world's 6.8 billion people, 1 billion live in affluent countries, and roughly 2.5 billion people live in developing countries where GDP has grown by 7 percent or more a year over a sustained period—a rate unimaginable in previous centuries.

At the same time, the last decade has left many developing countries even farther behind: 23 countries have seen GDP grow more slowly than that of the advanced countries, and even more have seen per capita incomes fall amid faster population growth. More than one billion people continue to live on less than

$1.25 a day, and 2.5 billion—almost 40 percent of the world population—live on less than $2.00 a day.

So, progress is still far from universal and fairly widespread, and sustained progress in the developing world is fairly new. What the recent period has shown beyond doubt, however, is that, given the availability of technology, developing countries in every region of the world can grow extremely rapidly if they establish the domestic conditions necessary to adopt advanced techniques. But this can happen only if they learn from other economies that stabilized their macroeconomic conditions, opened to the world, exhibited higher rates of savings and investment, and depended on both the state and markets for growth. It is now generally understood that while private actors working through markets provide the essential driver of economic progress, an effective state that enables the market economy, with secure property rights, the rule of law, and adequate education, is just as crucial.

In 2050—A world transformed

Once the basic conditions for absorbing advanced technology become established, developing countries can grow faster than advanced countries, which have the more arduous task of innovating at the frontier.

An empirical examination of the drivers of growth among the G20 countries, half of them developing, suggests that developing countries tend to grow faster for four reasons. First, their total factor productivity tends to advance 1 to 4 percentage points faster than that of advanced countries as they absorb existing technology. Second, they invest a higher share of their income—27 percent, compared with 20 percent in advanced countries over the past decade. Third, their labor force is growing 1 to 2 percentage points faster than that of industrial countries. And fourth, their exchange rates tend to appreciate in real terms (reflecting their faster labor productivity growth), increasing their purchasing power in world markets and making them more attractive, bigger markets.

These trends are particularly evident in the differing economic trajectories within the G20. Under a plausible scenario (all long-term forecasting has to be taken with a pinch of salt) the developing country members of the G20 are projected to grow by an average of 4.6 percent a year to 2050, more than twice the 2 percent for the advanced countries. By then, developing countries will account for 56 percent of world GDP at market exchange rates and 68 percent at purchasing-power-parity exchange rates. The projected growth of developing countries is about 2 percentage points lower than they exhibited over the last 10 years, reflecting the fact that, as they advance, their economic structure tends to resemble that of advanced countries. For example, China is projected to grow at

5.6 percent over the next 40 years, having grown at nearly twice that rate over the last 10.

But even as developing countries of the G20 rise among the world's largest economies, they will remain relatively poor. China will be the largest economy by 2050, but under this scenario its per capita income will be 37 percent that of the United States at market exchange rates. India, the third largest economy by 2050, will have a per capita income just 11 percent that of the United States at market exchange rates.

This scenario does not cover a large group of developing countries that remain very poor today and that have seen their per capita income diverge further from the advanced countries over the last 20 years. Still, the developing countries of the G20 today account for nearly half the world's poor living on less than $1.25 a day, and, under plausible assumptions (see chapter 3), poverty will fall substantially across the world. Growth in the G20 alone will reduce the number of people living on less than $1.25 a day by 600 million, from 1.3 billion in 2005.

To repeat, these advances will occur only if the business climates and educational systems of developing countries continue to improve. Meanwhile, advanced countries will have to show greater flexibility and even greater capacity to innovate to ensure that their living standards continue to improve as well. Globally, markets will have to stay open and trade relations will have to strengthen to enable progress.

Trade—The great development arena

Even in the largest developing countries the domestic economy is dwarfed by global markets in size and sophistication. In recent years developing countries have risen remarkably in importance both as importers and as exporters, and in most instances trade has been central to their economic success. Indeed, though rapid export growth does not always guarantee success, no country has sustained growth without increasing exports. In this sense, while the conditions for growth have to be established at home, the global trade arena (measured by increased exports and imports) is often where development succeeds or fails.

Part of the expansion in the trade of developing countries came on the back of liberalizing trade, but it also reflects structural changes. Developing countries have diversified their exports from primary commodities to manufactures, which offer better prospects for export earnings growth and provide greater price stability. Inflows of foreign direct investment (FDI) have increased, supporting the participation of developing countries in supply chains, the provision of services at a distance, and the exploitation of natural resources. And the growing middle class in developing countries has boosted demand for advanced goods—such as automobiles and consumer durables—and services.

These trends are expected to continue over the next 40 years; by 2050, developing countries, particularly China, will be a dominant force in world trade. Their share of world exports will more than double from 30 percent in 2006 to 69 percent in 2050, and advanced countries will depend more on them as export markets. China will be the largest export destination for Europe (excluding intra-European trade), and Latin America and China will be, respectively, the first and second export destinations for the United States, outpacing Europe.

While the GATT/WTO system has been pivotal in getting us here, having supported an open and rules-based trading system over the past several decades, it no longer appears able to achieve new trade liberalization at the global level. A huge unfinished agenda remains in opening trade in agriculture and services, in investment, and in temporary movement of workers. Tariffs on manufactures in developing countries remain especially high and dispersed. The Doha Round's failure to conclude 9 years after its launch and the limited (in the view of many) liberalization during the Uruguay Round have been profoundly disappointing. Although previous rounds of multilateral negotiations opened export markets for developing countries, the bulk of their liberalization has come through autonomous policy choices. More recently, bilateral and regional accords, negotiated outside the World Trade Organization (WTO) and not effectively bound by WTO disciplines, have come to play an increasing role.

The expected changes in the global economy are likely to further hinder progress through the WTO, as now constituted. The WTO requires a single undertaking achieved by consensus, implying that all countries must agree to the whole package of trade commitments for any commitment to pass. This means that objections to any provision—or to the failure to include some provision—can torpedo a tortuously negotiated agreement, leading to either a breakdown of negotiations or a watered-down agreement that fails to achieve significant change.

A leader willing and able to push through multilateral trade agreements is not likely to emerge from this increasingly multipolar world. Advanced countries —which, at best, will shed the unemployment and debt burdens of the crisis very slowly in the coming years—will be focused on rebuilding their battered economies. And developing countries will be preoccupied with addressing their large poverty gaps and developing their backward regions. At the same time, many complex issues (including services, investment, agricultural subsidies, and imports of manufactures by developing countries) are likely to remain outside binding multinational disciplines, due both to technical complexity and to the problems in imposing effective disciplines in a highly varied and rapidly changing development context.

Further progress in trade liberalization will thus require alternatives to cumbersome multilateral processes. Autonomous reform is likely to remain the chief driver, particularly as the trade barriers in developing countries increasingly hurt other developing countries, and they still have ample space for improvement. Their trade-weighted most-favored-nation applied tariffs, for example, remain close to 10 percent, more than triple the 3 percent in advanced economies.

Bilateral and regional agreements are also likely to proliferate further, given their greater ability (compared with multilateral approaches) to achieve reforms in such specialized areas as services, investment, and government procurement. Highly specialized, plurilateral agreements are set to rise in importance as well, as major countries find deeper integration (for example, in regulating finance or in mitigating climate change) impossible while catering to the demands of numerous smaller players.

The WTO needs to work with—rather than against—these emerging trends. It must encourage autonomous trade liberalization, support plurilateral agreements, and promote more inclusive approaches with dispute settlement mechanisms that protect the poorest countries. In addition, it should encourage well-designed regional agreements rather than view any regional approach as a threat. Finally, it must look for opportunities that consolidate the progress already made under a multilateral umbrella, including eliminating all tariffs under 3 percent, banning export subsidies in agriculture, adopting a unified—or at least voluntary—code on rules of origin, and providing duty-free, quota-free access to least-developed countries.

Finance—Harnessing the beast

Like trade, finance—the second channel of global integration—is a natural driver and complement to development. As their incomes rise, firms and residents in developing countries can take advantage of liquid international markets to borrow money, raise equity more abundantly and cheaply, invest abroad, and diversify their portfolios. At the same time, international investors look to exploit the opportunities afforded by the fast growth in developing countries. But much more than in trade, the potential benefits of financial integration must be weighed against the enormous costs and risks associated with financial instability.

But as incomes rise and countries become connected through trade, travel, and communication, financial integration becomes very difficult to stop. Thus, the task of policy is to limit its potential for instability through regulation and a hopefully judicious set of constraints on risky transactions.

In recent years developing countries have not only become more integrated into international financial markets—they have also played a crucial role in foreign reserve accumulation and capital flows. They already hold more than 50 percent of foreign exchange reserves, account for 33 percent of inward FDI, and are an increasingly important source of FDI. Private capital inflows to developing countries have risen substantially over the past 25 years, growing from 1.3 percent of their GDP in the mid-1980s to 5 percent in recent years. This trend is expected to persist and perhaps accelerate as developing countries become the world's largest economies, though advanced countries are expected to remain the principal centers of finance for an extended period.

Developing countries' increased financial integration could have immense implications both for them and for the world economy—not all of them good. Many developing countries have relatively weak financial sector institutions; for example, their monitoring of risk-taking by banks and corporations and their auditing and accounting services are inadequate. And their government's limited ability to effectively respond to a crisis can greatly increase their vulnerability. In the past, financial crises in developing countries that were open to external capital markets have imposed huge costs. Recent events demonstrate the weaknesses and vulnerability of rich countries' financial systems, but the impact of crisis on them has been smaller (though hardly negligible).

As developing countries' weight in global finance increases, the potential for extremely costly systemic crises could rise. A financial crisis in one of the largest developing countries would have immediate global repercussions, introducing a fairly new source of systemic risk. The U.S. financial collapse had enormous implications for the world economy because the United States is the largest economy and a center of finance. When China becomes the largest economy and its participation in global finance rises, a crisis there could have similar implications, with the added complication that the ability of its financial and political institutions to manage a major domestic financial crisis has not been tested.

The risks in financial integration underline the need for strong financial policies. Developing countries should err on the side of prudence when liberalizing restrictions on capital markets and devote more resources to financial regulation. The combination of financial restrictions and regulatory scrutiny will vary by country, but caution should be the byword. Advanced countries should seek and support improvements in the regulatory capacity of developing countries, which will reduce the probability of costly global crises.

The possibility of larger and more frequent crises also increases the importance of coordinating financial policies around the world, since a loose network of uncoordinated regulations could create volatile financial flows and increase regulatory arbitrage. The differences in country sizes, incomes, and policy objectives will, however, make such coordination challenging to say the least.

Agreements on financial regulation need to adequately reflect the interests and abilities of developing countries; gentlemen's agreements among the club of rich countries are no longer adequate for ensuring global financial stability. Global agreements also need to focus on restricting risk-taking and encouraging cooperation in monitoring financial institutions.

In addition, a legitimate lender of last resort with access to adequate resources is needed, as highlighted by the Great Recession. Developing countries should be expected to increase their contributions to international financial institutions, but even with that added weight, a lender with the resources to address a large crisis is unlikely to emerge. In its absence, national governments must cooperate in crisis management. The potentially large commitments to finance the deficits of crisis-afflicted countries, and the difficulties of imposing adequate conditions on them, raise the likelihood of—and the importance of accepting—sovereign default as one approach to resolving a crisis.

Migration—The neglected pillar of globalization

International migration, the third major channel of global integration, stands in sharp contrast with trade. While barriers to global trade have broadly fallen over the past 150 years, barriers to immigration have progressively increased. In economic terms this is perverse, as the gains from international migration surpass the gains from trade.

These divergent policy trends can be rationalized (though not necessarily justified) by the fact that migration has more important social consequences: accepting a new immigrant has much greater implications for society than does importing a new machine. It is perceptions of these social effects (which the majority typically perceives as negative)—and not of migration's economic benefits or distributional implications—that play the larger role in determining policy.

The primacy of social issues has led destination countries to jealously guard their prerogatives in immigration policy, while origin countries have little to offer in the form of reciprocal concessions. So, international agreements have little influence over immigration policy. Despite the considerable lip service paid to the principle of the free movement of workers, regional agreements have done little to lower barriers (except in the European Union). Bilateral agreements have facilitated legal migration by low-skilled workers, but recent agreements have covered only a small number of workers, particularly in comparison to the number of illegal migrants coming from the same origin countries.

The high barriers to immigration have had perverse results. In many destination countries, restrictions are only partially effective, resulting in significant illegal immigration, reduced welfare gains from migration, and eroded respect for the law and social values. That produces an extremely curious situation: rich countries choose to forgo the substantial economic gains from immigration in an effort to achieve social objectives, but they create an enormous social problem—illegal immigration—in the process, and they waste resources on pitiful enforcement efforts while making immigrants more vulnerable to physical danger and abuse. Today's immigration policies create enormous social problems while severely reducing the gains for rich countries, poor countries, and migrants.

Ineffective policy frameworks are set to become all the more destructive as the demand for, and supply of, migrants rises. The aging of populations in rich countries will increase the demand for the services that immigrants can provide, while the relatively young populations in many developing countries will create a large reservoir of potential émigrés. Technological progress in transportation and communication will likely further reduce the cost of migration, as will the availability of extensive networks of immigrants in destination countries. Rising incomes in developing countries will create vast opportunities for workers to emigrate, while the international wage gaps that encourage emigration will persist.

As developing countries become more important in the global economy, their ability to better the migration experience for their nationals will improve as well. They will be able to provide them with consular representation, for example, as well as information on the risks and opportunities in emigration. And their continuing urbanization will increase the supply of migrants by spreading information on migration opportunities and disrupting social networks.

Individual developing countries will develop their own immigration policy, and many are becoming an important destination for migrants. But the onus for fixing the broken frameworks lies squarely on the shoulders of the rich countries. More rational immigration policies could not only immeasurably improve global welfare—they could also help establish more peaceful and productive societies in the rich countries. In particular, destination countries need to integrate society by embracing their immigrants rather than penalizing them. In Europe this means affording the descendants of immigrants genuine economic opportunities. In the United States it means eschewing the increasingly popular but entirely bankrupt reliance on police action to control illegal immigration. In this, international coordination can play only a secondary role, though progress is possible in areas that enjoy widespread support, like protecting migrants from human traffickers.

The global commons—A twenty-first century tragedy?

Conflicts over the global commons—resources owned by no one but exploited by many—provide the most dramatic examples of the challenges that the rise of developing countries poses for international cooperation. These issues—which include limiting climate change, maintaining air quality, avoiding the exhaustion of ocean resources, and efficiently using network telecommunications—cross national boundaries and cannot be dealt with efficiently through markets, which fail to capture the cost to society of depleting public goods. They thus require cooperation within countries (a difficult enough task) and among governments. This is becoming more challenging as developing countries' rapid growth and large populations mean that they are more active in exploiting resources, but their incomes, technological capabilities, political structures, and social values differ greatly from those in advanced countries.

This tension is clear in climate change, the most critical issue. Developing countries' annual carbon emissions now exceed those of rich countries, making their participation in any agreement critical. But they are understandably unwilling to sacrifice future growth to control emissions, because the stock currently in the atmosphere—which drives climate change—is largely due to the rich countries, and developing country emissions remain much lower per capita.

Developing countries' differences with advanced countries—as well as among themselves—can impede global cooperation in other areas as well. Their weak administrations make it difficult to protect forest resources within their borders, to conserve migratory fish that pass through their jurisdictions, and to cooperate in detecting and controlling contagious diseases. As for telecommunications, authoritarian governments limit Internet access in the interest of political control or conservative social values.

But as developing countries rise in economic importance, efficient and equitable solutions to most global commons issues will require their participation. Therefore, the challenge is to structure global negotiations in ways that encourage developing countries to participate but also lead to an effective agreement. One approach that can help balance the concerns for legitimacy with those of effectiveness of agreements is to limit participation to the main actors, while also including protocols for the treatment and eventual inclusion of nonparticipants. Providing technology and perhaps other incentives for participation could also help, as would including some provision for amending agreements as technology and other circumstances change.

Experience suggests that success in negotiating international agreements will depend on some specific characteristics of the problem. Not surprisingly, reaching agreement is easiest when broad consensus exists that there is a problem (not always the case!), a small number of countries are the major contributors, the costs of not reaching agreement are borne by the main perpetrators, the agreement is about increasing efficiency (a win-win game) rather than limiting the use of a resource, and negotiations start off on the right foot.

Viewed from this perspective, the likelihood of reaching agreements to limit carbon emissions is distant. For climate change the threat is heavily disputed, the number of significant emitters is large and growing, the damage to each country is not closely related to its share of emissions, and any effective agreement will need to limit energy consumption and thus growth.

Still, the threat is so large that a way forward must be found. Some limits on emissions are being achieved through local, country, and regional initiatives. Agreements initially crafted among the largest emitters and subsequently extended may provide a way forward. Technology can clearly play a much more important role, and there is much that advanced countries can do to help developing countries improve their efficiency in the use of energy.

In contrast to climate change, efforts to control infectious diseases, for example, appear easier: as the nature of the threat is evident to all, each country has a strong incentive to control epidemics within its own borders, and, though control requires government expenditures, it rarely involves severe limitations on the resources required for growth.

Sub-Saharan Africa—Will it break through?

The global economy will likely be transformed by the rise of several emerging giants—Brazil, China, India, Indonesia, Mexico, and Russia. Will the countries in Sub-Saharan Africa, home to nearly 900 million people, also play a major role? The answer is not known. But there is reason for hope, and the prospects for growth in a continent where about half the population lived in absolute poverty in 2005 will be no less important in human terms even if the region's impact on the world remains limited.

Growth accelerated in Sub-Saharan Africa in the decade prior to the crisis: 17 African economies grew at 5 percent or more in the decade leading up to 2008, up from only 7 economies in the previous decade. While Africa's growth rates remained in the bottom half of developing economies, the continent finally ended its long period of declining per capita income. Higher commodity prices, particularly for oil, supported faster growth: GDP in resource-rich economies rose 6 percent a year from 1999 to 2008. But natural resources were only part of the story. The region's 36 non–resource-rich economies nearly doubled their growth rate, mainly due to rapidly expanding services. Supporting the faster growth in many countries were policy improvements, including lower inflation and government debt, reduced trade barriers, an improving business climate, increased investments in education, and reduced incidence of conflict.

Sub-Saharan Africa faces many challenges and opportunities in sustaining rapid growth. Low savings (constrained by low incomes and underdeveloped financial sectors) and limited access to external finance kept the investment rate below 20 percent of GDP in the past decade, well below the 30–35 percent in the most successful developing regions. Productivity growth remains low due to poor education outcomes, weak governance, and inadequate infrastructure, despite recent improvements. Dependence on commodities may subject the region to falling terms of trade and high volatility. On the bright side, the rise of emerging economies will increase the demand for Africa's exports and the supply of finance, and the rising number of middle-class consumers will boost domestic demand for high-quality goods.

The coming increase in the labor force driven by high fertility and large numbers of young people is the wild card. With adequate health care, nutrition, and education, the coming bulge in young workers could generate a sharp acceleration in income growth. But without better provision of these public goods, more workers could simply mean higher unemployment and more poverty, and perhaps social unrest. To a very great extent, Africa's future depends on its governments' ability to provide the services essential for human welfare.

Confronting change—The need for a global conscience

We live in extraordinary times. The recent unprecedented improvement in global welfare is poised to continue, potentially lifting hundreds of millions of individuals out of extreme poverty and improving living standards throughout the world.

But rapid growth in the developing world may generate severe threats to future progress—from awakening the tensions associated with great power transitions to increasing the risk of financial crisis and protectionist backlash. Unequivocally, higher living standards have increased carbon emissions and heightened the potential for environmental disaster. And the rise of developing countries has made global cooperation to cope with all these issues more difficult, while the multilateral frameworks to facilitate it appear incapable of handling present challenges, not to mention the bigger ones to come.

Whether the future brings greater prosperity or calamitous political and economic crises and climate disaster depends critically on policies—those pursued at home and those designed to further cooperation globally. In general, international negotiations must recognize the growing importance of developing countries if they are to achieve effective results. But in most areas, attempts to achieve comprehensive agreements based on consensus (as UN Conventions and the WTO purport to do) are doomed either to failure or to irrelevance.

In some areas—trade, for example—carefully designed regional and bilateral negotiations are likely to generate considerable benefits, as are agreements in specialized areas among a critical mass of countries. In others—migration, for example—international agreements intrinsically have more limited influence. Countries appear destined to have to find their own paths to good migration policy, and the potential for more rational approaches—enabling greater economic efficiency and improved welfare of migrants—is great.

The new G20 summit of advanced and developing nations helped the world avoid a descent into depression, but as a mechanism to enhance global governance, it has many weaknesses. Because it has already become too large and unwieldy, it runs the risk of paralysis. Yet the grouping has already established itself as the preeminent economic forum, and it holds the best promise as a vehicle to make inroads into many of the issues that have so far eluded smaller and unrepresentative forums, such as the G7, and larger ones, such as the UN General Assembly.

But international cooperation to accommodate the rising economic weight of developing countries will require more than good design. Citizens of individual countries need to broaden their vision to the global stage. Just as the growth of national identity contributed to, and was reinforced by, the development of the nation-state, global concerns are not likely to be effectively addressed without the spread of some sense of a global conscience. As Benjamin Franklin said at a crucial moment in American history, "We must hang together, gentlemen . . . else, we shall most assuredly hang separately."

Notes

1. Williamson 1990.
2. For example, in trade in agriculture and in the governance of the Bretton Woods institutions.

References

Williamson, John. "What Washington Means by Policy Reform." In *Latin American Adjustement: How Much Has Happened?* ed. John Williamson. Washington, DC: Institute for International Economics, 1990.

CHAPTER 2

HOW WE GOT HERE

A SHORT HISTORY OF DEVELOPMENT

Economic stagnation has been the norm for much of recorded history. The Industrial Revolution marked the start of sustained economic advance but divided the world in two: Europe and its sparsely populated colonies, where incomes advanced rapidly, and the rest. Divergent incomes and levels of technology persist.

Japan was the first country that did not inherit European norms to break out of poverty, initiating rapid growth in the second half of the nineteenth century. But it was only after World War II that economic success spread more widely to several countries in East Asia and a few others in other continents.

In the last 20 years China and India joined the group of rapidly growing countries, and the conditions for advance were established in a much larger group of developing countries. When these conditions converge, extremely fast growth is possible.

For centuries, mankind made only sporadic advances in technology, economic output, and living standards. Great civilizations rose and then faltered. No advance lasted or propagated widely. In the mid-eighteenth to mid-nineteenth centuries, however, a convergence of apt institutions, favorable geography, growing empire, and a critical mass of technological discoveries produced the Industrial Revolution in Britain, enabling sustained advances in per capita income.

Following the Industrial Revolution, however, technology and growth again failed to spread evenly across the world. Success was limited to a few countries in

Europe and sparsely inhabited colonies, which essentially imported institutions, education, and technology from the metropolis. At the same time, Latin America, Asia, and Africa—which were more heavily populated and had more established indigenous institutions—fell further behind amid colonization and resistance to European influence.

In the late 1800s Japan—which was not colonized—became the first non-Western society to break out of its slow growth, reflecting favorable initial conditions, a concerted public and private sector effort, and a fierce desire to learn from advanced countries and industrialize. But Japan remained an exception until the second half of the twentieth century, when the conditions for strong, sustained advance proliferated across much, though by no means all, of the developing world.

The brief history of development that follows illustrates five crucial points. First, economic progress is not guaranteed. Indeed, stagnation has been the norm for most of history, and most advances have been short-lived. Second, the conditions that enable sustained economic advance—which together triggered the Industrial Revolution in England at the end of the eighteenth century—are multiple and complex; there is no single explanation or simple recipe. Third, sustained and widening divergences in income have been common throughout history and remain so today. Fourth, when favorable conditions emerge, however, large gaps in productivity and technology can be narrowed, facilitating extremely rapid economic growth. Fifth, the experience of the last 25 years suggests that the conditions for catch-up are becoming widespread—though far from universal—across large parts of the developing world, which today accounts for more than 80 percent of world population, setting the stage for unprecedented global growth.

A world without growth

Economic progress is by no means guaranteed—centuries of economic stagnation have defined most of human history. From the beginning of the first century to 1820, total world output grew less than seven-fold while world population more than quadrupled. In other words, over more than 1,800 years the income of the average person grew by only 50 percent, or less than one-fiftieth of a percent a year.[1]

These figures are subject to a great deal of uncertainty, but nearly all estimates yield the same conclusion: on average, no discernable economic progress occurred over an individual's lifetime from ancient times until the Industrial Revolution. Although the average conceals instances of temporary advance, it also conceals cases where wages may have actually declined. In Africa "per capita income was lower in 1820 than in the first century."[2] And immediately before the Industrial

Revolution, laborers' wages in England—one of the most advanced societies at that time—are estimated to have been lower than those in Ancient Babylonia and Athens.[3]

Despite this long-run stagnation in per capita income, the world's total economic output expanded slowly as populations grew and people spread from China to other parts of Asia and from Europe to the Americas. This "extensive" economic growth contrasts sharply with the "intensive" growth common in today's economies, which comes from rising productivity levels.[4] Increased trade also provided a channel for raising living standards, particularly in Rome and Europe and its colonies, though the advance of trade was also extremely slow (see chapter 4).

Why no improvement?

Although the causes of this prolonged economic lethargy are the subject of much academic debate and beyond the scope of this book, the stagnation, at its core, was likely associated with a lack of significant technological progress. Technology advanced at an excruciatingly slow pace before the Industrial Revolution—less than 0.05 percent a year,[5] compared with around 2 percent in advanced countries today and an even faster rate in emerging economies.

Throughout the centuries, there were major advances—the wheel, the plough, and the sail in ancient times, and the printing press more recently, for example—and minor technical improvements—agriculture gradually became more efficient, and banking and credit systems were introduced as early as the twelfth century. But the breakthroughs did not amount to a critical mass. For example, the speed at which information traveled at the time of the Roman Empire was roughly the same as that in Venice—an advanced society for its time—1,400 years later.[6] Some societies even showed evidence of technological regression. In the thirteenth century China impressed travelers with its modern ships, water clocks, and advanced coal mines; later visitors found that the Chinese were no longer able to produce any of these goods.

These gradual technological improvements allowed some societies to temporarily surge ahead. These improvements failed, however, to yield permanent gains. In Rome, which had roads, an advanced legal system, and active trading networks, living standards of artisans are estimated to have been as high as those of workers in Italy in 1929.[7] Around 1000 China flourished technologically, and its people enjoyed incomes among the highest in the world.[8] High incomes in both China and Rome also helped to sustain moderate population growth. These advances were not permanent, however. The Roman Empire declined and finally collapsed in 476, and China began to fall behind other regions around 1300.

The improvements also failed to reach other societies. Technology spread as the successful civilizations grew larger and more populous, but other cultures rarely adopted the improvements. So, when these societies began to falter, the surges in technology that had accompanied them receded as well.

Outside these isolated pockets of success, technology continued to stagnate, and living standards remained depressed. Some scholars, starting with Malthus' theories in the late eighteenth century and continuing today, argue that even when food production rose and populations increased—times absent of major conflict, disease, or famine—living standards actually declined. Without rapid technological progress the amount of food and other goods that can be produced on a given amount of land by a given number of people stays relatively constant. As populations increase, as when food production rises, the marginal returns of the land and each laborer diminish, depressing average living standards. This relationship, in which population size and living standards move inversely, is commonly known as the "Malthusian Trap." Its proponents argue that, in the absence of technological advance, marked increases in living standards can occur only if population declines, as during the great plague of the fourteenth century.[9]

Although some historians question the "Malthusian Trap," few dispute that incomes grew very little before the Industrial Revolution. The modest, steady economic growth so familiar to citizens in modern economies is a fairly recent phenomenon that—until even more recently—reached only a limited number of countries.

Breakthrough

The phenomenon of steady growth began with the Industrial Revolution in England, when multiple advances in technology and increases in per capita output and income not only lasted but also propagated selectively to other locales. For the first time in history, gradual and perceptible per capita income rises (0.5 percent or so a year) were sustained, even amid population increases,[10] and technological change and investment in capital—rather than population size and land availability—began to drive economic growth.

New technology—from the spinning jenny to the steam engine—modernized production processes for mass consumer goods, beginning with cotton, and increased the scale of enterprises. The cotton industry, initially smaller than the wool and linen industries, grew significantly. Rule-based, disciplined factories emerged. Coal output expanded as demand increased and mining technology improved,[11] and the invention of the steam engine improved the efficiency of coal as a source of energy, reducing the pressure on water. Agriculture's relative role fell, its productivity increased, and labor shifted from agriculture to other sectors.

While the range of dates assigned by different scholars to the Industrial Revolution varies, the process clearly took a long time. Even the relatively straightforward mechanization of just one industry, textiles, took more than 60 years: the first key innovation, the spinning jenny, was in 1766, and the last, a self-acting mule, in 1830.

Selective diffusion

Initially, the improvement in productivity growth and income per capita was largely unique to England.[12] By 1815 Great Britain, responsible for one-fourth of the world's industrial production, had become the leading commercial nation.[13]

No one characteristic of mid-1700s Great Britain enabled this shift. Instead, a unique confluence of institutional, geographical, and technological factors drove it. Commitments from the government to protect wealth and establish property rights created the incentives for investment and innovation.[14] England's island location provided access to cheap, dependable transportation via the water (the most efficient means of bulk transport before railways) and helped England gain a naval advantage.[15] Its abundant coal resources provided a ready source of power to drive the inventions of the Industrial Revolution.[16] And its empire enabled it to acquire new resources without having to use its own land or labor.[17] These factors played off of each other: Britain's colonization of cotton-rich territories like the United States, for instance, was crucial in part because institutional incentives had spurred inventions in the burgeoning cotton industry.[18]

Although the Industrial Revolution was initially centered in England, after several decades, the transformation took hold in other European countries and their least populated colonies—Australia, Canada, New Zealand, and the United States—which reproduced many of the conditions and institutions of the home country with the added benefit of abundant land and natural resources.[19] By the 1880s the United States had surpassed Britain in income per capita and industrial production. By 1913 northwestern Europe had come within about 80 percent of British incomes, and Argentina, Australia, Canada, and New Zealand were not far behind.

The mere existence of technological innovations was not enough to ensure economic progress, however, as their spread was gradual and highly selective. Although some scholars contend that other parts of the world—particularly China and Japan—had been as advanced as Europe before the 1800s,[20] all agree that, in short, the Industrial Revolution left most of Africa, Asia, and Latin America[21] in the dust. More than 150 years after the Industrial Revolution began, India still had 2 million handlooms and fewer than 1 percent of Indian workers were employed in modern factory industries.[22] Even by the end of the twentieth century, after growth in the developing world had accelerated sharply, the per capita income in the West and Japan was nearly 7 times that in the East.

Europe—Good institutions, quick diffusion

Initially, the Industrial Revolution spread to European countries, which benefited from institutions similar to those in Britain. First in France and then in Belgium, Holland, and parts of Italy and Germany, the Napoleonic Code codified property rights.[23] Markets and rational business organization also helped, as did strong systems of education, which built human capital and enabled further innovation. Across Europe, intellectual revolutions in the seventeenth century had encouraged scientific investigation, and public support for education was actually stronger in continental Europe than in Britain.[24,25]

Much like Britain, European countries also benefited from empires abroad, which eased the pressure on land, energy, and labor at home.[26,27] By 1900 European countries had colonized 35 percent of the world's land, gaining control of 20 million square miles in addition to its own meager 4 million.[28] Colonization increased the size and predictability of available markets and the scope for specialization.

Certain geographic characteristics also played a role. Abundant coal, cotton, and iron, for instance, made the spread of the Industrial Revolution easier in some countries. Belgium and Germany, which had abundant coal, could industrialize earlier than countries[29] without the same resources.[30] Proximity to England also helped: on average, the first known use of English innovations in Western Europe occurred 13 years after their introduction in England, compared with 52 years, on average, in Latin America.[31] Advances in technology, like the telegraph, and infrastructure, like the Suez and Panama canals, soon accelerated the speed of information travel, however.

Less populated colonies—Good climates, plentiful resources

Before the Industrial Revolution the colonies could be roughly separated into two groups: sparsely populated,[32] less developed territories with abundant natural resources, such as the United States, Canada, Australia, and New Zealand—and densely populated land with established cultures and institutions, including Asia, Latin America, the Middle East, Africa, and parts of the Caribbean.

The institutions that facilitated the spread of the Industrial Revolution arose naturally in the sparsely populated territories as Europeans settled there, but superimposing them in the more densely populated colonies was either not desired or proved far more difficult.

In the former, colonizers settled and established private property rights for most inhabitants, creating institutions that were, in effect, extensions of those in the home country, and thus more amenable to capitalism and per capita income growth for much of society (rather than only a select elite).[33] Education was also highlighted. In the northern U.S. colonies, the level of education surpassed that of the United Kingdom in the second half of the eighteenth century.[34] And by 1850 nearly every northern colony required the establishment of free schools open to all children and supported by general taxes.[35]

The climate and resources of the less populated colonies helped solidify these norms. In the northern United States, for instance, the climate was most conducive to grains, and yields were too low to promote exports or benefit from economies of scale. As a result, small, evenly distributed land holdings proliferated in the North. By 1900, 75 percent of U.S. households and 90 percent of Canadian households in rural areas owned land, while only 2.4 percent in Mexico did in 1910.[36] The more equal but smaller landholdings required many to develop technical self-sufficiency, encouraged innovation, and better aligned the incentives of those who worked the land with those who owned it.

This was not so in the southern U.S. colonies, however, where the land was most conducive to crops that benefited from economies of scale, and large landholdings with slave labor proliferated. Indeed, to an extent, the South reproduced some of the conditions of the densely populated colonies (discussed below) by importing African slaves. Perhaps as a result, the southern colonies failed to industrialize to the same extent as the northern ones and remained dependent on the North for industry and manufacturing long after the Civil War.

More populated colonies and non-European countries—Exploited for markets, cheap labor, raw materials

In the more densely populated colonies of Asia, Latin America, the Middle East, and Africa, colonizers destroyed indigenous institutions and designed frameworks to exploit the territories as markets for manufactures and providers of cheap labor and raw materials.[37] Given the already large populations and the lower number of colonizers, there were also no incentives to create institutions conducive to private property rights and equality. As a result, these colonies were less amenable to capitalism, and their populations remained largely uneducated, deprived of land ownership, and dependent on elites and foreign powers. Even the most progressive colonies in Latin America were more than 75 years behind the United States and Canada in providing broad segments of the population with access to education.[38] An extreme, more recent version of this model could be found in South Africa's dismantled apartheid system, which had effectively deprived the black population of any form of capital, education, or land.

Again, the abundant resources in these colonies reinforced the tendency of colonizers to establish exploitative institutions.[39] In Mexico key sectors like cattle-raising and forestry naturally required large swaths of land to be efficient, leading to less equitable land distribution and lower self-sufficiency. In Brazil sugar had a similar effect. Mineral extraction, one of Latin America's key industries, was conducted in a particularly oppressive manner, with Spanish colonizers forcing indigenous labor to work the mines, notably the Potosi mine in Bolivia.

Not all of the differentiation across colonies can be attributed to the colonizers' response to initial population density and development, however. Different colonizers had different tendencies that persisted even across the less or more densely populated line.

Of the empires, Britain's approach appears to have been the least damaging to long-term growth.[40] British colonizers conducted classes in the vernacular languages and trained people from the indigenous tribes to be teachers. Britain also tailored institutions more to individual colonies than did Spain or France, which had more centralized systems of empire. Furthermore, Britain's trade policy was the least restrictive—following its experience in the United States, where its tariffs encouraged revolt. Britain allowed colonies to determine their own tariff levels and had no import taxes itself—while Spain's strict system of mercantilism was the most limiting. As a result, territories like Argentina—which fit the "sparsely populated" bill with its relatively small population, varied climate, and prime land for raising cattle and cultivating cereals, sugar, and cotton—were held back by Spanish rule.[41]

Regardless of colonial practices, however, each colonial power affected the specialization patterns of its colonies and other non-European countries through its industrial success. Countries like China—which remained technically independent but had to bow to Europe on a plethora of issues—and colonies like India specialized in raw goods to pay for manufactured imports. Industrial output in both actually declined until 1913.[42] In India the British elites—whose consumption accounted for 5 percent of India's GDP—established a de facto preference for their own goods. Maddison estimates that Britain's drain on India—the colonial burden, measured by India's trade surplus—amounted to 0.9 to 1.3 percent of India's GDP from 1868 to the 1930s.[43]

These countries and colonies, which had pre-colonial cultures and institutions, were also often resistant to European norms and technologies. China, for instance, resisted European science and was indifferent to European advances in technology.[44] Its pre-colonial educational systems and institutions were less conducive to growth, however: China's "institutions for finding and learning—schools, academies, learned societies, challenges, and competitions," were lacking, as were its methods for holding on to the findings of previous generations.[45] In the Middle East, where some countries attempted to mirror the educational and industrial institutions of Europe, corruption obstructed progress.[46]

Some colonial practices also limited the spread of institutions and education. In Africa French colonizers forbade any teaching in vernacular languages and instead conducted classes in French, "result[ing] in large numbers of the population failing to achieve any kind of literacy."[47] In addition, by moving to the colonies, colonizers greatly increased the inequality there—particularly in the more heavily populated lands—reducing incentives for public education systems or universal suffrage.[48]

The special case of Japan—First non-Western industrializer

Japan deserves special attention because it became the first non-Western country to industrialize in the late nineteenth century, paving the way for the Asian Tigers and other developing countries that industrialized almost a century later. Although it did not initially share the institutions, empires, or scientific revolutions of the successful countries and colonies, it learned from Europe and demonstrated the speed at which undeveloped economies can modernize.

After the emperor was restored to power during the Meiji Restoration in the late 1860s, Japan's new leaders systematically pursued industrialization. Having witnessed the progress in Europe and the United States, they first established institutions to promote modernization, including a postal service, public education system, and universal military service requirements.

Their determination paid off. Production increased rapidly; in 1886, 62 percent of yarn consumed in Japan was imported, but by 1913 Japan imported almost nothing and provided one-quarter of the world's cotton yarn exports.[49] From 1875 to 1912 GDP per capita grew at 5.1 percent a year, more than twice as fast as in the United States over the same period.[50] World War I consolidated Japan's industrialization by greatly increasing the demand for exports.

Numerous explanations have been offered for Japan's success in industrializing as a non-Western country, from initial high literacy levels[51] to better-developed personal hygiene[52] to tight family structure, strong work ethic, self-discipline, and a sense of national identity and inherent superiority.[53] Japan also benefited from avoiding colonization, which not only kept its land and people from suppression and exploitation, but also allowed for centuries without war or revolution.[54]

Three other factors, all related to policy, may have played a more central role: a strong central state, a new commitment to economic openness, and a recognition of the importance of markets.

The support and will of an ambitious government made Japan's industrialization possible, highlighting the need for stable institutions in development. Under the shogun, Japan had been ruled by loosely connected lords, but the Meiji Restoration ushered in a more centralized government that combined the governmental structures of the shogunate with those of European states. This new government invested heavily in Japanese modernization, building model factories in a wide range of industries.

In addition to supplying physical capacity, Japanese leadership also helped provide the technical knowledge for industrialization by opening Japan to foreign ideas and trade. The government "purchased western technologies and equipment [and] employed skilled foreign labor" until the 1880s.[55] But rather than simply import foreign machines as many other countries did, Japan modified and improved Western machinery to fit its needs. The financial system was also imported from the West, and the Bank of Japan—modeled after the central bank of Belgium[56]—was established in 1881.

Despite the central role of the government, leaders appeared to understand the importance of markets—one of the government slogans at the time was "develop industry and promote enterprise."[57] The government encouraged "private enterprise by leading entry into targeted sectors with its pilot factories, acquiring and demonstrating new technologies, and supporting the opening of new markets."[58] When the factories and industries were suitably self-sufficient, they were sold to private entrepreneurs, often at a loss, suggesting that leaders were passing the baton of growth to the private sector.

The poorest countries fall farther behind

Despite the vast improvements in wealth, living standards, and technology in today's advanced countries over the past two centuries, as well as countless efforts by governments to copy or spread innovations, the income gap that emerged at the onset of the Industrial Revolution has not simply persisted—it has widened.

After centuries of stagnation, purchasing-power-parity (PPP) GDP per capita in Western Europe, the United States, and Japan has grown by an average of nearly 2 percent a year over the past 200 years.[59] Meanwhile, incomes in Africa grew only by an estimated 0.7 percent a year from 1820 to 2001, falling from 35 percent to 5 percent of U.S. incomes over that period[60] and resulting in "much wider income gaps today than at any other time in the past."[61] Even recent growth rates illustrate this: from 1980 to 2000 PPP per capita incomes grew by 190 percent in advanced countries, but only by 57 percent in Sub-Saharan Africa.[62]

More striking, not only have incomes in many of the world's poorest countries declined relative to those of their contemporaries, but some have even fallen below pre-industrial levels. For example, incomes in many countries, including Ethiopia, Nigeria, and Pakistan, are estimated to be less than those in eighteenth century England (and, by extension, those in ancient Rome); incomes in Tanzania and Burundi are around 75 percent lower.[63]

As the continued stagnation in these countries demonstrates, prolonged periods of little to no income growth are possible in many different contexts, even as other parts of the world race ahead. The same is true of technological progress: at the extremes, technology in some societies can remain centuries, if not millennia, behind others. Cuneiform, the oldest known written language, dates back as far as 2800 BCE,[64] yet the Piraha, an indigenous tribe currently living in the Amazon, lacks not only a written language,[65] but also words for precise numbers.[66] Even in today's interconnected world, economic convergence toward the world's most developed countries is anything but automatic. Although some countries have caught up to their industrialized counterparts—as Japan and South Korea did, and China, India, and Brazil now appear to be doing—many have not.

Decolonization may be partly responsible for this stagnation, particularly in Africa. While decolonization marked an economic upsurge for some countries, like the United States, many others suffered further after independence, left without solid institutions and with conflicts over territory, religion, and ideology. Bertocchi and Canova explain, "corruption, distorting government policies, political instability, and ethnic conflict, which are important in explaining the heterogeneity of Africa's growth, can . . . be viewed as a legacy of the colonial era."[67] The violence of the liberation process also took a toll on the physical capital of countries[68] and the timing of decolonization may have exacerbated its negative effects. During the Cold War, divisions among external powers supported internal conflict in Africa.[69] Countries that gained independence in the 1970s also had to confront the global economic slowdown.[70]

At the same time, empirical studies have identified an uptake in the growth rates of some former colonies following decolonization. Bertocchi and Canova find that, for one-third of the 18 African countries decolonized after 1960, independence marked a significant, positive structural break in their growth patterns.[71] Sylwester finds that, although decolonizing countries grew at slower rates than did already independent post-colonial states, they would likely not have grown any faster had they remained colonies.

Conditions for convergence become more widely established

Since World War II, growth has increasingly spread across the world, and the conditions for it appear to be becoming more widely established in developing countries. The spread of these conditions, though still far from universal, is setting the stage for unprecedented global growth.

What are these conditions? To address this question, the Commission on Growth and Development recently identified 13 countries whose GDP grew at 7 percent or more a year for at least 30 consecutive years (table 2.1)—a rate of advance unimaginable in previous centuries.

These countries, covering every region of the developing world, share several important characteristics—both with each other and with the countries most successful following the Industrial Revolution. They opened up to the world, learning from more advanced countries. They oriented their economies toward exports and grew partly on the back of global demand. They exhibited high rates of savings and investment, including public investment in infrastructure and education. And they depended on both the government and markets for growth. Macroeconomic stability—in the form of relatively stable inflation and exchange rates, as well as fiscal responsibility—was also central to their success.[72]

TABLE 2.1 COUNTRIES WITH SUSTAINED, HIGH GROWTH
(PERCENT)

	AVERAGE GROWTH	PERIOD
BOTSWANA	9.0	1961–2009
BRAZIL	7.4	1950–80
CHINA	8.1	1961–2005
HONG KONG SAR, CHINA	7.2	1960–2008
INDONESIA	7.1	1966–97
JAPAN	7.5	1950–83
KOREA, REP.	7.1	1961–2008
MALAYSIA	7.3	1961–97
MALTA	7.0	1964–96
OMAN	9.5	1961–2009
SINGAPORE	7.1	1961–2009
TAIWAN, CHINA	7.9	1965–2002
THAILAND	7.1	1961–97

Source: Growth Commission 2008; World Bank 2010; IMF 2010; IBGE 2010; Maddison 2003.

These conditions have become more common. Tariffs came down from an average of 15 percent in 1997 to 9 percent in 2007.[73] Inflation also fell, with rates averaging 5 percent or less from 1997 to 2007 in 64 developing countries,[74] more than twice the number in the preceding decade. Of the developing countries with data, average government debt fell from 58 percent of GDP in 1997 to 44 percent in 2007.[75] Over the same period, investment and savings rates increased. Developing countries' net national savings rose from an average of 7.7 percent of GDP in 1997 to 13.4 percent in 2007.[76] As globalization strengthens, best practices emerge, and technology spreads, more countries appear to fit the bill for high, sustainable growth. In fact, in the 10 years preceding the Great Recession, 26 additional countries saw GDP grow at the same high rate as the 13 identified by the Growth Commission (figure 2.1).

These success stories should not conceal the much less happy picture in the 23 developing countries, which fell farther behind advanced countries in GDP growth over the same period, and the even larger number that saw their per capita income fall. Many of these countries remain heavily dependent on official development assistance and migrant remittances from abroad. And more than

FIGURE 2.1 COUNTRIES WITH HIGH GROWTH FROM 1997 TO 2007, EXCLUDING THOSE IDENTIFIED BY THE GROWTH COMMISSION
(AVERAGE ANNUAL GROWTH RATE)

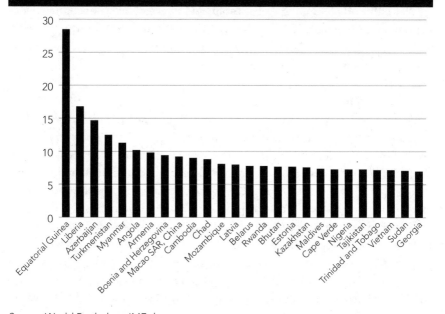

Source: World Bank data; IMF data.

1 billion people around the world continue to live on less than $1.25 a day; in Sub-Saharan Africa the number of people below this poverty line has almost doubled since 1981.

Although increased international integration is only one part of the successful growth mix the Commission identified—apt domestic policies are equally essential—it is clear that globalization in the postwar period has made many of the necessary conditions more accessible across the world. As foreign direct investment (FDI) flows increase, so does recipient countries' knowledge of foreign production techniques and overseas markets.[77] Similarly, as markets grow more integrated and trade more liberalized, foreign markets become more accessible, giving countries the opportunity to dramatically increase output and specialize in goods not necessarily favored by domestic consumers.

Open trade policies also give still-developing countries access to the technology—which needs only to be implemented, not invented—to catalyze growth. According to the World Bank, "low income countries employ only a quarter of the level of technology in developed countries."[78] While Hong Kong, Japan, Taiwan, and Thailand began to catch up to international best practice in the latter half of the twentieth century, Latin America and Africa fell even farther behind.[79] Fortunately, in the words of the Growth Commission, "it is easier to learn something than it is to invent it."[80] As the East Asian experience shows, technological catch-up at even low levels can reap many benefits.[81]

Not only will continuing globalization and international cooperation enable the rise of developing countries, but the increased toll on resources that will accompany their rise will also make such cooperation all the more essential—particularly for protecting the global commons (chapter 7).

Failed experiments

These twentieth century success stories stand in contrast to failed experiments, including import substitution and central planning. Under import substitution, favored by India and many countries in Latin America in the 1950s and 1960s, countries limited international trade to foster production for domestic rather than global markets. Although these policies temporarily encouraged growth in manufacturing, they failed to promote broader economic development.[82] Insulated from international markets, domestic markets were both too small to foster adequate specialization and economies of scale and too distorted by protectionist policies to promote efficient resource allocation or achieve world class standards. Plagued by inefficiencies, domestic industries produced high-cost, low-quality goods that were not competitive internationally.[83] The World Bank found that the performance of economies oriented toward international markets was broadly superior to those focused on domestic markets in "almost all respects."[84] So, development in import-substituting economies suffered.

Other countries elected to follow centrally planned, communist models of development. In their early stages communist economies were also remarkably successful, increasing their production by at least as much as capitalist economies.[85] The Soviet Union grew faster than the United States over many years and developed an impressive manufacturing sector, a powerful military, and a centralized education system. But this growth was grossly inefficient, powered principally by large injections of labor, capital, and natural resources. The centralized planning system could not cater to the complex needs of a modern economy, became increasingly susceptible to corruption and waste, and led to an enormous misallocation of resources; productivity failed to improve and Soviet goods and services remained of poor quality. Eventually, Soviet growth slowed and living standards stagnated or fell as global living standards rose. Economic policies lost their popularity, and, after attempts at reform failed, the Soviet economy—and state—collapsed.[86]

The spectacular failure of central planning should not be interpreted as meaning that government intervention is inevitably prone to failure. Again and again, governments have successfully catalyzed economic development, most notably in Japan (see above) and China—where remarkable market-based development and state control coexist—in recent decades. Instead, the failure of central planning, much like the failure of import substitution, highlights the dangers of too little competition. As Andrew Walder concluded when reflecting on Chinese development, "the task is not to revile state involvement but to change it."[87]

As an increasing number of countries join the "developed" ranks, the pool of best practices and lessons increases. While there is no "one-size-fits-all" approach to market or government policies, developing countries can learn from the success of countries as varied as Malta, where the population is well below 500,000, and China, where it is well over 1 billion, and the failed experiments elsewhere.

Conclusion

The overriding message from this thumbnail sketch of development history is that nothing is automatic or natural about sustaining growth in living standards. But in the presence of large gaps in technology and achievement, the establishment of certain conditions for enterprise and learning (including apt institutions, stability, and openness) can produce extraordinary advances in a short period. This lays the ground for our next chapter, which explores scenarios for the future of development.

Notes

1. Maddison 2001, appendix B.
2. Maddison 2001, 45.
3. Clark 2007.
4. Maddison 2001.
5. Clark 2007. Clark calculates growth in technology based on estimates of population growth, changes in per capita income (which he assumes to be minimal), and land rents. For a detailed explanation of this calculation, see Clark (2007).
6. Clark 2007
7. Cameron 1989.
8. Maddison 2001.
9. Conversely, in societies dependent on subsistence agriculture, higher life expectancy would be associated with declining living standards. The "Malthusian Trap" may help provide a partial explanation for the fall in incomes per capita in Africa in the 1980s and 1990s.
10. This version of the Industrial Revolution is more common today, though earlier scholars, including Landes and Ashton, argue that the Industrial Revolution marked a dramatic, relatively immediate transition to the rapid growth rates of modern times in Britain. The exact dates and scope of the Industrial Revolution are still debated, with the full range of dates assigned by different scholars spanning centuries.
11. Scholars disagree on technology's role in increasing coal output. Some, like Ashton and Pomeranz, argue that technological advances greatly improved the capacity of mines and were at the heart of the Industrial Revolution's productivity gains. Others, including Crafts, Harley, and Mokyr, argue that technology advances in mining were minimal and that production simply moved along the existing supply curve, increasing in response to growing demand
12. Some scholars argue that a similar episode of technological advances had already led to sustained productivity growth in the Netherlands by the time the British Industrial Revolution began (Clark 2001).
13. Cameron 1989.
14. North and Weingast 1989.
15. Cameron 1989.
16. Cameron 1989.
17. Pomeranz 2000.
18. Pomeranz 2000.
19. Referred to as the "West" for simplicity.

20. See, for example, Pomeranz (2000). Bairoch (1993) suggests that, before to the Industrial Revolution, the income gap between the poorest and richest country was likely only 1 to 1.5—that is, the GDP of the richest country was either equal to or 1.5 times the size of that in the poorest country—and the per capita income gap may have been even smaller. For the opposite opinion, see Landes and Maddison.
21. Similarly, the "East."
22. Clark 2007.
23. Cameron 1989.
24. Cameron 1989.
25. Pomeranz (2000) challenges the idea that this was a uniquely European characteristic, pointing to China's similar interest in science and mathematics in the seventeenth century.
26. Pomeranz 2000.
27. Some scholars dispute that colonizing nations benefited from their empires. O'Brien and Prados de la Escosura argue that empires were economically irrelevant for long-term growth in Europe and that, in some cases, capital would have been better allocated in domestic economies than in colonies. Others, including Grossman and Iyigun, have noted that by the middle of the twentieth century, colonies may have been a net burden on their metropolitan governments.
28. Clark 2007.
29. Switzerland, the Netherlands, Scandinavia, and the Austro-Hungarian and Russian empires.
30. Cameron 1989.
31. Clark 2007.
32. Even in the sparsely populated territories, "the indigenous population was uprooted repeatedly to make way for land-hungry newcomers" whose weapons, diseases, and diplomacy made the expansion possible (Landes 1999, 311).
33. Engerman and Sokoloff similarly find that education systems and other institutions in less populated areas were more conducive to per-capita income growth, but suggest that this was because they were designed to encourage immigration.
34. Maddison 2001.
35. Engerman and Sokoloff 2005.
36. Engerman and Sokoloff 2005.
37. Acemoglu, Johnson, and Robinson 2002.
38. Engerman and Sokoloff 2005.

39. Bairoch (1969, 1975) argues that the different climate also limited the spread and relevance of the earlier agricultural revolution to these countries and colonies, asserting that a revolution in agriculture is a necessary precursor to a strong revolution in industry.

40. Grier 1999.

41. Landes 1999. This does not imply, however, that every British colony outdid every non-British colony, or that every Spanish colony underperformed non-Spanish colonies. For instance, India grew more slowly than Mexico until the 1970s and than the rest of Asia (excluding China) until 1989.

42. Clark 2007.

43. Maddison 2001.

44. Landes 1999.

45. Landes 1999, p. 343.

46. Landes 1999.

47. Grier 1999, p. 319.

48. Engerman and Sokoloff 2005.

49. Landes 1999.

50. Tang 2008.

51. Cameron 1989.

52. Clark 2007

53. Landes 1999.

54. Landes 1999.

55. Tang 2008, p. 1.

56. Cameron 1989.

57. Cameron 1989, p. 271.

58. Tang 2008, p. 4.

59. Maddison 2003.

60. Maddison 2003.

61. Maddison 2001, p. 27

62. IMF 2010.

63. Clark 2007.

64. Adkins 2003.

65. Hespos 2004.

66. Gordon 2004.

67. Bertocchi and Canova 2002, p. 1864.

68. Bertocchi and Canova 2002.

69. Young 1986.

70. Sylwester 2005.

71. Bertocchi and Canova 2002.

72. Commission on Growth and Development 2008.
73. World Bank 2010.
74. IMF 2010.
75. World Bank 2010.
76. World Bank 2010.
77. Commission on Growth and Development 2008.
78. World Bank 2008, p. 17.
79. Page 1994.
80. Commission on Growth and Development 2008, p. 22.
81. Page 1994.
82. Krugman and Obstfeld 2006.
83. World Bank 1987.
84. World Bank 1987, p. 85.
85. Yusuf 2009.
86. Curtis 1998.
87. Walder 1995, p. 979.

References

Acemoglu, Daron, Simon Johnson, and James A. Robinson. "Reversal of Fortune: Geography and Institutions in the Making of the Modern World Income Distribution." *Quarterly Journal of Economics*, 117 (2002): 1231–94.

Adkins, Lesley. *Empires of the Plain: Henry Rawlinson and the Lost Languages of Babylon.* New York: St. Martin's Press, 2003.

Bairoch, Paul. *Agriculture and the industrial revolution.* Translated by M. Grindrod Collins, London: Collins, 1969.

———. *Economics and World History: Myths and Paradoxes.* Chicago, IL: University of Chicago Press, 1993.

———. *The Economic Development of the Third World since 1900.* Translated by Cynthia Postan. Berkeley, CA: University of California Press, 1975.

Bertocchi, Graziella, and Fabio Canova. "Did colonization matter for growth?: An empirical exploration into the historical causes of Africa's underdevelopment." *European Economic Review*, 46 (2002): 1851–71.

Cameron, Rondo. *A Concise Economic History of the World.* New York: Oxford University Press, 1989.

Clark, Gregory. "The Secret History of the Industrial Revolution." University of California Davis, 2001, www.econ.ucdavis.edu/faculty/gclark/papers/secret2001.pdf.

———. *A Farewell to Alms: A Brief Economic History of the World.* Princeton, NJ: Princeton University Press, 2007.

Commission on Growth and Development. *The Growth Report: Strategies for Sustained Growth and Inclusive Development*. Washington, DC: World Bank and International Bank for Reconstruction and Development, 2008.

Curtis, Glenn E., ed. *Russia: a Country Study*. Washington, DC: Federal Research Division, Library of Congress, 1998.

Engerman, Stanley L., and Kenneth L. Sokoloff. *Colonialism, Inequality, and Long-run Paths of Development*. NBER Working Paper 11057. Cambridge, MA: National Bureau of Economic Research, 2005.

Gordon, Peter. "Numerical Cognition Without Words: Evidence from Amazonia." *Science*, 306 (2004): 496–9.

Grier, Robin M. "Colonial legacies and economic growth." *Public Choice*, 98 (1999): 317–35.

Hespos, Susan J. "Language: Life without Numbers." *Current Biology*, 14 (2004): R927–8.

IBGE (Instituto Brasileiro de Geografia e Estatística). *Estatísticas do Século XX*. Rio de Janeiro, Brazil, 2010.

IMF (International Monetary Fund). *World Economic Outlook: Rebalancing Growth*. Washington, DC, 2010.

Krugman, Paul, and Maurice Obstfeld. *International Economics: Theory and Policy*. 7th ed. Boston, MA: Pearson Addison Wesley, 2006.

Landes, David S. *The Wealth and Poverty of Nations: Why Some Are So Rich and Some So Poor*. London: W. W. Norton, 1999.

Maddison, Angus. *The World Economy: A Millennial Perspective*. Paris: Development Center of the OECD, 2001.

———. *The World Economy: Historical Statistics*. Paris: Development Center of the OECD, 2003.

Mokyr, Joel. "The Industrial Revolution and the New Economic History." In *The Economics of the Industrial Revolution*, edited by Joel Mokyr, 1–51. Totowa, NJ: Rowman and Allanheld, 1985.

North, Douglass C., and Barry R. Weingast. "Constitutions and Commitment: The Evolution of Institutional Governing Public Choice in Seventeenth-Century England." *Journal of Economic History*, 49 (1989): 803–32.

Page, John. "The East Asian Miracle: Four Lessons for Development Policy." *NBER Macroeconomics Annual*, 9 (1994): 219–82.

Pomeranz, Kenneth. *The Great Divergence: China, Europe, and the Making of the Modern World Economy*. Princeton, NJ: Princeton University Press, 2000.

Sylwester, Kevin. "Decolonization and Economic Growth: The Case of Africa." *Journal of Economic Development*, 30 (2005): 87–101.

Tang, John P. "Financial intermediation and late development in Meiji Japan, 1868–1912." U.S. Census Bureau, Washington, DC, 2008.

Walder, Andrew G. "China's Transitional Economy: Interpreting Its Significance." *China Quarterly*, 144 (1995): 963–79, www.ln.edu.hk/mkt/staff/gcui/andrew.pdf.

World Bank. *World Development Report: Barriers to Adjustment and Growth in the World Economy*. Washington, DC, 1987.

———. *Global Economic Prospects: Technology Diffusion in the Developing World*. Washington, DC, 2008.

———. *World Development Indicators*. Washington, DC, 2010.

Young, Crawford. "Africa's Colonial Legacy." In *Strategies for African Development*, eds. Robert J. Berg and Jennifer S. Whitaker. Berkeley, CA: University of California Press, 1986.

Yusuf, Shahid. *Economics through the Decades: A Critical Look at 30 Years of the World Development Report*. Washington, DC: World Bank, 2009.

CHAPTER 3

IN 2050

A WORLD TRANSFORMED

In 2050 the developing countries will, under plausible assumptions, account for the bulk of global economic activity and trade. Their rise will create great opportunities, including a much larger global middle and rich class and the decline of absolute poverty to a fraction of today's. But it also carries great risks of increased political strife, financial crises, protectionism, greatly increased migration pressures, and demands on the global commons.

Changes in country policy and enhanced international collaboration will be necessary to mitigate these risks. But the fact that developing countries will be among the largest economies while remaining relatively poor will complicate international cooperation.

The world economy is undergoing a historic transformation, reflecting the rapid growth of developing countries and their integration into global markets. Contrary to some predictions, the resilience of developing countries during the Great Recession suggests that they will persist with market-oriented policies that underpin their growth and integration. And the crisis—whose epicenter was in the United States and Europe—may well accelerate their rising share of global economic activity.

The world's economic balance of power will shift dramatically. China will overtake the United States as the world's largest economic power, and India will join both as a global leader. Other emerging economies in Asia and Latin America will outpace Europe, driving a vast expansion of global trade, financial integration, and migration.

It is impossible to project with any claim to precision over 40 years. It is possible, however, to discern likely long-term economic trends conditional on certain assumptions, and to sketch the broad contours of the world economy that would result from them. So, the discussion that follows, even though it will contain hard numbers, should be interpreted as painting a plausible scenario, not as a point forecast.

Rather than show a large number of alternative futures, the chapter tries to identify this "central tendency" or baseline—on the assumptions that market-oriented policies persist and that major political, economic, and ecological disasters are avoided. It then briefly discusses the main risks. This approach has the defect of suggesting precision that is frankly illusive. But it helps focus on the analysis of the baseline, economizes on the attention span, and gives the critical reader a clear target to shoot at and disagree with.

The chapter begins with a brief discussion of the long-term implications of the crisis. It next presents the main scenario: long-term growth projections for the world's major economies, the G20, and four large countries in Sub-Saharan Africa from a new model that uses a Cobb-Douglas production function as the base. It then draws some implications for the main channels of international integration: trade, financial flows, relative prices, migration, and capital flows. The chapter also reviews risks to the forecast, including climate change, and concludes with some policy implications.

The crisis and its implications

In the run-up to the Great Recession, many developing countries, though not all, saw remarkable economic advances and a rise in living standards. Better policies, less debt, and higher reserves helped them weather the crisis.

Growth in the developing countries in the aggregate has exceeded that of the industrial countries by 2–3 percentage points a year since the turn of the century, 400 million people have been lifted out of poverty since 1990, and average life expectancy has risen to 70 years in many of them. Developing countries have integrated into the global markets for goods, capital, and labor. Tariffs have been cut to a third of their level in the early 1980s, trade has risen by 15 percentage points of GDP over the last 15 years, and FDI's share of GDP has more than doubled. Remittances have surged. This rapid growth and integration has been associated with a cumulative and mutually reinforcing adaptation of various technologies imported from advanced countries. Growth has also been associated with better macroeconomic management: in the years before the crisis, developing countries saw a large decline in external debt to GDP, smaller fiscal balances, and a large increase in foreign currency reserves.

The effects of the Great Recession were severe, but the developing countries were damaged less than industrial ones. Many developing countries saw relatively small decelerations in growth, and some continued to grow quite rapidly, including three countries—China, India, and Indonesia—that account for nearly half of the developing world's population. Exceptions include Russia and several developing countries in Eastern Europe, hit worse than the industrial countries. The crisis was most pronounced in the United States and a few countries in Europe.

While the trade and financial shocks initially affected every country in the world, the banking systems of most developing countries were relatively insulated. The prudent macro stance many of them adopted in recent years allowed them to adopt countercyclical policies and mitigate the crisis. Flexible exchange rates helped. Once the global panic subsided, confidence in emerging markets returned quickly, and capital flows were reestablished, if well below those of the pre-crisis period.

But even if there is no relapse and a robust recovery ensues, the legacy of the crisis will be profound. The postcrisis world is likely to be characterized by lower growth in the countries worst affected by the crisis, and by greater volatility as massive government intervention is withdrawn. Rising public sector debt in advanced countries due to the crisis, estimated by the IMF to be in the region of 100 percent of GDP, will constrain macroeconomic policies for years, demanding a structural adjustment in taxes and spending in many countries.

Contrary to the proclamations of some skeptics, it appears unlikely that the crisis will lead to a fundamental change in policies supporting free markets and global economic integration, partly because developing countries weathered the crisis well. Some of the institutional planks of the dominant policy paradigm, including the development banks and especially the IMF and the Financial Stability Board, emerged reinforced by the crisis. WTO disciplines, though porous, also proved their value. Central bankers, perhaps the most consistent proponents of the current policy paradigm, were absolutely central in fighting the crisis, also emerging stronger. They can be expected to be more active in financial regulation and surveillance.

Baseline scenario

Before the Great Recession the balance of economic power in the world was gradually shifting to the South and the East. Now, as industrial countries slowly resume growth along their precrisis long-term paths but do not recover the output lost during the crisis, developing countries—whose output losses were much lower—will accelerate out of the recession. In the coming years the most successful of them, especially in Asia, will converge even more rapidly toward their advanced counterparts.

GDP projections through 2050 for the world's major economies—the 19 nations of the G20 (the European Union is excluded) and several large countries in Africa—are presented here. Based on a standard Cobb-Douglas output model, the projections build on a long history of studies, dating at least to the early 1970s. The idea of the Big Five developing countries—China, India, Indonesia, Brazil, and Russia—and their effects on the world economy through 2020 was introduced in the World Bank's 1997 Global Economic Prospects.[1] Some years later Goldman Sachs unveiled the BRIC acronym to denote the Big Five, minus Indonesia, which was then in deep crisis (but has since recovered). In the early 2000s Goldman Sachs[2] and PricewaterhouseCoopers[3] developed their own projections.

Technological change, the single most important driver of economic growth, is incorporated in these models exogenously; in other words, it is a given number generated outside the model. This is hardly satisfactory, and modern growth theory has attempted to identify the factors that drive technological change— such as competition among firms and the skills of workers—and to incorporate them in endogenous growth models.

The model used in this book tries to incorporate the theory of technological change by making it dependent on an underlying set of factors, which include the initial gap with the most advanced countries, openness to foreign technology, contestability in markets competition, quality of the business climate, and levels of education (see annex).

Based on the model, rapid growth in developing countries will result from a high, though slowing, population increase, as well as advances in total factor productivity (TFP) from technology absorption (conditional on the quality of education, governance, business climate, and infrastructure, and declining over time as the gap with advanced countries closes). While investment rates in developing countries will also be higher than in industrial countries, technology will be more important than capital accumulation in both.

The large shift in economic power that these projections imply will have far-reaching consequences for global economic governance and for relationships among countries and geographic regions. Kenichi Ohmae's 1980s concept of a Triad—a world economy led by the United States, Europe, and Japan—will be eclipsed by a new order, consisting of China, the United States, and India. And as foreshadowed by the recently ratified Lisbon Treaty, Europe will have to operate increasingly under an EU banner in order to retain its historical influence. International organizations whose governance structures still reflect the world as it was in 1945 must either adjust or be relegated to the margin.

Before presenting the projections, we consider the underlying assumptions for labor force growth, investment, and technology improvement.

Drivers of growth favor developing countries

Labor force growth

According to the UN, the global population will rise from 6.8 billion in 2009 to 9.2 billion in 2050, and the global labor force will expand by 1.3 billion. Developing regions will see their work forces expand by 1.5 billion people, mostly in Africa and Asia, while the labor force in developed areas will shrink by more than 100 million workers. The working age population in developed regions will fall from 62.8 percent of the population in 2009 to 52.0 percent in 2050. It will also decline in developing regions, but only from 61.1 percent to 59.5 percent.

Capital stock

Physical capital stocks will continue to accumulate as incomes rise and rates of savings cover depreciation and allow for new investment. But as the marginal contribution of capital to output declines, the incentive to invest will fall. In industrial countries, savings as a share of GDP will likely decline as populations age and the dependency ratio rises. In developing countries, where capital-to-output ratios are much lower, capital stocks will rise substantially as the working population increases. China stands out as an exception: despite a shrinking population, investment is expected to remain high.

Historically, developed countries have invested about 20 percent of GDP in fixed capital formation each year. Developing countries have invested significantly more, with investment in some countries peaking at around 35–40 percent.

Japan provides a useful case, because its investment in capital stock can be traced through the different stages of development. Japan's yearly investment rate peaked at 36 percent when its economy was growing rapidly and has moderated toward 20 percent in recent years. South Korea had a similar experience, with yearly investment peaking at 40 percent in 1992 before declining to just below 30 percent since then (figure 3.1).

Over the next 40 years China and India are expected to have the highest average investment rates—33.8 and 33.5 percent a year, respectively. The United Kingdom and Germany are projected to invest at the lowest rates—17.7 and 18.3 percent, respectively.

Technological progress and productivity

Technological innovation will become a more important driver of growth as the means of production shift from labor-intensive to capital-intensive. As in a comprehensive World Bank report on technology and development explains, "Part of the strong projected performance for developing countries derives

FIGURE 3.1 INVESTMENT CONVERGING TOWARD 15–20 PERCENT FOR MATURE ECONOMIES
(PERCENT OF GDP, FIVE-YEAR MOVING AVERAGE)

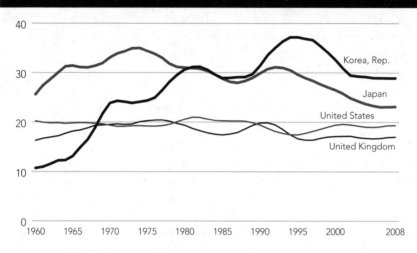

Source: World Bank data; IMF data.

from stronger labor force growth, but much can be attributed to technological progress."[4]

Developing countries will continue to absorb well-established technologies, such as electricity and sanitation. While the largest urban agglomerations and elite firms and individuals in developing countries typically have access to such technologies, rural areas and less favored segments of society often do not.

But newer technologies, such as mobile phones and the Internet, are spreading rapidly to developing countries, partly because they are relatively inexpensive and require little government spending on infrastructure. Although advanced countries will remain the source of cutting-edge technological innovation, some developing countries will innovate by modifying technologies to suit local conditions.

The potential for technological catch-up is greater when TFP and per capita income are low. Thus, convergence of the poorest countries could be the fastest. But actual rates of catch-up will depend on each country's educational attainment, communication and transportation infrastructure, governance, and business and investment environment. These factors hold technological progress significantly below potential in low-income countries, but as educational attainment and openness to world trade rise, technologies spread faster. In this sense, our model incorporates some features of endogenous growth theory.

An examination of the relevant indicators suggests that, among major developing countries (those in the G20), Russia, China, and Mexico are well prepared for faster adoption of foreign technologies, largely because of fairly high levels of educational attainment and supportive infrastructure. But governance indicators in Russia and China are weak, suppressing technological convergence (adjusted for initial income), other things being equal.

Contrary to India's high-tech image, its spread of technology and speed of convergence (adjusted for initial income) are assumed to be among the lowest in the G20. It exhibits the lowest education indicators and worst business climate in the G20, while Indonesia has the G20's weakest communication infrastructure. Education, infrastructure, and governance must improve before rapid technological advancement can occur in India and Indonesia.

The degree to which these factors will hold countries' technological growth below the potential is suggested by their income gap alone, with a score of 10 representing maximum ability to take advantage of technological catch-up to the United States (figure 3.2). (For a complete description of the initial growth conditions and the relevant indicators, see annex table A2.)

Projections—The "rise of the rest"

As developing countries house a larger share of people, capital, and technology, their share of global GDP will increase, dramatically shifting the economic balance of power. By the midpoint of this century the United States and Europe, long the traditional leaders of the global economy, will be joined in economic size by emerging markets in Asia and Latin America.

But as these countries become the world's largest economies, as well as the most populous, they will not rise to be among the world's richest, breaking the decades-old correlation between economic size and per capita income. This notion of a low- or middle-income country becoming the world's largest economy— dating to at least 1993, when China was predicted to rise as a world power—now appears more likely.[5] The recent promotion of the G20 as the world's principal economic forum will likely mark the end of wealthy country dominance over the world economy and usher in a more integrated and complex economic era.

The baseline scenario assumes that markets stay open and macroeconomic policies remain sound; and catastrophes—economic, natural, or geopolitical— are assumed not to occur. For these reasons the projections represent only an educated assessment of the present direction of the international economy.

To account for more immediate risks, such as a slow recovery and unfavorable debt dynamics in many advanced economies following the financial crisis, projections for the first 5 years are provided by the IMF's *World Economic Outlook*. For each of

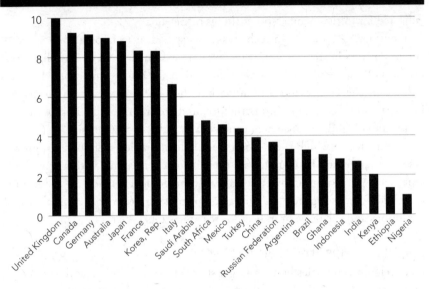

FIGURE 3.2 THE UNITED KINGDOM HAS THE GREATEST ABILITY TO CATCH THE UNITED STATES, NIGERIA THE LEAST
(INDEX OF TECHNOLOGICAL CATCH-UP CONDITIONS, 0 DENOTES SLOWEST CONVERGENCE TO THE UNITED STATES, 10 DENOTES FASTEST)

Note: The index above is an aggregate of indices that measure the following factors: educational attainment, communication and transportation infrastructure, governance, and business and investment environment. The United States has been omitted; the U.S. index score is 10.
Source: World Bank 2009; authors' calculations.

the 10 years that follow until 2025 the predictions are an average of the model and the recorded growth rate during 1997–2007. By nudging the projections toward the trends of the pre-crisis decade— roughly the length of two complete business cycles—factors that affect growth in the medium term, such as political disruptions or natural resource windfalls, but are not incorporated in the long-term growth model can be partly accounted for. Beyond 2025, the projections are entirely model-driven.

2050—A new economic order
The weight of global economic activity is already shifting substantially from the G7 countries toward emerging economies in Asia and Latin America. Over the next 40 years, this trend is expected to accelerate (table 3.1).

As labor productivity in the developing countries increases relative to that in the developed countries, wages will increase and the price of nontradables

TABLE 3.1 AVERAGE ANNUAL GDP GROWTH

	PERCENT CHANGE (YEAR ON YEAR)			REAL GDP (2005 $)		
	PRECRISIS TREND (1997–2007)	CRISIS YEARS (2007–09)	PROJECTIONS (2009–50)	2009	2030	2050
ARGENTINA	2.6	2.0	4.1	223	527	1,267
AUSTRALIA	3.6	1.5	2.9	787	1,501	2,257
BRAZIL	2.8	2.2	4.1	1,011	2,440	6,020
CANADA	3.3	−1.0	2.6	1,171	2,083	3,154
CHINA	9.6	8.8	5.6	3,335	21,479	46,265
FRANCE	2.4	−1.0	2.1	2,203	3,323	4,528
GERMANY	1.6	−2.1	1.4	2,833	3,593	4,535
INDIA	7.0	6.3	5.9	1,065	5,328	15,384
INDONESIA	2.7	5.0	4.8	354	1,073	2,975
ITALY	1.5	−3.1	1.3	1,732	2,197	2580
JAPAN	1.1	−3.1	1.1	4,467	5,786	6,216
KOREA, REP.	4.3	0.6	2.5	945	2122	2,812
MEXICO	3.3	−3.1	4.3	866	2,397	5,709
RUSSIAN FEDERATION	5.7	−1.2	3.3	869	2,487	4,297
SAUDI ARABIA	3.2	1.7	4.8	348	896	2,419
SOUTH AFRICA	3.7	0.4	4.3	271	791	1,919
TURKEY	4.0	−2.9	4.4	509	1,437	3,536
UNITED KINGDOM	2.9	−1.9	2.1	2,320	3,597	4,997
UNITED STATES	3.0	−1.2	2.7	12,949	22,258	38,646

Source: IMF data; authors' projections.

relative to tradables will rise in developing countries, as predicted by the Balassa-Samuelson effect.[6] These changes, which imply an appreciation of real exchange rates in developing countries, will increase the importance of developing economies as export markets.

The total economy of the G20 is expected to grow at·an average annual rate of 3.5 percent, rising from $38.3 trillion in 2009 to $160.0 trillion in 2050 in real dollars (constant prices). More than 60 percent of this $121 trillion dollar expansion will come from six countries—Brazil, Russia, India, China, Indonesia, and Mexico (the Big Five+M)—to eclipse the G7. U.S. dollar GDP in these six economies will grow at an average of 6 percent a year; their share of G20 GDP

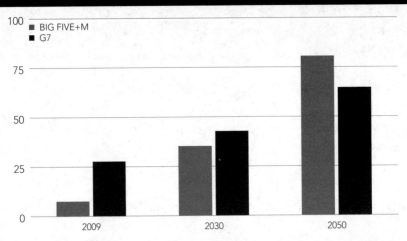

FIGURE 3.3 THE BIG FIVE+M WILL ECLIPSE THE G7
(GDP, REAL $, TRILLIONS)

- BIG FIVE+M
- G7

2009   2030   2050

Source: Authors' projections.

will rise from 19.6 percent in 2009 to 50.6 percent in 2050. By contrast, GDP in the G7 will grow less than 2.1 percent a year, and their share of G20 GDP will decline from 72.3 percent to 40.5 percent (figure 3.3).

In purchasing power parity (PPP), the shift is even more dramatic. Today developing countries claim only 41 percent of the G20's GDP in PPP terms; by 2050 their share will rise to more than 68 percent. Again, the Big Five+M economies will be responsible for most of this growth, with their share rising from 36 percent to 62 percent.

The new triad

China, India, and the United States will emerge as the world's three largest economies in 2050. Rapid annual growth of 5.6 percent and a strengthening currency—the renminbi's real exchange rate against the dollar is predicted to appreciate by more than 1 percent a year—will drive China's U.S. dollar GDP up from $3.3 trillion in 2009 to $46.3 trillion in 2050, 20 percent larger than that of the United States in real dollar terms and 90 percent larger in PPP terms. Of all G20 countries India is predicted to post the fastest growth—5.9 percent a year, and its rapidly growing population—to become the world's most populous nation in 2030—will push its U.S. dollar GDP to $15.4 trillion in 2050, more than 14 times its current level (figure 3.4). And its PPP GDP will be nearly 90 percent that of the United States.

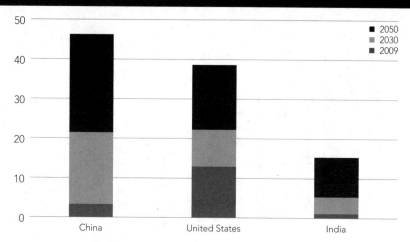

FIGURE 3.4 2050'S NEW TRIAD
(GDP, REAL $, TRILLIONS)

Source: Authors' projections.

Despite these dramatic increases in total GDP, U.S. per capita GDP will be nearly three times China's and more than eight times India's, complicating the U.S. role in the global economy. U.S. technological advantages will likely help it maintain its position as a leader of the international community, but China's and India's much lower per capita incomes, combined with their large size, may reinforce their authority as their conditions will be perceived as more representative of the vast majority of the world population.

A more balanced world

The economic balance of power within the rest of the G20 will tilt toward emerging markets, as slowing growth in high income countries—1.6 percent annually—is met with rapid expansion in the developing world—4.6 percent annually. But excluding China and India, emerging markets will not supplant Europe and Japan as economic powers, but they will add new authoritative voices to the international dialogue.

Real GDP in Brazil and Mexico is expected to increase by more than 4 percent a year, nearly matching the GDP of Japan, today's second largest economy, in 2050; Russia and Turkey are both expected to be larger than present-day China (figure 3.5).

Japan's influence in Asia will likely recede with China's rise and Indonesia's rapid expansion. Japan will grow by a sluggish 1.1 percent a year, the slowest of all G20 economies. Japan, Asia's most powerful nation in the twentieth century, will be pressed to develop ever closer economic ties with China, an economy

FIGURE 3.5 BRAZIL AND MEXICO CLOSE IN ON JAPAN
(GDP, REAL $, TRILLIONS)

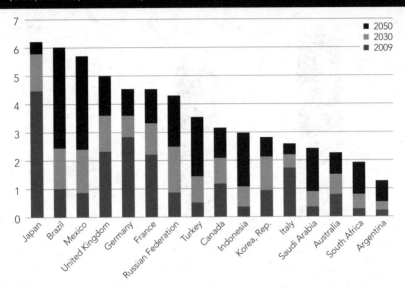

Source: Authors' projections.

that will be more than 7 times larger than Japan's in U.S. current dollar terms (market exchange rates) in 2050, and with India, which will be 2.5 times larger. Like Britain in past centuries, Japan will seek to promote a regional balance of power, implying continued close political and security ties with the United States.

The four largest countries in Europe are expected to grow by only 1.5 percent annually as their share of G20 GDP shrinks from 24 percent in 2009 to 10 percent in 2050. To retain their historical influence, European nations will likely need to collaborate and conduct their foreign policy increasingly under an EU banner. If the EU follows the 1.5 percent growth average of its four largest countries, real U.S. dollar GDP will increase from $14.1 trillion to $25.8 trillion in 2050, placing it among the world's three largest economies.

Russia, historically a great power, may become a political outlier under this scenario. The world's largest country, and enormously rich in natural resources, its population in 2050 will be down to 109 million from 140 million today. With China, India, and the United States, not only the world's three largest economies but also the world's three most populous, to its south and east, Russia may face mounting pressure to increase its economic and security ties with Europe if it is to maintain a voice in world affairs.

TABLE 3.2 AVERAGE ANNUAL GDP GROWTH

| | PERCENT CHANGE (YEAR ON YEAR) | | | | REAL GDP (2005 $) | |
	PRECRISIS TREND (1997–2007)	CRISIS YEARS (2007–09)	PROJECTIONS (2009–50)	2009	2030	2050
ETHIOPIA	5.7	9.5	6.5	28	109	366
GHANA	5.0	5.9	6.7	17	91	337
KENYA	3.8	2.1	5.4	30	98	287
NIGERIA	7.6	4.4	5.0	213	733	1,636

Note: Ghana's particularly rapid growth will be driven in part by the recent discovery of the Jubilee oil field off Ghana's coast.
Source: IMF data; authors' projections.

Can Africa break through?

The impressive advance in the G20 developing economies depicted by the baseline scenario conceals the plight of many of the poorest and less successful developing economies, which have been falling behind even as growth accelerated among a large part of the world's population. Because of macroeconomic and political instability, barriers of distance and transport, environmental degradation, inadequate capacity, and explicit policy choices not to integrate in global markets, these countries remain outside the mainstream.

Among the outliers are the Democratic Republic of Korea, Haiti, and Myanmar, but most are in Africa. Can they do better? The answer—according to our model—is yes. Applying the projection methodology to the four large countries in Sub-Saharan Africa—Ethiopia, Ghana, Kenya, and Nigeria—suggests that, in the absence of major conflicts, they could exhibit rapid growth over the next 40 years. Africa's rapidly increasing population will help drive growth in the near term, while large technological improvements can potentially sustain the expansion over coming decades, despite unfavorable (though improving) initial conditions in education, governance, and infrastructure.

The Africa 4 countries are projected to grow at an average of 5.5 percent a year from now until 2050. Relative to past decades' dismal performance, these growth rates represent a major acceleration, but they are not out of line with outcomes since the turn of the century (table 3.2).

With rapid growth and exchange rate appreciation, Nigeria could surpass the smallest G20 economy in 2005 U.S. dollars (figure 3.6). Nevertheless, in 2050, per capita income in these countries is expected to be only 13 percent of that in the G20 in U.S. dollars (figure 3.7).

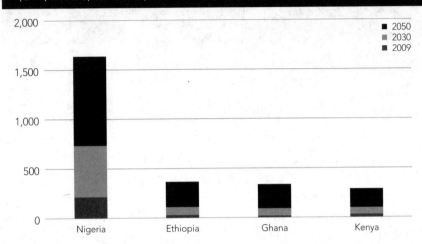

FIGURE 3.6 NIGERIA IN 2050 COULD SURPASS THE SMALLEST G20 COUNTRY TODAY
(GDP, REAL $, BILLIONS)

Source: Authors' projections.

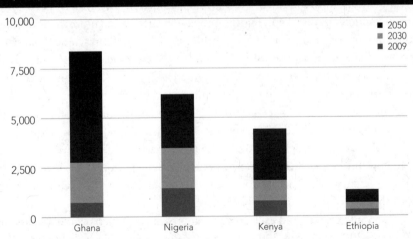

FIGURE 3.7 THE AFRICA 4'S PER CAPITA INCOME WILL BE LESS THAN HALF OF INDIA'S
(GDP, REAL $, BILLIONS)

Source: Authors' projections.

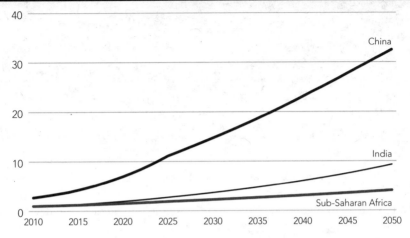

FIGURE 3.8 CHINA AND INDIA CAN BECOME EXPORT DESTINATIONS FOR AFRICA
(GDP, REAL $, TRILLIONS)

Note: The value for Sub-Saharan Africa is a weighted average of per capita GDP in Ethiopia, Ghana, Kenya, and Nigeria.
Source: Authors' projections.

Under this scenario the average per capita income in these countries will be less than half of India's and a fraction of China's, raising the possibility that African countries could become competitive with the Asian giants in labor-intensive manufactures, as well as destinations for outsourcing.

As incomes in China (and to some extent India) diverge from those in Africa, China and India could become major export destinations for Africa not only in raw materials but also in basic manufactures (figure 3.8). There is, of course, nothing automatic about this outcome, as the ability to compete in the international market for manufactures will require a big improvement in the quality and predictability of the business climate and efficient investments in education, which may or may not be forthcoming. The prospects for growth in Sub-Saharan Africa are discussed in detail in chapter 8.

The fall in extreme poverty and the rise of the global middle class

Not only will the economic landscape be dramatically changed by 2050, but the world will also be profoundly different in human terms. Over the next 40 years, millions, if not billions, of people around the world will be lifted out of the harshest forms of poverty (table 3.3). Accompanying this trend will be the emergence of a new global middle and rich class (GMR)—the segment of the

TABLE 3.3 PERCENTAGE OF POPULATION LIVING IN POVERTY

LIVING ON LESS THAN $1.25 A DAY	2005	2010	2020	2030	2050
CHINA	15.9	7.9	3.1	2.0	1.2
INDIA	41.6	34.5	10.4	4.1	2.5
INDONESIA	27.4	18.1	7.4	4.1	2.3
SUB-SAHARAN AFRICA	45.8	39.7	26.2	16.1	8.4
LIVING ON LESS THAN $2.00 A DAY	**2005**	**2010**	**2020**	**2030**	**2050**
CHINA	36.3	19.5	5.1	3.2	2.0
INDIA	75.6	64.1	40.5	19.6	4.0
INDONESIA	55.9	47.4	29.8	13.0	3.7
SUB-SAHARAN AFRICA	69.6	62.5	49.0	35.8	16.9

Source: World Bank data; authors' projections.

global population that can demand advanced goods and services—in developing countries.[7]

In 2005 the World Bank estimated that more than 1.3 billion people—more than a quarter of the world's population—lived in extreme poverty, consuming less than $1.25 a day in PPP terms. Nearly twice this number, or half the world's people, lived on less than $2.00 a day. By 2050 no country in the G20 will have more than 5 percent of their people in extreme poverty, though significant portions of society will still live on less than $2.00 a day. (See annex for the methodology behind these poverty projections.)

Poverty rates are expected to come down significantly in Indonesia, Brazil, Mexico, and Turkey, but growth in China and India—nations home to 48 percent of the world's people living on less than $1.25 a day in 2005—will be the driving force behind this shift. Over the past 25 years, more than 600 million people have emerged from poverty in China. (Excluding China, global poverty has actually increased since 1981.) From 2005 to 2050 China and India will lift 600 million more people from the most extreme forms of poverty.[8]

Economic growth will also bring relief to millions of poor in Sub-Saharan Africa, but the region will remain the most impoverished. The benefits of the area's strong growth will be diffused across a rapidly expanding population, holding per capita incomes down in a region where just under half the population consumed less than $1.25 a day in 2005. Although the next 40 years will bring marked improvements, poverty will remain relatively high: in 2050, 8.4 percent of the population will still live on less than $1.25 a day, and 16.9 percent, on less than $2.00 a day.

These trends certainly offer hope. They do not imply, however, that poverty will no longer be a serious economic and humanitarian concern. The higher poverty line—$2.00 a day—will satisfy basic human needs, but it will mean a miserable existence. Nor is absolute income the only measure of the human condition. Both within and across countries, enormous relative income disparities will severely limit the poorest segments' political voice, social integration, and access to economic markets and opportunities.

Many of those lifted from poverty will join the new GMR class. Estimates, discussed in further detail in chapter 4, show that the GMR population in the developing G20 economies is likely to grow from 739 million in 2009 to 1.9 billion in 2050 (table 3.4).[9] Today, 24 percent of the global GMR population resides in developing countries; by 2050, about 60 percent will.[10] But the purchasing power of the GMR in advanced countries will be about 60 percent bigger than that of the GMR in developing G20 countries.

TABLE 3.4 SIZE OF THE GLOBAL MIDDLE AND RICH (GMR) CLASS
(POPULATION, MILLIONS)

	2009	2020	2030	2050
ADVANCED ECONOMIES	1,193	1,225	1,254	1,284
DEVELOPING G20 ECONOMIES	368	740	1,295	1,958
CHINA	118	375	779	1,092
BRAZIL	66	80	110	170
RUSSIAN FEDERATION	57	82	93	98
INDIA	37	69	121	273
MEXICO	37	51	72	111
TURKEY	17	29	46	70
INDONESIA	11	20	33	81
ARGENTINA	17	21	28	40
SOUTH AFRICA	9	13	14	23
LARGE AFRICAN ECONOMIES				
NIGERIA	4	6	10	22
KENYA	4	7	10	26
ETHIOPIA	3	6	11	34
GHANA	1	3	5	18

Source: World Bank data; authors' projections.

Trade and financial integration

Assuming that the world does not retreat into protectionism, the role of developing countries as exporters and importers will increase significantly over the next 40 years, reflecting their high growth rate and the rise of their middle classes. Their share of global exports will more than double. In addition, their dependence on developed country markets is projected to weaken as trade among developing countries overwhelms that among advanced economies. Patterns of comparative advantage will shift as well, as incomes, wages, capital-labor ratios, and education levels increase faster in successful developing countries than in industrial ones. These trends are discussed in further detail in chapter 4.

Financial integration will increase, and developing countries' share of capital flows will rise along with their participation in trade. Robust global growth, a favorable financing environment, and domestic policy improvements led to a surge in private capital flows to developing countries before the financial crisis. Going forward, continuing policy improvements and rapidly expanding trade (which will attract FDI, as well as other flows thanks to improved creditworthiness) are likely to continue the upward trend in private capital flows. Even assuming that FDI grows in line with GDP, and not faster as in recent history, the share of developing countries in the world's net FDI inflows will jump from 25 percent in 2005–07 to 66 percent in 2050. Many low-income countries will cross the ratings threshold to attract private portfolio flows and will see increased bank lending. Developing countries will also become larger investors, in both each other and industrial countries.

The greater financial integration of developing countries will present new opportunities. In Africa, for example, the prospects for aid flows have become even less certain with the advent of the crisis, but the potential for private capital inflows remains relatively untapped.

But greater financial integration will also present new challenges for macroeconomic and regulatory policies. These policies need to ensure that capital is used effectively and does not simply respond to artificial distortions or market euphoria—and that safeguards are built against sudden stops and reversals in capital flows (see chapter 5).

Prospects for relative prices

Commodity prices in the coming years will likely continue their gradual downward path relative to manufactured goods (the price surge in the mid-2000s notwithstanding). A broad array of empirical studies shows that primary commodity prices have declined historically relative to manufactured goods, with estimates of long-term decline ranging from –0.6 to –2.3 percent a year.[11]

The reasons for the secular decline have also been widely explored—and include the low demand elasticity for primary commodities relative to manufactures and services, the growth of substitutes, and the rapid technological advances that have reduced the cost of growing or extracting these materials.

In addition, the price of basic manufactured goods may be expected to continue to decline relative to knowledge-intensive goods and services. The declining price of manufactured goods relative to services is a well-documented feature of economic development. From 1950 to 2000 manufacturing productivity in the United States increased at an average annual rate of 2.8 percent, compared with 2.0 percent in nonfarm business overall. From 1990 to 2002 manufacturing productivity's relative pace was even more impressive: 3.9 percent a year, compared with 2.3 percent. This strong productivity differential lowers the cost of producing manufactured goods, and thus their price, relative to services.

At first glance, the downward trend in primary commodity prices appears to be threatened by massive increases in demand from the acceleration of growth in large developing countries, including China and India, that are net importers of energy, materials, and many agricultural commodities. But consider three offsetting effects. First, technological advances in both the production and use of commodities in a broad range of developing countries will increase supply and reduce demand. For example, the Food and Agriculture Organization (FAO) and the Organisation for Economic Co-operation and Development (OECD) argue that agricultural productivity is likely to increase in the medium term and note that, in Central and Eastern Europe as well as in Sub-Saharan Africa, it can rise significantly if existing technologies are implemented.

Second, investments in commodities also will rise. This is clearest in agriculture, where the potential for bringing more land under cultivation is huge. Currently, 1.4 billion hectares are used for crops. Recent FAO and OECD estimates show that an additional 1.6 billion hectares could be cultivated. Found in Africa and Latin America, the majority of this land is highly suitable for rainfed crop production, though it requires large infrastructure investments and institutional improvements before it can be put to effective use. And as new land is cultivated, it may take longer for yields there to catch up. Moreover, investment in the production of raw materials (including that financed directly by China and India) is also likely to rise, increasing supply.[12]

Third, global population growth is expected to slow, even as absolute numbers rise, which will directly translate into reduced demand growth for commodities. And while a rise in per capita income will likely increase demand for other products, after a certain threshold income is reached, it should have no significant impact on demand for agricultural products.

Fundamentally, GDP growth has consistently outpaced the demand for commodities. While this downward trend in commodity intensity is not immutable, a major external change would be required to break it—nor is it clear what that change might be.[13] Some of the more disruptive technologies on the horizon, including biotechnology and miniaturization, could both reduce the demand for some commodities and greatly increase their supply. The drive to reduce carbon emissions could also begin to make a dent in energy use. But oil may be an important exception to the downward trend in commodity prices, as the exhaustion of easily accessible reserves places a floor on oil prices. And prospects for prices depend critically on the severity of the effects of climate change, which could cause shortages of food and land in some areas of the world.

Despite this long-term downward trend, commodity prices are likely to remain highly volatile, and price spikes such as the ones in the mid-2000s may recur, as they have today. The reasons for high volatility of commodity prices have also been widely explored. They include low short-term income and price elasticities of demand and supply, long lead times before investment and supply respond to changing demand conditions, weather factors in agricultural commodities, and policy-induced distortions that impede the orderly adjustment of markets. Newer sources of instability may include more variable weather due to climate change and increased use of commodities and commodity derivatives for speculation.

Increasing migration

Migration is already significant, with more than 200 million people residing outside their countries of birth today. Migration pressures have been reduced drastically by the Great Recession and its effects on labor demand. But pressures for increased migration are likely to intensify in the coming years. Demographic trends, wide and in some cases widening gaps in economic opportunity, spreading networks of migrants, more intensive communication, and greater ability to afford the cost of migration will increase the mobility of workers. In the longer term, the effects of climate change may greatly increase the need to migrate out of the worst affected regions in developing countries (for a discussion of the prospects for increased migration, see chapter 6).

Risks

Even though the last 40 years have been relatively free of shocks compared with the previous 40 (which saw the Great Depression and World War II), they nevertheless included at least three major financial crises (the Debt Crisis of the 1980s, the Asian Financial Crisis, and the Great Recession of 2007–09), the fall of the Berlin Wall, and the emergence of China.

At least four classes of risk could introduce major discontinuities that would undermine these projections, each addressed briefly here.

Climate change

While natural resources are by and large not a constraint, climate change could severely reduce the prospects for global growth. Climate change is already occurring, but the timing and extent of its most severe effects remain very difficult to pinpoint. It is assumed in the baseline that the positive growth factors discussed above will outshine any negative effects. But even a modest rise in temperatures of 2 degrees Celsius could sharply reduce welfare, particularly in developing countries. And without concerted efforts to control carbon emissions, much greater increases are likely, with particularly catastrophic implications for many developing regions (see chapter 7 for a discussion of the potential impact of climate change).

Climate change may drive large migration flows from the most affected regions (South Asia, East Asia, and Africa) to the industrial countries, which are best able to cope with its effects and could even benefit from modest rises in temperatures.[14]

It could also exacerbate protectionist measures. Border adjustments to compensate firms for tighter emission standards have been incorporated in draft legislation in the U.S. Congress, and are explicitly supported by at least one prominent European leader. They are perceived as profoundly inequitable by China, India, and many other developing countries whose emissions are a fraction of those in industrial countries. The legitimacy of these border adjustments under WTO rules is questionable, and if enacted, they risk a large deterioration in international trade relations with unpredictable consequences.

Geopolitical breakdown

The next 40 years may see one of the greatest shifts in economic and military power in history. China's influence will rise, compete with, and perhaps overtake that of the United States. And major power shifts will occur within regions, with China and India relative to Japan, the great European powers continuing on a path of relative decline, and Brazil and possibly Mexico becoming more ascendant in Latin America.

History documents that these transitions have rarely been easy and that there is a high likelihood of hitting any number of flashpoints along the way. Even if major disputes over territory or regional influence are resolved peacefully, economic relations could be undermined by trade disputes, differences over dealing with climate change, and many other issues related to the global commons, and major economic crises.

In short, globalization does not exist in a vacuum. Maintaining the cohesion of the international community is crucial to its continuation.

Financial crisis and depression

The world economy's near demise at the turn of 2009 should remove any sense of complacency about the dangers lurking in international financial integration when adequate regulatory mechanisms and sound macroeconomic policies are lacking even in the world's most advanced economies.

Yet the ability of countries to turn the many lessons of the Great Recession into effective reforms remains unproven and even highly suspect. The reasons are multiple—they include the financial industry's resistance to reform, ideological differences about the appropriate role of regulation and market discipline, the difficulties of internationally coordinated action, the complexity of modern financial markets, and the weak capacities of both domestic and international regulators. Furthermore, the political challenges of dealing with macroeconomic imbalances of various kinds are formidable.

Arguably, the world economy emerges from the crisis a more, and not less, dangerous place, reflecting large public debts, difficult-to-reverse financial sector support policies, large overhangs of liquidity, and greatly increased moral hazard, particularly in financial institutions deemed "too big to fail." These vulnerabilities will not soon disappear—indeed, they may become greater with the passage of time as the financial industry's appetite for risk returns once memories of the disaster begin to fade.

Protectionism

A relapse into protectionism presents perhaps the single most important risk to this forecast, since the growth projections are grounded in assumptions about technological catch-up and increased efficiency that depend on open international markets.

Given the densely interwoven fabric of today's global economy, and the vast set of rules under WTO and regional agreements, including international legal redress procedures, a large relapse into protectionism is likely only in the presence of the other risk factors discussed above. International markets could become closed in the event of a deterioration of great power relations to the point of open military or economic hostilities; an economic depression and rise in mass unemployment (as narrowly avoided in 2009); or profound divisions over climate change and the attempt to resort to trade sanctions as an enforcement mechanism. The risks to open trade would be compounded if more than one of these conditions occurred together: in general the risks of geopolitical breakdown, financial crisis, and protectionism tend to rise in the presence of the others.

An alternative, lower-growth scenario

If any or all of the above risks materialize, growth may be significantly slower than estimated. Under a lower-growth scenario, growth in industrial countries is expected to be 0.3 to 0.5 percentage points lower than in the base case, 1 to 1.3 points lower in China and India, 0.5 to 0.8 points lower in other emerging economies, and 1.5 point lower in non-G20 economies in Sub-Saharan Africa. Under those assumptions, the G20 GDP will reach $109 trillion in 2050, 32 percent less than its baseline GDP. China and India will emerge as two of the three largest economies in the world, but both will remain smaller than the United States in dollar terms; But China's PPP GDP will still surpass that of the United States to become the largest in the world. The relative weight of emerging markets in the global economy will still rise, with an average annual growth rate of 4.5 percent for the "Big Five+M", compared with 1.6 percent growth in the G7. (For complete results, see annex table A1.)

Slower global growth will imply much slower progress on poverty reduction, particularly in Sub-Saharan Africa. Relative to the baseline, extreme poverty (less than $1.25 a day) in 2050 is only moderately higher in India and Indonesia, but the 2050 poverty rate in the five Sub-Saharan countries including South Africa analyzed here will be near 15 percent—or 95 million people—compared with 8 percent in the baseline. By comparison, 148 million people lived in extreme poverty in these five countries in 2005. The headcount for $2.00 a day poverty can be expected to be 32 percent in Sub-Saharan Africa, holding a total of 205 million people below the poverty line, only a small reduction from the 225 million in 2005.

Slower growth would also have a modest impact on the growth of the global middle and rich class (GMR) in developing countries. The GMR class in developing G20 countries would be about 15 percent lower in 2030 and 2050 than under the baseline projections. In China and India it could be 20 percent and 30 percent lower, respectively, in 2030.

The weight of developing countries in world trade will, however, still rise sharply. The share of developing countries in world exports will be about 61 percent, 8 percentage points less than their share under baseline projections. Export shares of advanced countries will be slightly higher under this low-growth scenario but not large enough to displace China as the world's leading exporter. China's exports will account for about 20 percent of world exports, followed by the EU's 17 percent.

Assuming no efforts to reduce emissions, carbon concentrations under this low-growth scenario would be less than that expected under the baseline growth rates, making the mitigation of climate change less daunting. But slower growth could also reduce the space for necessary investments and make other trade-offs more difficult. Upholding the commitments put forth at Copenhagen would require a smaller reduction in emissions-to-GDP ratios, but the cost of these reductions (relative to GDP) could be even greater.

Conclusion

This chapter has argued that the world economy is undergoing a profound transformation, reflecting the acceleration of growth in developing countries, home to the vast majority of the world's population, and their increased integration into global markets. Although many countries have been left behind, large opportunities for greater efficiency have been exploited in recent years with the surges in international flows of trade, capital, labor, and technology. But the potential gains to come are much larger, with productivity and living standards in developing countries still a fraction of those in advanced countries, which are innovating at a rapid rate.

These opportunities could open new avenues for development in both the richest countries, which will find they can address vast new markets for their advanced products, and the poorest, which may find that the climb up the technological ladder through manufactures exports is possible as the giant economies of Asia migrate to more sophisticated products and present large new markets for both commodity and basic manufactures exports.

These favorable prospects are, however, far from a forgone conclusion, and no country can expect to capture the prize automatically. Sound domestic policies that favor integration into global markets—including macroeconomic stability, a sound business climate, and appropriate investments in education—will be necessary for success. But even more will be needed. The community of nations will need to work together to continue to build the international integration frameworks essential for trade, capital, people, and technology to continue to flow. They will jointly need to build stronger safeguards against massive financial crises. They will need to find a way to avert environmental catastrophe in the form of uncontrolled climate change. Above all, they will have to manage the historic power shift toward new actors from the developing world without resorting to war or protectionism.

Notes

1. World Bank 1997.
2. Wilson and Purushothaman 2003.

3. Hawksworth 2006.
4. World Bank 2008, p. 45.
5. Armington and Dadush 1993.
6. Balassa 1964; Samuelson 1964.
7. All individuals with a per capita income above $4,000 in 2005 PPP terms are considered members of the global middle and rich class (GMR). This follows the World Bank definition, which defines the middle class as those with per capita incomes between $4,000 and $17,000. Those with incomes above $17,000 are considered members of the rich class.
8. Poverty models are based on studies by Ravillion (2001), Ahluwalia and others (1978), and Anand and Kanbur (1991). Poverty data are from World Bank (2009) and the United Nations University World Institute for Development Economics Research (2008).
9. These include China, India, Russia, Brazil, Mexico, Argentina, Indonesia, Turkey, and South Africa. Although Saudi Arabia is also a developing G20 economy, it was not included in these calculations because data were not available for its distribution of income.
10. This is the ratio of the GMR population in developing G20 countries to the total that includes the GMR in all advanced countries. It is assumed that more than 95 percent of the population in advanced countries is in the GMR class.
11. Grynberg and Newton 2007.
12. OECD/FAO 2009.
13. World Bank 2008.
14. The Intergovernmental Panel on Climate Change estimates that in Europe, Australia, and New Zealand, growing seasons will lengthen, frost-risk will fall, and new crops will become viable (Parry and others 2007).

References

Ahluwalia, Montek S., Nicholas G. Carter, and Hollis B. Chenery, "Growth and Poverty in Developing Countries." *Journal of Development Economics*, 6 (1978): 299–341.

Anand, Sudhir, and Ravi Kanbur, "International Poverty Projections." Policy Research Working Paper Series 617. World Bank, Washington, DC, 1991.

Armington, Paul, and Uri Dadush, "The Fourth Pole." *International Economic Insights*, May/June 1993, 2–4.

Balassa, Bela. "The Purchasing Power Parity Doctrine: A Reappraisal," *Journal of Political Economy*, 72 (1964): 584–96, http://burbuja.udesa.edu.ar/materias/kawa/ecintmon/balassa64.pdf.

Grynberg, Roman, and Samantha Newton, eds. *Commodity Prices and Development.* New York: Oxford University Press, 2007.

Hawksworth, John. *The World in 2050.* London, PricewaterhouseCoopers, 2006.

OECD/FAO (Organisation for Economic Co-operation and Development/Food and Agriculture Organization). "OECD-FAO Agricultural Outlook 2009–2018." Paris, 2009.

Parry, Martin, Osvaldo Canziani, Jean Palutikof, Paul van der Linden, and Clair Hanson, eds. *Climate Change 2007: Impacts, Adaptation and Vulnerability.* Cambridge, UK: Cambridge University Press, 2007.

Samuelson, Paul. "Theoretical Notes on Trade Problems." *Review of Economics and Statistics*, 46 (1964): 145–54, www.clarku.edu/faculty/mcallan/Econ308/Readings/samuelson.pdf.

United Nations University World Institute for Development Economics Research. World Income Inequality Database, Version 2.0c. 2008, www.wider.unu.edu/research/Database/en_GB/database/.

Wilson, Dominic, and Roopa Purushothaman. "Dreaming with BRICs: The Path to 2050." Global Economics Paper 99. Goldman Sachs, New York, 2003.

World Bank. *Global Economic Prospects and the Developing Countries.* Washington, DC, 1997.

———. Global Economic Prospects: Technology Diffusion in the Developing World. Washington, DC, 2008, http://siteresources.worldbank.org/INTGEP2008/Resources/complete-report.pdf.

———. *World Development Indicators 2009.* Washington, DC, 2009.

CHAPTER 4

TRADE

THE GREAT DEVELOPMENT ARENA

Trade will continue to outpace the growth of output by a wide margin, and the rise of developing countries will transform it. Today's 30/70 share in world trade of developing and industrial countries is projected to switch to 70/30 in 2050. China will be at the center of global trade flows, and developing countries will dominate trade in manufactures, and be the largest destination for FDI and perhaps its most important source.

Trade is the arena of globalization where international collaboration and rules are best established. But the demands on an open and rules-based trading system are bound to increase, and the sharp rise in competition from all sources could accentuate protectionist pressures.

The world will need an effective and vibrant WTO to govern the increased trade flows, but the institution risks becoming marginalized due to the proliferation of regional arrangements and the inability to strike multilateral deals among more than 150 countries.

To remain relevant the WTO will need to promote agreements among a critical mass of players.

The rising economic weight of developing countries and their integration into global markets are transforming world trade. In the last 12 months China became the world's largest exporter, manufacturer, energy consumer, and car market—on a path to becoming the dominant trading partner of most countries within a generation. And Brazil, India, Indonesia, and Mexico will likely join it in the ranks of the 10 largest trading nations.

By 2050 developing countries are projected to account for nearly 70 percent of world trade in goods—more than twice their share today—while the shares of Europe and the United States will be cut in half. Unlike the second half of the twentieth century, when a handful of rich countries dominated, the world trading system will increasingly be governed by giant developing and developed economies.

At least four important structural changes underlie the rapid growth of developing countries' trade. They are very rapidly increasing their participation in trade in manufactures. They are becoming home to the global middle class. They are attracting a rising share of FDI and becoming integrated into global value-added chains. And they are taking a leading role in forging new trade policies, especially through regional and bilateral trade agreements.

All this will create great new trading opportunities—and major governance challenges, especially for the WTO, the ultimate regulator of world trade. Of the four channels of globalization, trade is where international collaboration has made the most progress. But with the U.S. and EU shares of world trade rapidly declining, who will lead global trade negotiations? Will the onslaught of lower wage competition from giant developing economies be accommodated, or will protectionist pressures escalate? How will the WTO's cumbersome consensus process deal with the complex and fast-changing nature of modern trade relations?

This chapter describes the main trends and prospects for international trade as developing countries rise, reviews the policy challenges raised for the world trading system, and proposes ideas for its reform. It begins by briefly reviewing the history of developing country participation in world trade.

Developing country trade in history

Today's developing economies dominated some major trade routes dating at least to Roman times [1] The Silk Road, a direct link between two of the major civilizations at that time—China in the east and the Roman Empire in the west—was one of the most important trade routes. Silks, gemstones, perfumes, and other luxury goods (high value relative to weight) were carried along this route from 300 BC onward. China and India were also engaged in overland trade with Eastern Europe and the Islamic world. The caravan routes of the Middle East and the shipping lanes of the Mediterranean were also among those dominating international trade until about 1500.

Following the epic fifteenth century European voyages of discovery across the Atlantic and Pacific, culminating in the rounding of the Cape of Good Hope and the circumnavigation of the globe, new trade routes, especially those across the Atlantic, began to overshadow the established Europe-Mediterranean-Asian connections. Trade accelerated, if at a rate that pales in comparison to the more recent, extraordinary expansion. From 1500 to 1815 the volume of intercontinental trade grew by about 1 percent annually—faster than the 0.25 percent annual growth of world population over that period (figure 4.1).[2] But that was half the rate from 1870 to 1915, and a snail's pace compared with more recent rates, like the near 7 percent over the 35 years preceding the Great Recession.

Just as the long-term trend of trade volumes since 1500 was one of marked acceleration, so the range of goods traded between continents widened steadily. Trade in bulkier goods, made possible by declining transport costs due to improvements in navigation and sail technology, became much more important. Originally, developing economies exported only high-value spices and silk. As the period progressed, trade in bulkier commodities, such as sugar and raw cotton, became possible and profitable. Reflecting this, India's exports of cotton textiles accounted for more than half of the English East India Company's exports to Europe in the 1750s.

New commodities from the Americas also grew. While silver was the most important European import from the New World in the sixteenth century,[3] sugar accounted for roughly 50 percent of Europe's imports from America in the eighteenth.[4,5] The supply of primary commodities from the New World,

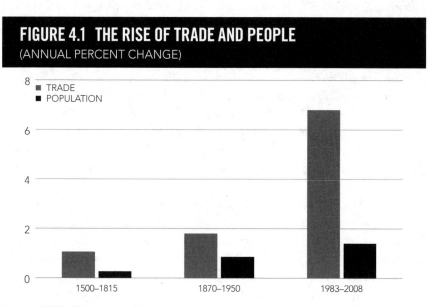

FIGURE 4.1 THE RISE OF TRADE AND PEOPLE
(ANNUAL PERCENT CHANGE)

Source: OECD data; Maddison 2007.

especially cotton, proved essential as the Industrial Revolution took hold in Britain and continental Europe. As its exports of textiles and other manufactures grew, Britain became more active in international trade; the share of exports in its national income rose from 8.4 percent in 1700 to 15.7 percent in 1801.[6]

In response to the cotton, sugar, and tobacco boom, the slave trade surged in the eighteenth century; two-thirds of the 9–10 million persons trafficked over the history of the slave trade were transferred in that century.[7] Meanwhile, Europe used the resale of American gold and silver and the proceeds from the slave trade to help pay for its imports of spices, Chinese porcelain, silk, tea, and cotton textiles.

Although the advanced countries of Europe exported more manufactures as the nineteenth century progressed, the exports of developing economies in Asia, Latin America, and Africa remained overwhelmingly primary products. The revolutions in canals, steamships, and railways in the nineteenth century increased the expansion of world trade—at around 3.5 percent annually between the 1820s and the end of the century. But their main effect was to enable developing countries to export an even broader range of bulk commodities, such as wheat, iron, and other minerals.

Developing countries also were important as export markets, with Asia absorbing nearly 40 percent of world silver production between 1600 and 1800.[8] Around 1880 developing economies in Asia, Latin America, Africa, and Oceania imported about 50 percent of the world's manufactures, while they exported nearly 40 percent of primary commodities.

It wasn't until the twentieth century that developing country trade in manufactures began its rise. As the demand for manufactures grew faster than that for commodities, and the price of commodities fell relative to manufactures, the share of primary commodities in world merchandise trade fell sharply, from about 63 percent in 1913 to 18 percent at the end of the twentieth century.[9] At the same time, developing countries absorbed technologies from the advanced countries, whose wages rose steadily. Eventually, many developing economies in Asia and parts of Latin America began to export labor-intensive manufactured goods.

The last few decades have also seen a substantial increase in global trade in services, which rose from 7 percent of world GDP in 1975 to 12 percent today. The developing country share of global service exports reached 27 percent in 2008, up from 24 percent in 2000. About two-thirds of their exports of commercial services come from developing Asia.

The composition of global trade in services has also changed—with transportation and travel services growing, and the share of developing economies in those sectors also rising. From 2000 to 2008 developing countries gained 5 percentage points of world share in transportation and travel services, reaching 30 percent in the former and 34 percent in the latter. The last 10 years have also seen a surge in the remote provision of services from developing countries, in areas ranging from call centers, to such back-office functions as accounting and order processing, to such high-value-added services as software development.

Developing economies have held a significant share of world exports for more than a century.[10] According to Maddison their share hovered near 20 percent from 1870 to 1990. Though it reached as high as 30 percent in the wake of World War II, it fell back to 20 percent in 1990. Since then, however, developing countries have increased their share by more than half.

World trade today

Developing countries have contributed much to the acceleration of world trade since the 1980s. The enormous increase in their relative weight over the last 10 years (from 19.5 percent of world merchandise exports in 1996 to 30 percent in 2006)[11] reflects not only China's meteoric rise as an exporter, but also surging oil prices and rapid export growth in regions that have only recently become integrated in global trade: Eastern Europe and Central Asia. By contrast, export growth in some countries still lags behind. India's share of global merchandise exports, for example, remained little more than 1 percent in 2006, though its share in commercial service exports advanced from 0.6 percent to 2.5 percent over the same period (figure 4.2).

As oil prices rose, oil exporters also experienced large increases in their shares of world exports. MENA's share went from 1.4 percent to 4.5 percent, Sub-Saharan Africa's from 0.7 percent to 1.6 percent. Having transitioned into market economies, the Eastern European and Central Asian countries also saw large increases in export shares, matched by even larger increases in imports and rising current account deficits.

In contrast, the export share of most industrial countries fell, with the U.S. share falling from 13.9 percent to 9.5 percent. Japan's decline was particularly stark: from 8.6 percent in 1996—significantly more than the total share of Brazil, China, India, and Russia—to 5.4 percent in 2006, less than China's share alone (see figure 4.2).

The importance of developing countries as an export market has grown as well, due to rising incomes and populations, which have made foreign exchange more available to those in developing countries and have enabled them to purchase the quality and diversity available in the global marketplace. The EU's exports to China more than quadrupled from 1996 to 2006, while its exports to

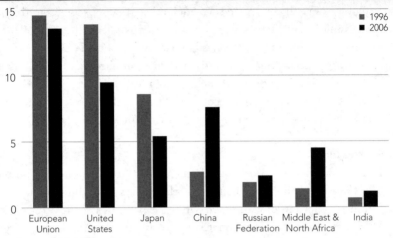

FIGURE 4.2 EXPORT SHARES FALL FOR THE DEVELOPED, CLIMB FOR THE DEVELOPING
(PERCENT OF WORLD MERCHANDISE EXPORTS)

Note: European Union is extra-trade.
Source: UN Comtrade database.

Central Asia, Eastern Europe, Russia, and Sub-Saharan Africa more than tripled. But over the decade, its exports to Japan were unchanged at about 2 percent of the total, while exports to other industrial countries fell from 9 percent to 7 percent. The United States also increased its exports to developing countries—from 31 percent of its total exports in 1996 to 38 percent in 2006.

The Great Recession reduced global trade by 11 percent in 2009, and despite an impressive rebound, trade only recently recovered to its precrisis peak and remains 10–15 percent below its 20-year trend path. Even so, developing countries' share in world trade continued to rise through the crisis. For example, China overtook Germany as the leading global exporter, its share of world exports having reached 10 percent in 2009, up from 7.6 percent three years before.

Four current trends
Four mutually reinforcing trends help explain the growth of developing countries' trade and characterize the ongoing transformation of world trade today. The first trend—toward policy liberalization—underpins the other three, reflecting in part structural changes associated with the development process. The diversification of developing country exports into a wide range of manufacturers greatly increases the potential size of their markets. The emergence of a large middle and rich

class in developing countries makes them more important customers. And greater integration through financial markets and foreign direct investment facilitates and stimulates trade, including trade in components and intracompany trade.[12]

Liberalization

The fundamental changes in developing economies' role in trade over the past quarter century have been associated with global reductions in trade barriers. Since the end of the 1980s advanced economies have cut their trade-weighted, average most-favored-nation tariff rate in half, from 6 percent to 3 percent, while developing countries have cut theirs from 19 percent to 7 percent. The larger absolute decline in tariffs from a higher level undertaken by developing countries is likely to have had a much greater welfare benefit than the larger percentage decrease from a lower base in advanced countries.[13]

Multilateral agreements—the General Agreement on Tariffs and Trade (GATT) negotiations and the formation of the WTO—were instrumental to past trade liberalization and set the stage for more recent unilateral (autonomous policy action), regional, and plurilateral liberalization. The GATT rounds reduced both applied and bound tariffs in advanced countries and bound tariffs in developing economies (which tended to reduce actual tariffs unilaterally to levels well below their bound tariffs). The Uruguay Round, the last general multilateral agreement of the eight rounds of multilateral liberalization, yielded cuts of about 40 percent in bound tariffs on industrial products. This agreement made cuts from much lower initial levels—an average of 6.3 percent—to 3.8 percent and involved 123 member countries, standing in stark contrast with the first round, which involved 23 members and resulted in cuts in bound tariffs of 26 percent from very high levels.[14]

While tariffs in advanced countries had been reduced substantially in previous rounds, the Uruguay Round established significant tariff commitments on the part of developing countries. Developing countries as a whole agreed to upper limits—or "bindings"—for 72 percent of their tariff line items, up from 22 percent before the Uruguay Round. And sectors previously considered too sensitive, such as agriculture, textiles, and apparel, were brought under the multilateral framework. New areas—notably trade-related intellectual property rights and services—were also brought into the system.

Progress on multilateral disciplines in these sectors since the Round has been excruciatingly slow, however, leading many to view the Uruguay Round as a disappointment. The Doha Round has been an even clearer case of nondelivery. In fact, no significant new liberalization of trade in goods, or reductions in bound tariffs, has come from multilateral negotiations since 1995, when the

Uruguay Round was concluded and the WTO was created. Companies appear to be increasingly disengaged from the WTO processes.

Lack of progress in the Doha Round is partly attributed to agriculture, and agreement on agricultural policy is seen as critical to breaking the deadlock. Previous negotiations failed to deliver significant reforms in this sector, and it remains one of the most highly protected sectors in international trade, with high import tariffs, export subsidies, and quotas in advanced economies. Agricultural tariffs by high-income countries are about five times higher than tariffs on merchandise products, and eight times higher than for manufactured goods (excluding textiles and apparel).[15] In addition, direct subsidies to farmers in OECD economies in the form of producer support amounted to $250 billion on average in 2002–04.[16] The high cost of this protection for developing economies, where agriculture accounts for a much higher share of output, exports, and employment than in high-income economies, has made agricultural market access a critical issue in the Doha talks.

But negotiations have yet to make satisfactory progress on the goals of reducing trade-distorting domestic subsidies, eliminating export subsidies, and substantially increasing market access to agricultural products. Unless high-income economies increase market access to agricultural products, developing economies seem unwilling to progress with negotiations on other areas, such as market access to services, of interest for high-income economies.

Nonetheless, the WTO has been pivotal in securing trade since it was established in 1995. Its influence is clearest in the accession of China and other countries and in its settlement of disputes. In addition, economically significant agreements in telecommunications and financial services, under the General Agreement on Trade in Services (GATS), have been achieved, and the Aid for Trade initiative has become a significant vehicle in several development agencies.

Despite the stall at the WTO, world trade continues to advance at unprecedented rates. Over the last 25 years it has grown about 5 percentage points faster than has world population, compared with about 1 percentage point faster from 1870 to 1950. While many factors help account for this, including transport innovations, communication technologies, and economic growth, liberalization was clearly instrumental.

Various studies confirm the significance of trade liberalization in boosting global trade. According to Baier and Bergstrand, 25 percent of world trade growth between 1960 and 1990 can be attributed to trade liberalization.[17] Adler and Hufbauer attributed a similar share (25 percent) of U.S. merchandise trade growth since 1980 to trade liberalization, with unilateral trade liberalization twice as important as the multilateral.[18]

Around the world, autonomous policy changes have accounted for the lion's share of tariff liberalization in recent decades. Most of the comprehensive trade reforms in large countries (Argentina, Brazil, and China in the early 1990s, and more recently, India) were primarily unilateral. Since the mid-1980s more than 60 developing countries have unilaterally lowered barriers to imports. Unilateral reforms accounted for two-thirds of the 21 percentage point cut in average weighted tariffs of all developing countries between 1983 and 2003.[19] A similar study showed that only 25 percent of the reductions of applied tariffs on trade in goods since 1995 is attributable to the implementation of the Uruguay Round, 10 percent to regional agreements (figure 4.3).

To be sure, an American exporter to Chile may not feel that its business is quite as secure as if it were selling inside the United States, and a U.S.-Chile free trade agreement, or Chilean commitments under the WTO, would make it more secure. But these are differences of degree, and they depend on the rule of law in Chile and how it differs from the United States. An exporter from Russia, which scores low on the rule of law and remains outside the WTO, may feel that exporting to the United States or Chile is as safe as selling at home in Russia, even without any trade agreements. Nor is protection under multilateral agreements—which include safeguards and provisions for countervailing duties and antidumping, but where redress under dispute settlement can only be sought cumbersomely through nations—perfectly certain.

FIGURE 4.3 UNILATERAL REFORMS ACCOUNTED FOR TWO-THIRDS OF THE 21 PERCENT AVERAGE CUT IN DEVELOPING COUNTRY TARIFFS
(PERCENT OF TOTAL TARIFF REDUCTION BY TYPE OF LIBERALIZATION, 1983–2003)

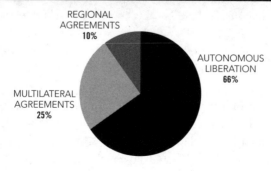

REGIONAL AGREEMENTS
10%

AUTONOMOUS LIBERATION
66%

MULTILATERAL AGREEMENTS
25%

Source: Martin and Ng 2004.

Regional trade agreements (RTAs)[20] have greatly expanded since the 1990s, over the same period that developing countries were undertaking autonomous liberalization policies and meeting their commitments under the Uruguay Round of the GATT. A total of 462 RTAs had been notified to the WTO as of February 2010, with 271 in force at that time (some having lapsed, while others were in the process of negotiation or ratification and entry into force).[21] Just as the number of RTAs has increased, so the percentage of world trade covered by them has expanded sharply: according to the UN Conference on Trade and Development (UNCTAD), more than half of world trade in goods is conducted through RTA partners.

While the boom in RTAs in part reflects the reintegration into the global economy of countries in transition from socialism, the slow progress in the Doha negotiations and the frustration with the multilateral trading system seem to have further strengthened interest in regional approaches. Indicating the large increase in RTA activity since the establishment of the WTO, notifications of RTAs averaged 20 a year between 1995 and 2006, compared with less than three notifications a year during the 47 years of the GATT regime.

The majority of the regional agreements are between developed (North) and developing (South) countries, but with the emergence of several major RTAs in the developing world, the importance of South–South RTAs has increased. New RTAs not only address issues concerning trade in goods and services, but also issues such as investment, trade facilitation, government procurement, environmental and labor standards, competition policy, and particularly protecting intellectual property.

WTO disciplines helped keep protectionism in check during the crisis, allowing world trade to recover at the same spectacular rates at which it had fallen. But in keeping with recent trends, the proliferation of regional agreements must also have also been important. The growing worldwide dependence on trade for production (trade in components and intrafirm trade have soared) as well as consumption (consumers have become accustomed to a diversity of imported products) likely also helped.

Despite the progress, further liberalization of trade policy will be critical to the continuing growth of global trade. Binding and biting WTO disciplines on trade in services (the bulk of economic activity today) are still in their infancy. Massive distortions of agricultural trade persist, including tariffs, quotas, and subsidies estimated to represent a cost to consumers in industrial countries in excess of $250 billion.[22] Developing economies still have wide scope for further unilateral liberalization of tariffs and nontariff trade barriers. Trade-weighted most-favored-nation applied tariffs in manufacturing, for example, remain high in developing economies—just under 10 percent, more than triple the roughly 3 percent in advanced economies.

Developing countries will dominate trade in manufactures

Countries that moved up the ladder of development diversified from primary commodities to manufactured goods, which offer better prospects for export earnings growth and provide greater price stability, allowing countries to avoid the volatile terms of trade that commodity-dependent economies experience. Sometimes this transition happened spontaneously, but often countries actively pursued it through export-led economic growth policies.

Following the historical pattern, today's developing countries have increased their presence in manufactured exports.[23] The share of developing economies in the export of global manufactured goods increased from 21 percent in 1996 to 33 percent in 2006. China's share tripled over that period, reaching 9.8 percent and surpassing both the United States and Japan. Other developing countries have also diversified and increased their manufactured exports, with the share in Sub-Saharan Africa's total exports rising from 7.1 percent to 18.7 percent.

Exports of manufactured goods from developing countries might have increased even more and export diversification progressed even further if exports of minerals had not surged as substantially as they did, driving up the exchange rate and diverting investment to minerals. Due largely to higher prices, but also because of new natural resource discoveries and greater efficiency in production, developing countries significantly increased their exports of mineral fuels and chemicals, the two product groups that exhibited the highest export growth rates over 1996–2006, from 54 percent to 63 percent. Sub-Saharan Africa's mineral fuels exports rose from $14.5 billion to $80.9 billion, and Middle East and North Africa's from $36.9 billion to $360 billion.

Foreign direct investment drives the globalization of production

Developing countries' rapid trade growth in the decade preceding the Great Recession was supported by their impressive progress in financial integration. The broader implications of financial integration of developing countries are explored in chapter 5. Here, the focus is on FDI, a crucial vehicle for integrating developing countries into global value-added chains and trade in services (banking, retailing, wholesaling, transportation, telecommunications). Over the decade before the Great Recession, FDI inflows to developing economies nearly quadrupled.

Trade integration facilitates financial integration. Openness encourages capital inflows as investors take advantage of outsourcing and exporting opportunities, makes importing inputs easier, and is associated with efficiency improvements that make exporting easier as well.

The reverse is also true: financial integration facilitates trade integration. FDI is heavily associated with slicing up the value chain—locating various stages of production in different geographical locations, based on comparative advantage. Specifically, efficiency-seeking FDI invests in foreign operations to create the most cost-effective production network. Such investment is now crucial in the trade of developing countries. An estimated 60 percent of China's exports are from factories owned by foreign investors. According to some estimates, the share of domestic content in China's exports is only about 50 percent.[24] Furthermore, the value added in complex manufactured products today is often attributable to components sourced in a dozen or more countries.

Advances in information and communication technology (ICT) have made such slicing up possible. As a result, the globalization of the production process has also increased the role of intermediate goods—parts and components—in global merchandise trade. According to the WTO the share of intermediate manufactured products in nonfuel world trade was around 40 percent in 2008 and, according to an OECD study, trade in intermediates represented more than half of total trade in every region in 2006.[25] Integration into low-wage manufacturing platforms either as producers or service providers has allowed some smaller economies, such as Malaysia, Singapore, and Hong Kong, to join the super-traders, with extremely high trade-to-GDP ratios.

FDI plays a central role in developing country trade in at least three other ways: to exploit large new markets (market-seeking FDI), to exploit natural resources (resource-seeking FDI), and to outsource the provision of services, such as call centers. While a growing proportion of FDI is efficiency-seeking, the majority of investment in developing economies is market-seeking, attracted by factors like developing countries' market size, per capita income, and market growth, as with Wal Mart opening stores in Mexico. According to a global survey by UNCTAD on the motives of multinational companies to internationalize their production, 51 percent referred to market-seeking as the most significant motive, compared with 17 percent for resource-seeking and nearly 10 percent for efficiency-seeking.[26]

As developing economies have become more integrated through FDI, their state-owned enterprises have emerged as major sources of such investment. A growing number of state-owned enterprises are becoming key players in outward FDI in resources, telecoms, and other sectors. The major investment tools for states include sovereign wealth funds (SWFs), national oil corporations, and other state-owned enterprises. SWFs, mainly driven by large current account surpluses, invested $23 billion in FDI in 2009—more than double the level in 2005—accounting for more than 2 percent of global FDI flows.[27] Such investments are dominant in outward FDI from emerging economies. For example, the 10 largest Chinese multinational enterprises are state-owned.[28] The world's 13 largest energy companies, in reserves, are also owned by governments, and state-owned companies control more than 75 percent of global crude oil production.

The emergence of states as major players in FDI has implications for the global economy. Given their rising assets and modest involvement in FDI thus far, state-owned enterprises could become much bigger sources of investment. According to UNCTAD, SWF assets—estimated at $3 trillion in 2007—are projected to reach $12 trillion by 2015, but only 0.2 percent of SWF assets are involved in FDI so far. But growing state-sponsored foreign investments has raised concerns that they may destabilize financial markets, because such investments may be motivated by political objectives rather than maximizing economic growth. A recent study also suggests that such investments could threaten developed economies' competitive edge in the market-based system and slow economic growth in the long term because they distort markets through the political motives, bureaucracy, waste, and corruption associated with state-run companies.[29]

Developing countries will be home to most of the (consuming) global middle and rich

As noted by the World Bank and others, the rapid economic growth of developing countries has already produced a large global middle and rich (GMR) class, those with annual incomes of at least $4,000 in 2005 PPP. They can demand more overall and increase the demand for advanced goods and services in particular, rapidly expanding the markets for internationally traded products, such as automobiles and consumer durables. They also demand more and better education, health, and international tourism services.

This GMR class will grow dramatically over the next 40 years, almost exclusively in developing countries. Based on forecasts in chapter 3, the GMR population in the developing G20 economies will grow from about 368 million people in 2009—roughly equal to the total population of the EU—to 1.3 billion in 2030, and reach 1.9 billion in 2050 (see table 3.4).[30] At present, 24 percent of the global GMR population resides in developing countries, a share forecast to rise to about 50 percent by 2030 and 60 percent by 2050.[31] But the average income of the GMR class in advanced countries will then be about 60 percent bigger than that of the GMR class in developing G20 countries.

The GMR class will account for a bigger share of the population of the G20 developing countries, rising from 11 percent in 2009 to 48 percent by 2050. Even in Brazil, where income inequality is particularly high, the GMR class' share of the country's population will almost double by 2050. In some African countries, such as Ghana, Nigeria, and Ethiopia, where the middle class accounted for less than 5 percent of the population in 2009,[32] 100 million will be in the GMR class by 2050.

The rise of the GMR class in developing countries will have far-reaching implications for trade. Not only will the major consumer markets for many products and services be in developing countries, particularly for the more standardized "stripped down" versions, but there will also be a tendency for both the design and manufacture of those products to occur closer to the markets there. A natural next step will be the establishment of globally recognized brands in developing countries, as Corona beer or Lenovo computers have already done today. Advanced countries should remain competitive in highly sophisticated consumer products and luxury goods, the demand for which will grow rapidly in developing countries.

World trade in 2050

Barring geopolitical or climate-induced catastrophes and assuming that the world does not retreat into protectionism, the share of world trade held by developing countries could more than double over the next 40 years, reaching nearly 70 percent by 2050 (figure 4.4). In addition, developing country dependence on developed country markets will weaken. Reflecting high growth rates and the rise of the middle class, emerging economies will come to dominate international trade.

As indicated by the GDP projections in chapter 3, the weight of global economic activity is shifting from advanced countries toward emerging economies. Based on these projections, and consistent with the current trend, developing countries' share of world exports is expected to increase from 30 percent in 2006 to 69 percent in 2050,[33] with China's share tripling (to 24 percent) and India's rising fivefold (to 6.2 percent). Conversely, the industrial countries' share will decline, with that of the United States falling from 9.5 percent to 7 percent and that of Japan from 5.4 percent to just 2.4 percent.

Developing country imports will significantly increase as well. Based on a conservative elasticity of trade to GDP of 1.3, their share of exports from advanced economies will increase from 24 percent in 2006 to 58 percent in 2050. China will emerge as the second largest export destination for EU exports (49 percent of the EU's exports will be intra-regional), and Latin America will be the United States' largest export market (accounting for 27 percent of U.S.

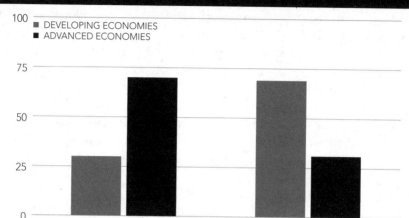

FIGURE 4.4 FROM 30–70 TO 70–30
(PERCENT OF WORLD TRADE, 2006–50)

■ DEVELOPING ECONOMIES
■ ADVANCED ECONOMIES

Source: Authors' projections.

exports), followed by China. These forecasts, based on a fixed elasticity to GDP growth, do not take into account the effect of changes in sectoral demand shifts. Because U.S. and EU exports appeal to the middle class, and this group will be expanding rapidly in China and other developing giants, even these numbers likely underestimate developing countries' rise in importance as export markets for advanced countries. .

Developing countries will also become more important export markets for one another. In 2006 South–South exports accounted for about 31 percent of total exports from the South, and about 10 percent of world exports. In 2050 their share in the South's total exports will double, and their share in world exports will rise more than four-fold. By 2050 China will surpass the EU as the leading export market for India, accounting for 22 percent of India's total exports, while East Asia and the Pacific and the Middle East and North Africa will together account for about 35 percent of India's exports. Only 27 percent of Africa's exports will go to the United States and the EU in 2050, down from more than 50 percent in 2006. Instead, intra-African trade will account for 25 percent of the region's total exports; this could increase further if infrastructure and trade logistics constraints are addressed. In addition to reducing developing economies' vulnerability to a growth slowdown in advanced economies, this increase in South–South trade flows increases opportunities to learn from other developing countries about how to best adapt technology to local conditions.

The escalation of competitive pressures originating in developing economies that appear destined to take their place among the world's largest trading nations are bound to give rise to protectionist pressures. Protectionism of the "creeping" variety is a constant temptation and threat, but protectionism is most dangerous in times of economic crisis, when it tends to escalate sharply—as it did in the Great Recession and, much more devastatingly, in the Great Depression of the 1930s. Clearly necessary for the realization of the projections discussed here is maintaining open international markets and strengthening rules that govern trade.

A more demanding international context for multilateral processes

Looking to the next 40 years, it is difficult to see how a slow-moving WTO, dependent on consensus and the single undertaking principle, can produce timely results in a rapidly-evolving international context, even if a heavily diluted Doha deal is concluded (albeit a decade or more after it began).[34]

Four features of the postcrisis world economy will make achieving results under the current WTO setup even more arduous. First is the inability of the advanced countries to lead the process, as they have done historically. Slow domestic growth, unaffordable entitlement spending, and high and rising public debts will make the United States, Europe, and Japan more self-absorbed and defensive than they have been in the past. Large internal imbalances in Europe exposed by the Greek crisis will exacerbate this trend.

Second is the greater multipolarity and diversity of the trading system. China, Brazil, and India are playing much larger roles in the world trading system, reflecting their relative ease in navigating the crisis and their rising economic weight. These countries are, however, more focused on development priorities and huge internal poverty gaps than on leading a free trade offensive. Even if the advanced countries were inclined to pass the baton to the developing countries, they would be equally unlikely to take it.

Third, though the rise of these economies presents great opportunities and vast new markets, advanced countries increasingly view them as powerful commercial rivals in areas of traditional comparative advantage, not as poor cousins needing assistance—directly counter to the declared motivation of the Doha Development Agenda.

Fourth, many complex issues, such as services, investment, agricultural subsidies, and imports of manufactures in developing countries, de facto remain largely outside the reach of binding multilateral disciplines. Although most of these issues are not new and are technically part of the WTO, imposing effective disciplines on them in a highly differentiated and rapidly changing development context is likely to prove even more difficult.

These trends toward slow growth in advanced countries, multipolarity, perceived trade rivalry, and increased complexity are likely to be with us for a long time.

The future of the world trading system

How, then, will the trading system evolve over the next generation? Here is a plausible "business as usual" scenario:

- Trade will continue to grow rapidly, driven mainly by the rise of living standards in developing countries and their adoption of existing technology. Autonomous liberalization will remain the main driver of trade reforms in areas as varied as the EU's common agricultural policy, financial sector liberalization in India and China, and opening the poor countries to FDI.

- Bilateral and regional agreements will also continue to proliferate, and the more successful ones will seek ways to deepen and broaden reforms to cover services, investment, and government procurement. But selective agreements among the largest economic blocs, such as an agreement on services trade and regulations between the United States and the EU, may be the next wave of regionalism, further undermining the multilateral process.

- An increasing number of highly specialized plurilateral agreements may be negotiated outside the WTO, including deeper and more encompassing financial regulation and agreements on clean energy and on climate change mitigation and trade. Plurilateral agreements may also come to address specific needs that remain unmet within the WTO—for example, the granting of duty free and quota free access to LDCs in a stepped up effort to achieve the Millennium Development Goals.

- Russia—the only G20 member that remains outside the WTO—will eventually come into the fold, and the WTO will continue be an enforcer of legacy agreements, which may at some point also include a diluted Doha deal. But the WTO will progressively lose share in enforcement to national courts and arbitration mechanisms pertaining to regional and plurilateral agreements. It will probably remain an important forum for discussing trade matters and a source of analysis of trade trends, but multilateral liberalization will become an activity very much at the margin of rapidly evolving trade relations. G20 and G8 Sherpas, for example, will resist pressures to set deadlines that embarrass their leaders and undermine the credibility of their broader agendas.

This scenario is certainly not optimal for the WTO, but will it be bad for world trade? It will clearly mean greater complexity, many lost opportunities to make broader trade-offs and to establish multilateral disciplines, and a higher possibility of serious backsliding in any economic crisis that is deeper and longer lived than the Great Recession. But given the progress in liberalization through other channels, and judging by the experience of the last 20 years, such a scenario will not necessarily spell disaster for world trade—or for the world trading system.

Can the world improve on this outcome? Almost certainly yes, but only if the WTO membership adopts a very different business model in negotiations.

Outlining the WTO reform agenda

Because the WTO is driven entirely by the political and economic interests of its many member states, there is, not surprisingly, no agreed-upon blueprint for reform. But the following needed steps would amount to a wave of progress that would bring the WTO back to the center of global economic integration.

Crucially, the WTO must break away from its splendid isolation amid a sea of fast-changing trade relations. It must move from a single-minded focus on reciprocal multilateral concessions based on consensus—negotiations bearing too little fruit—and find ways to contribute actively in arenas where actual liberalization is taking place. This implies addressing the following four issues.

First, the WTO must support autonomous reform. Experience shows that countries are inclined to engage in autonomous reform, and—contrary to the prevailing mercantilist logic of negotiators—trade theory and empirical evidence point overwhelmingly to the benefits that countries derive from opening to global markets. The WTO must therefore draw on the experience of the World Bank and the International Monetary Fund and work with them to institute programs of trade and complementary reforms at the country level. In this regard, the WTO should exploit its Trade Policy Review Mechanism, which is now a useful diagnostic instrument but has the potential to provide the basis for an ongoing dialogue on trade reform.

Second, the WTO should reduce its reliance on the consensus rule and instead promote agreements among a critical mass of members. The purpose of such "plurilateral" agreements would be to establish new rules or achieve new market access in important sectors. Examples of sectors covered by plurilateral agreements include government procurement, telecommunications, and financial services.

Such agreements would likely be challenged—especially by the smallest and poorest countries—on the grounds that they discriminate or that they can preempt the broader agenda. Yet the alternatives of vacuous global deals are surely worse. Moreover, small and poor countries may find that there are agreements of primary interest to them. The answer is not to forbid plurilateral agreements—it is to proceed on a small set of such agreements that reflects the interests of smaller and poorer countries as well as those of larger and richer ones.

More flexible agreements could be structured to comply with well-identified criteria to minimize the adverse effects on nonmembers and to make them less exclusive by extending membership on reasonable terms, including favorable treatment for the poorest countries. The agreements would be subject to WTO dispute settlement, so that signatories of the agreements could find redress against other signatories, and nonmembers could also challenge signatories if they do not live up to due process as they apply to nonmembers—for example, in accession to the agreement.

Third, in addition to promoting autonomous and plurilateral reform, the WTO should also harness the energy behind regional agreements. Research has shown that many regional agreements are badly designed and implemented (and that some exist only on paper). But it has also shown that others—starting with the EU, the North and Central American free trade agreements, and even some South–South agreements, such as the Pan-Arab Free Trade Area, the Gulf Cooperation Council, and the Southern Africa Customs Union—have been genuinely successful in removing barriers, increasing the certainty of access, and creating trade. Regional agreements can also deal more easily with difficult behind-the-border impediments to trade, and they provide fertile ground for experimentation and advancing disciplines that can be adopted more broadly.

The WTO must cease viewing regional trade agreements solely as a threat and start treating them—as large segments of the business community do around the world—as an opportunity to advance trade. A large body of research has identified the essential characteristics of welfare-enhancing regional agreements that minimize discrimination: a low external tariff, simplified rules of origin, and coverage of all forms of trade.[35] The WTO must promote and even encourage— rather than ignore or frown upon—the formation of such well-designed, welfare-enhancing regional and bilateral agreements among its members. It should facilitate the harmonization and reduction of their external tariffs, and foster RTA accession for smaller and poorer countries that might otherwise be excluded. Establishing effective rules to govern regional agreements should be the WTO's long-term objective, but its constructive engagement with regional processes is a prerequisite to achieving that goal.

Fourth, the WTO must decide how the progress along the unilateral, plurilateral, and regional channels can eventually be "multilateralized" and translated into a set of enforceable rules. Over many years, great advances in open trade have been made on the basis of autonomous and regional processes alone, but the WTO can make a big contribution by consolidating the gains under these agreements and complementing them with plurilateral approaches.

Recent experience demonstrates conclusively that a good way not to do this is to have a big comprehensive trade round. A more realistic approach must first recognize that the principles of multilateralization (such as most-favored-nation status and nondiscrimination) exist only as ideals. WTO agreements, not least the current Doha drafts, are rife with exceptions, special treatment, and nonreciprocity. So, the real choice is not between partial agreements and all-encompassing agreements that treat everyone the same; it is between partial agreements negotiated separately among a subset of members or partial agreements bundled together into one package that everyone agrees to.

There are at least three nonexclusive ways to multilateralize. One approach is to encourage the "flexible geometries" of agreements to become wider when possible, by extending plurilaterals to a larger group of members. China and the United States, for example, have agreed to pursue China's inclusion in the WTO's Government Procurement Agreement.[36]

Another response is to seek specific opportunities to consolidate liberalization that has already occurred or that requires only modest steps across the board. WTO members might, among other things, agree to eliminate all tariffs under 3 percent; ban export subsidies in agriculture; adopt a unified code for rules of origin (or at least a voluntary one); or provide duty-free, quota-free access to least developed countries. More than one of these steps could be promoted simultaneously to address a diversity of interests without forcing a full-fledged negotiation on everything.

Yet another approach is to promote agreements in which one country or a group of countries bind actual tariff levels or service schedules in specific sectors, both as a self-restraint and as an inducement to others to do the same. One could imagine, for example, a G-6 group consisting of the United States, the EU, Japan, China, India, and Brazil—which together account for more than 80 percent of world trade—agreeing on such a step and adopting a common approach to induce other countries to do the same by, for example, providing a defined accession procedure that includes preferential terms for the poorest countries.

This outline of a reform agenda is intentionally limited to badly needed reforms that go to the heart of the WTO's mission. A more comprehensive treatment of WTO reform would include improvements in areas where the institution is already delivering. One is dispute settlement (making it faster, less costly, and less reliant on trade sanctions). A second is accession (making negotiations more transparent and achieving a better balance between the acceding country's commitments and the benefits it receives). That would require a more independent and effective idea-driven secretariat.

Conclusion

The trade projections here point to significant opportunities—from shifts in comparative advantage to a large expansion of world trade to ever deeper integration. But if the full potential on any of these fronts is to be realized, policy must be reformed on both the national and international levels.

The extent to which comparative advantage will shift in manufactured goods and developing countries will serve as markets for one another will depend largely on reforms in developing countries. These reforms are particularly important in the poorest countries. To bolster exports, the quality and predictability of their business climate must be improved. While such improvements are important for all sectors, including primary commodities, they are absolutely essential for stimulating investment in manufacturing, where deficiencies cannot be offset by abundant or unique resource endowments.

If done gradually and with supportive measures, reducing the high import protection still prevalent in many sectors in developing countries would also foster efficiency, exposing firms to international competition and easing their access to imported inputs. By making trade less expensive, reducing customs and logistical impediments would have similar effects. Forging new South–South links in trade and finance through regional agreements and institutions—which can share information, promote common regulations, and support cross-border projects—would also harness the expanding complementarities in South–South trade.

The success of developing countries in manufactures will force rich countries to accelerate the pace at which they innovate and differentiate, as well as require them to make their business environment more flexible and predictable. Private investments in specialized skills and R&D are likely to increase, and governments can support the trend in various ways.[37] Advanced countries have their own trade reforms to complete as part of this process, including opening their service markets in areas ranging from professional services to maritime and air transport, and eliminating their wasteful and distorting agricultural support regimes.

The projections suggest that a large expansion in world trade, as well as marked increases in efficiency, innovation, and ultimately human welfare, are likely in the coming 40 years. Of all the arenas of globalization, trade is where international collaboration is most advanced. But an open, rules-based system appropriate for this new world economy is still a work-in-progress, as shown by the floundering Doha process. Incorporating the diverse interests of developing countries in trade rules and liberalization agreements is crucial—but the WTO's consensus requirement cannot be allowed to dilute agreements to the lowest common denominator. Far-reaching reforms of the WTO are needed to make multilateral negotiations more flexible and responsive to individual countries and regional groups or "clubs" interested in making progress in specific areas. Disciplines must be strengthened to ensure that the progress of world trade is not hampered—or worse, reversed—in the midst of another crisis.

Notes

1. Although countries have shifted ranks over the course of history—China and India were among the world's high-income economies in the sixteenth century, for example, as was Argentina in the early part of the twentieth. We refer to advanced and developing countries based on their situation today. According to the World Bank, developing economies are those whose gross national income per capita was less than $12,195 in 2009.
2. Findlay and O'Rourke 2001.
3. Barret 1990.
4. Steensgaard 1995.
5. The New World refers to the Western Hemisphere, specifically the Americas.
6. Crafts 1985.
7. Barret 1990.
8. Davis 1962.
9. Findlay and O'Rouke 2001.
10. Maddison's definition of developing countries includes Asia (excluding Japan), Latin America, Eastern Europe and the former USSR, and Africa.
11. This discussion of past trends compares 1996 with 2006, unless otherwise noted. Projections, explored later in the paper, compare 2006 levels with those expected in 2050.
12. This section draws heavily on the GDP projections in chapter 3. Estimates of financial integration and the global middle and rich (GMR) class come from those projections, while the trade projections are based on them as well, using a method discussed below.
13. Martin 1997.
14. Chapter 9 further explores the tension between inclusion and achieving significant change through multilateral negotiations.
15. Anderson and Martin 2006.
16. OECD 2005.
17. Baier and Bergstrand 2001.
18. Adler and Hufbauer 2009.

19. World Bank 2005.
20. These are agreements among a group of countries that reduce barriers to trade on a reciprocal and preferential basis for those in the group.
21. World Trade Organization members are bound to notify the World Trade Organization about their regional trade agreements. Notifications may also refer to the accession of new parties to an agreement that already exists, such as the accession of Bulgaria and Romania to the European Union Customs Union.
22. OECD 2005.
23. Unless otherwise specified, the figures for manufactured goods are based on UN Comtrade's classification, which excludes machinery and transport equipment.
24. Koopman, Wang, and Wei 2008.
25. Miroudot, Lanz, and Ragoussis 2009.
26. UNCTAD 2007.
27. Investment vehicles established by states with large foreign currency holdings to maximize the state's return on investment.
28. OECD 2008.
29. Bremmer 2010.
30. They include Argentina, Brazil, China, India, Indonesia, Mexico, Russia, South Africa, and Turkey. Although Saudi Arabia is also a developing G20 economy, it was not included in these calculations because data were not available for its distribution of income.
31. The share is defined as the ratio of the GMR population in developing G20 countries to the total, which includes the GMR in all advanced countries. It is assumed that more than 95 percent of the population in advanced countries belongs to the GMR class.
32. The average income of the highest decile (assumed to be the 95th percentile) was less than the $4,000 cut-off for the GMR class.
33. To project trade flows, we assume that imports into a given country will grow at the rate of GDP times an elasticity of 1.3 (a conservative estimate, given that the elasticity of world trade to world GDP from 1960–80 was 1.7) and that exports will grow proportionally to the GDP of the exporting country. For simplicity, trade deficits and surpluses as a share of GDP are assumed to stay constant, at the rate of the base period.
34. The single undertaking principle requires that virtually every item of the negotiation is part of a whole and indivisible package and cannot be agreed upon separately.
35. Newfarmer 2006.

36. The WTO Agreement on Government Procurement is a plurilateral agreement, and its goal is to open countries' nondefense government procurement markets to international competition. It mandates that procurement-related rules be transparent and that procuring entities do not discriminate against foreign suppliers.
37. World Bank 2008.

References

Adler, Matthew, and Gary Hufbauer. "Policy Liberalization and U.S. Merchandise Trade Growth, 1980–2006." Working Paper 09-2. Peterson Institute for International Economics, Washington DC, 2009.

Anderson, Kym, and Will Martin. *Agriculture, Trade, and the Doha Agenda.* Washington, DC: World Bank, 2006.

Baier, Scott, and Jeffrey Bergstrand. "The Growth of World Trade: Tariffs Transport Costs, and Income Similarity." *Journal of International Economics,* 52 (2001): 1–27.

Bremmer, Ian. *The End of the Free Market: Who Wins the War between States and Corporations.* New York: Portfolio, 2010.

Crafts, Nicholas F. R. *British Economic Growth during the Industrial Revolution.* Oxford, UK: Clarendon Press, 1985.

Davis, Ralph. "English Foreign Trade, 1700–1774." *Economic History Review,* 15 (1962): 285–303.

Evenett, Simon J. "No Turning Back: Lock-in 20 Years of Reforms at the WTO." In *What World Leaders Must do to Halt the Spread of Protectionism,* ed. Richard Baldwin and Simon Evenett. Centre for Economic Policy Research, London, 2008.

Findlay, Ronald E., and Kevin H. O'Rourke. "Commodity Market Integration 1500–2000." CEPR Discussion Paper 3125. Centre for Economic Policy Research, London, 2001, http://ssrn.com/abstract=298023.

Koopman, Robert, Zhi Wang, and Shang-Jin Wei. *How Much of Chinese Exports is Really Made In China? Assessing Domestic Value-Added When Processing Trade is Pervasive.* NBER Working Paper 14109. Cambridge, MA: National Bureau of Economic Research, 2008.

Martin, Will. "Measuring Welfare Changes with Distortions." In *Applied Methods for Trade Policy Analysis,* eds. Joseph Francois and Kenneth Reinert, Cambridge, UK: Cambridge University Press, 1997.

Martin, Will, and Francis Ng. "Sources of Tariff Reductions." Background paper for *Global Economic Prospects: Trade Regionalism, and Development.* World Bank, Washington, DC, 2005.

Miroudot, Sébastien, Rainer Lanz, and Alexandros Ragoussis. "Trade in Intermediate Goods and Services." OECD Trade Policy Working Papers 93. Organisation for Economic Cooperation and Development, Paris, 2009.

Newfarmer, Richard. "Regional Trade Agreements: Designs for Development." In *Trade, Doha and Development*, ed. Richard Newfarmer. Washington, DC: World Bank, 2006.

OECD (Organisation for Economic Co-operation and Development). "Agricultural Policies in the OECD Countries: Monitoring and Evaluation 2005, Highlights." Paris, 2005, www.oecd.org/dataoecd/33/27/35016763.pdf.

———. *Moving Up the Value Chain: Staying Competitive in the Global Economy. A Synthesis Report on Global Value Chains*. Paris, 2007, www.oecd.org/dataoecd/24/35/38558080.pdf.

———. "China's Outward Foreign Direct Investment." OECD Investment News, March 2008, www.oecd.org/dataoecd/28/10/40283257.pdf.

Reinhart, Carmen M., and Kenneth S. Rogoff. "Is the 2007 U.S. Subprime Crisis So Different? An International Historical Comparison." *American Economic Review*, 98 (2008): 339–44.

Steensgaard, Niels. "Commodities, Bullion and Services in Intercontinental Transactions Before 1750." In *The European Discovery of the World and its Economic Effects on Pre-Industrial Society*, ed. H. Pohl, Stuttgart: Franz Steiner Verlag, 1995.

UNCTAD (United Nations Conference on Trade and Development). *World Investment Prospects Survey 2007–2009*. Geneva, 2007.

World Bank. *Global Economic Prospects 2005: Trade, Regionalism, and Development*. Washington, DC, 2005, http://siteresources.worldbank.org/INTGEP2005/Resources/gep2005.pdf.

World Bank. *Global Economic Prospects 2007: Managing the Next Wave of Globalization*. Washington, DC, 2006.

World Bank. *Global Economic Prospects 2008: Technology Diffusion in the Developing World*. Washington, DC, 2008.

World Bank. *Global Development Finance 2009: Charting a Global Recovery*. Washington, DC, 2009, http://siteresources.worldbank.org/INTGDF2009/Resources/gdf_combined_web.pdf.

CHAPTER 5

FINANCE

HARNESSING THE BEAST

With development and trade come pressures for capital mobility. Financial integration cannot be stopped indefinitely. Yet finance-driven crises can impose mammoth costs, particularly for developing countries with weaker institutions. So, opening to volatile capital flows must be undertaken cautiously and managed carefully to ensure effective controls on risk-taking.

As developing countries come to represent a large share of trade and financial transactions, their participation in international agreements on financial regulation will be essential to their effectiveness and to avoid regulatory arbitrage. And as developing countries come to dominate the global economy, they will present a larger share of systemic risk. It is in the vital interests of advanced countries to support improvements in financial regulation in developing countries.

Developing countries are becoming more important actors in global financial markets, with momentous implications for their own development and for the global economy. International financial integration will inevitably accompany the higher incomes and increased trade and international communication as residents and firms in developing countries seek to diversify their assets and tap liquid global markets. As such, it can bring many benefits.

It can also expose a country to extraordinary risks and greatly accentuate boom-bust cycles. The Great Recession has shown that, even in the most advanced financial systems—such as the United States and the United Kingdom, where the capacity to regulate and formulate policy is supposedly strongest—the risks associated with financial speculation are enormous. These risks are even greater in countries with weak institutions and low regulatory capacity, where the economy is less diversified and more volatile, and where creditworthiness is low and access to international capital markets can suddenly stop. That is why developing countries need to be particularly cautious about the free flow of capital—especially external debt and portfolio equity flows, which tend to be much more volatile and pro-cyclical than foreign direct investment (FDI). In short, financial integration brings many benefits and cannot be stopped—but to avoid disaster, it must be harnessed.

Strengthening the regulatory framework for financial integration will become all the more essential as the importance of developing countries rises in foreign direct investment, bank loans, and portfolio flows. The increasing weight of developing countries in the global asset portfolio will help residents of advanced countries earn higher returns on their foreign investments and improve diversification. But the rise of poor countries with weaker institutions will also increase systemic risks. For example, a financial crisis in China or Brazil would already have major global implications today. As these countries grow to be much larger than nearly all of today's international financial centers, the risks become that much greater as well.

So, the rise of developing countries in a financially integrated world has two important policy implications. First, because weak institutions are a major source of crises, it is in the interest of advanced countries to support improvements in the institutions and rules governing developing country financial sectors. And second, the rapid integration of developing countries increases the urgency of international agreement on rules to restrict risk-taking—including capital requirements, limitations on the kinds of business commercial banks can conduct, transparency requirements, and rules governing derivative transactions. The rise of developing countries also increases the need for an adequately resourced lender of last resort. All this can work only if developing countries are included in the rule setting—and the sooner, the better.

Finance contributes both to growth and to crises

The growth of financial institutions can increase the volume of savings and the efficiency of investment. Greater access to banks can increase the returns on savings, reduce the risks involved in holding wealth, facilitate diversification, and improve welfare through the delivery of numerous financial services. And banks can help direct savings to activities with high returns by disseminating information and increasing the role of investors with specialized knowledge. While the relationship is not necessarily causal, the size of the banking system increases with the level of development: banking deposits in low-income countries equaled 26 percent of GDP in 2008, and in high-income countries, 103 percent (figure 5.1).

Nevertheless, systemic crises generated by failures of confidence in financial institutions are as old as capitalism, and highly leveraged institutions have often magnified the losses—and the implications for the broader economy—of declines in economic activity. Hence the importance of supervising financial institutions to prevent them from taking on excessive risks, and the need for a lender of last resort to either support or manage the closure of bankrupt institutions, thus minimizing the fallout.[1]

Financial development has supported growth and generated crises since the rise of capitalism

Banking goes back to ancient Egypt and Babylon,[2] and industrial development and the growth of trade have been intricately connected to financial innovation for many centuries. Goldsmith's discovery that banks could profit through issuing notes backed by, but larger in value than, their gold holdings often contributed to an expansion of economic activity. The most famous of them developed into prominent banking firms (such as Gosling and Sharpe, which became part of Barclays).[3] Credit

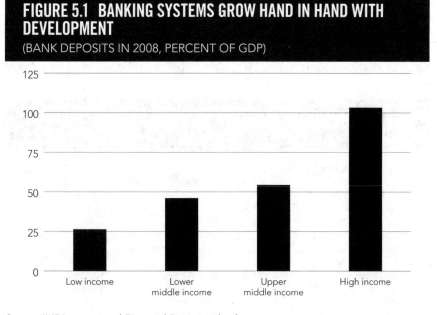

FIGURE 5.1 BANKING SYSTEMS GROW HAND IN HAND WITH DEVELOPMENT
(BANK DEPOSITS IN 2008, PERCENT OF GDP)

Source: IMF International Financial Statistics database.

supported trade in both Europe and the Middle East during medieval times, by substituting for scarce coinage, avoiding costly and unsafe transport of money across long distances, and facilitating risk sharing.[4] Bankers were particularly important (as they are today) as intermediaries who were in a better position than traders to enforce compliance with commitments for future payment for receipt of goods.[5] But in olden times, like today, financial expansion could be dangerous. The Dutch tulip mania in the 1630s, where the price of rare tulip bulbs reached astronomical levels and subsequently collapsed, was fueled by the provision of credit from sellers.[6] Financial crises were frequent in eighteenth century England,[7] and France contributed John Law's Mississippi Company (box 5.1).

Financial development also supported the acceleration of the Industrial Revolution and the rapid expansion of technology in the nineteenth century. Bank lending and the issuance of stocks and bonds were essential in amassing the considerable resources for major infrastructure investments. But the failure of some of these investments drove the banking panics and severe economic downturns that plagued the century.[8] For example, in the early 1820s the sale of stock to finance gas lighting, canals, and railroads in England—plus gold and silver mines, along with government debt, in Latin America—contributed to a rapid expansion of economic activity, supported by the Bank of England's easy money policies. Euphoria encouraged a further runup of stock prices (including bond issuances from imaginary countries) and higher risk loans, all of which ended with the 1825 crash, with attendant bank failures and a global recession.[9]

Rapid growth in finance was an antecedent to the Great Depression. The rapid expansion in economic activity in the 1920s was accompanied by a sharp rise in financial development (measured by bank deposits to GDP) in the major global

BOX 5.1 THE MISSISSIPPI COMPANY AND FRANCE'S FINANCIAL DEBACLE

In 1716 John Law employed a now-familiar financial innovation in establishing a bank with paid-in capital that could issue notes, largely in the form of loans to the French government. The initial result was to stabilize government finances and to raise prices, which contributed to a revival of business. Unfortunately, Law went on to issue further loans to the government. His declared intention was to increase the bank's reserves to support these loans by mining gold in Louisiana, for which purpose he established and sold stock in the Mississippi Company, which held the mining concession. The eventual discovery that the proceeds from the sales of stock were devoted to government loans rather than mining activities led to the bank's collapse and a severe decline in business activity.

Source: Galbraith 1975.

economies. This indicator peaked in 1929 (a level that remained unmatched through the end of the century) before plummeting sharply in the 1930s.[10] While the causes of the Great Depression are still debated, there is little doubt that the banking failures in the United States prolonged the collapse in output and employment.[11] The Great Depression was a valuable, if enormously painful, lesson in the importance of effective government management of modern financial systems.

The controls on financial speculation that followed the Depression were gradually eased

It is testimony to the ability of democratic societies to adapt their financial rules to reflect such lessons that the web of regulation and supervision constructed after the Depression considerably dampened the role of the financial sector as a driver of instability in the real economy. In a view that Paul Krugman has championed in recent articles, banking became a boring business.[12] And while financial sector profits were restrained and opportunities for finance to contribute to growth forgone, the global economy was more stable: banking crises were rare until financial innovation and deregulation loosened these controls. A compendium of banking crises lists one crisis from 1945–60 (India around the time of partition), one in the 1960s, 7 in the 1970s, 19 in the 1980s, and 25 in the 1990s.[13]

Several forces combined to unravel the web of controls built up following the Depression and unleash the forces of financial capital. The growth of offshore centers reduced the reach of supervision and eroded the profits of banks still subject to domestic controls, spurring calls for an easing of restrictions. Global financial institutions sought to operate in lightly-regulated jurisdictions, thus reducing the ability of all governments to impose controls. One example is the steady erosion, and eventual elimination, of the U.S. Glass-Steagall Act, as other jurisdictions allowed single firms to provide commercial banking, investment banking, and insurance services.[14]

Pressures for weaker regulation were also a byproduct of the Great Moderation, the period of declining inflation and (largely) sustained growth ushered in during the 1990s. The absence of serious crises in the rich countries reduced risk premia, encouraging investors to increase risk in order to maintain yields. Prolonged stability reduced the perceived need for many of the traditional restrictions on financial activities. And to the extent that moral hazard was a motive for the rise in risk taking (with investors in large institutions counting on public bailouts in the event of insolvency), the availability of foreign savings from countries that might bailout distressed firms further boosted excessive investment globally.[15]

Financial innovations enormously increased the complexity of financial transactions. Government supervisors (as well as bank boards of directors and investors) faced growing difficulties in monitoring the degree of risk, increasing reliance on private-sector regulation (such as incorporating ratings by private firms into regulatory criteria and relying on self-assessments of the quality of bank portfolios). Financial institutions that did not take deposits and thus were less strictly supervised, such as investment banks and hedge funds, accounted for a growing share of financial transactions.

Unfortunately, the developing country crises of the late 1990s were viewed in G7 policy circles as arising from policy mistakes and the failure to adopt Anglo-American financial standards in the affected countries—not as a sign of increasing financial instability in an era of rapid innovation and weakening regulation. So these crises did nothing to limit the reliance on private-sector risk assessments as a basis for supervision.[16] Despite occasional reminders, memories of the potentially devastating implications of unbridled finance dimmed, restrictions on financial sector activity dwindled, financial sector profits skyrocketed, and the share of the financial sector in economic activity grew rapidly.

The Great Recession has exposed the enormous costs—in higher unemployment, rising poverty levels, and greater government debt required to support economic activity—that can come from relying on the private sector to ensure financial stability. Major regulatory authorities have emphasized the need for greater public scrutiny of both banks and non-bank financial institutions. There is some hope, but no guarantee, that the recent crisis will encourage stricter controls on financial speculation and reduce investor appetite for underwriting excessive risks.[17] Efforts by the rich countries to raise capital requirements, improve the transparency of financial markets, and ensure that large institutions that pose systemic risks are effectively regulated should be the first priority for reform.

In appreciating the dangers of finance, remember that severe constraints on finance can also be destructive. The miserable economic performance of economies where the financial sector was severely repressed is a testimony to the importance of finance. For example, during the 1960s and 1970s many African and Latin American countries imposed strict controls on interest rates, which, accompanied by significant inflation, severely reduced the profitability, size, and efficiency of the financial sector.[18]

Developing countries are integrating into global financial markets

Similar to financial development, integration with global financial markets tends to rise with development. Developing countries' policies toward the inflow and outflow of capital have become more open in recent years, reflected in a much larger number of transactions.

Developing countries are opening to external capital flows

An index that summarizes various indicators of openness to external financial transactions (for example, limits on capital inflows, restrictions on the transfer of funds abroad) has risen substantially since 1990.[19,20] But for developing countries it slowed following the crises of the late 1990s, as policymakers became more concerned about the potential costs of allowing unrestricted external capital transactions. And financial openness in developing countries remains well below that of high-income countries (figure 5.2).

After declining with the crises of the late 1990s and the global growth slowdown in 2000–01, external capital flows to developing countries rose sharply during the boom in global finance before the recent crisis (figure 5.3). Developing country foreign direct investment inflows rose from 2.2 percent of their GDP in 2003 to 3.7 percent in 2008, while net long-term lending from private sources increased by 1.6 percentage points of GDP and portfolio equity investment by 0.5 percentage points. The expansion of foreign capital inflows contributed to the rapid increase in domestic financial development (figure 5.4), as credit from the banking system and stock market capitalization in developing countries increased relative to GDP after the early 1990s (until the huge losses with the financial crisis).

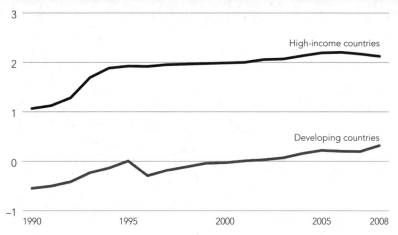

FIGURE 5.2 FINANCIAL OPENNESS, MUCH LESS IN DEVELOPING COUNTRIES
(AVERAGE OF COUNTRY INDICATORS)

Note: Each line represents the simple average of the countries in that income group with complete data for 1990–2008.
Source: Chinn and Ito 2008.

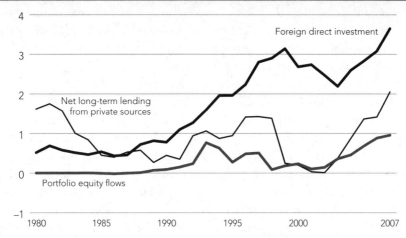

**FIGURE 5.3 FINANCIAL FLOWS TO DEVELOPING COUNTRIES—
RISING BEFORE THE GREAT RECESSION**
(PERCENT OF GDP)

Foreign direct investment

Net long-term lending
from private sources

Portfolio equity flows

Source: World Bank data.

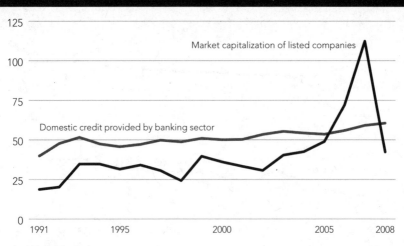

**FIGURE 5.4 FINANCIAL DEVELOPMENT IN DEVELOPING COUNTRIES
EVIDENT IN MARKET CAPITALIZATIONS OF LISTED COMPANIES**
(PERCENT OF GDP)

Market capitalization of listed companies

Domestic credit provided by banking sector

Source: World Bank data.

Developing countries are accumulating foreign assets

The most striking impact of developing countries on the global financial system has been the rise in their official reserve assets (figure 5.5), up from 16 percent of global reserves in 1990 to 57 percent in 2009. China accounts for a little more than half of the approximately 40 point rise in developing countries' share of reserves, with the bulk of the remainder attributable to other East Asian countries and the oil exporters in Europe and Central Asia. Latin America, Sub-Saharan Africa, South Asia, and the Middle East and North Africa have seen more modest increases. Developing country reserves have generally risen relative to exports and GDP (figure 5.6), partly reflecting the ability of the United States and several other industrial economies to consume beyond their current income.

For the United States, the overhang of $3.3 trillion in Treasury securities held by foreigners (44 percent by China and Japan) may constrain U.S. policy, as the sale of these securities could exert pressure on the dollar and on U.S. interest rates.[21] But the ability of foreign holders of U.S. Treasuries to destabilize the dollar or the U.S. economy is limited. The stock of financial assets of U.S. households and nonprofit organizations equaled $42.5 trillion in the first quarter of 2010, and their net worth (including only financial assets and liabilities) was $23 trillion. Thus, so long as U.S. residents (not to mention other foreigners) have confidence in U.S. policies, the potential supply of funds to purchase U.S. Treasury securities is substantial.

FIGURE 5.5 DEVELOPING COUNTRY RESERVES SURPASS THE HIGH-INCOME SHARE
(PERCENT)

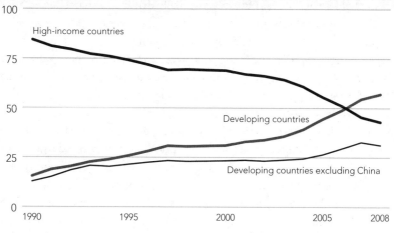

Source: IMF data.

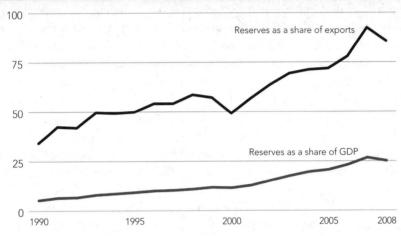

Source: IMF data.

The impact on U.S. interest rates of strategic sales of U.S. Treasury securities could be significant, though the demand for U.S. Treasuries is likely elastic: very small increases in yields would attract substantial demand, limiting the rise in interest rates. This does not mean that a run on the dollar is inconceivable. Concerns over unsustainable policies, coupled with moves by foreign holders to dump Treasuries, could precipitate a rush to other currencies by both foreign and domestic holders of dollars. But the most likely driver of a sharp depreciation of the dollar would be the failure to adopt policies sufficient to achieve a sustainable fiscal position, not strategic moves by foreign countries.

Developing countries also have good reason to avoid massive sales of their dollar reserves. About 60 percent of developing country reserves are denominated in dollars, so a sharp depreciation of the dollar (driven, say, by initial efforts to move reserve holdings into other currencies) could imply massive losses.[22] One estimate of dollar reserve holdings by Asian economies implies that a 20 percent depreciation of the dollar would result in a decline in wealth equivalent to 10 percent of their GDP.[23] And despite grave concerns over the sustainability of U.S. policies, most of the alternatives have serious drawbacks that will restrain pressures for a decline of the dollar as a reserve currency, at least in the short term (box 5.2).

The external assets of developing countries' private sector have also grown sharply in recent years. Here, data are hard to come by. Recorded capital outflows

BOX 5.2 THE END OF THE DOLLAR AS A RESERVE CURRENCY?

Despite the surge in trade and output growth from emerging markets over the past two decades, the dollar remains the world's dominant reserve currency. While the U.S. share of world GDP and trade has been declining, the share of international reserves denominated in dollars rose from 59 percent in 1995 to 71 percent in 2000, before falling to 64 percent in 2008. Reserves have risen as a share of world trade, so the world economy remains heavily dependent on the dollar.

From the perspective of U.S. firms and residents, the use of the dollar as a reserve currency provides seignorage income, reduces transaction costs, and shifts exchange risk to creditors and foreign trade partners.[1] There are also disadvantages: a stronger dollar helps U.S. consumers but makes producers less competitive and reduces the Federal Reserve's ability to use monetary policy to control domestic economic activity.

The forecasts in chapter 3 envision a continuing, and cumulatively very significant, decline in the importance of the United States in the global economy: by 2050 its share of G20 GDP is projected to fall to 24 percent (from 34 percent in 2009) and its share of international trade to 9.2 percent (from 12.8 percent in 2006). This process will inevitably feed pressures for alternative monetary arrangements. But which currency will gain share in reserves?

The euro accounts for the second largest share of international reserves, but its share remains below that of the currencies of EMU members in the 1980s and early 1990s.[2] Even before the European debt crisis, the euro's potential as a reserve remained doubtful largely because European financial markets are not as deep as in the United States (no instrument is comparable to U.S. Treasury bills in market size and liquidity).[3]

Slowing growth and high debt levels make it unlikely that the yen's use as an international currency will increase in the future.

Only about 1 percent of international reserves are SDRs.[4] And they are not held by the private sector, impairing their usefulness as a means of intervention in currency markets.[5] Negotiations over the size of SDR issuance and the terms of converting existing dollar reserves to SDRs are likely to be difficult.

The importance of the renminbi is set to continue to rise. However, China's shallow financial markets, the lack of full convertibility for capital account transactions, limitations on currency trading, and perhaps more fundamentally, potential for instability and weak institutions limit the use of its currency as the denomination of international reserves.[6]

So, the dollar will remain an important reserve currency for a significant period.

Notes
1. There are some offsetting costs not included in this calculation, such as controlling counterfeiting and maintaining stocks of dollars (Goldberg 2010).
2. Galati and Wooldbridge 2009.
3. Cohen (2008) argues that the euro also is less attractive than the dollar as a reserve asset because its value depends on political agreement among states, rather than a single authority capable of taking policy decisions.
4. Carbaugh and Hedrick 2009.
5. Countries with dollar holdings are committed to providing them to monetary authorities in return for SDRs, so holding SDRs and then converting them to dollars for the purposes of intervention is a feasible strategy (Williamson 2009). However, the expanded use of SDRs would likely require further international agreement.
6. See, for example, Bowles and Wang 2008.

in the balance of payments statistics are notoriously understated, due to the lack of statistical capacity in many countries and to efforts to avoid reporting (either to evade remaining controls on outflows or to avoid declaring income earned illegally or not reported to the tax authorities). "Illicit financial flows" from developing countries may have exceeded $1 trillion in 2006.[24]

One very rough indicator of the magnitude of private capital outflows from developing countries reflects the difference between their current account deficit and the sum of net capital inflows and changes in reserves.[25,26] This "balancing item" rose from outflows of $91 billion in 2003 to $658 billion in 2008. By this measure, the cumulative rise in developing private sectors' holding of capital abroad over this period totaled $2.3 trillion. Another measure of total external assets of developing countries (including official reserves and the holdings of sovereign wealth funds) is 15 percent of global GDP,[27] which was estimated at about $61 trillion in 2008.

Developing countries' share of global FDI flows more than tripled during 2003–08, reflecting much tighter global production links between developing and high-income countries (see chapter 4). Developing countries' share of stock market capitalizations also increased sharply. By contrast, their share of international bank assets (measured by the assets of banks reporting to the Bank for International Settlements) was fairly stable (figure 5.7). Indeed, developing countries are less important in international banking than their 25 percent share of BIS-reporting banks' assets in the early 1980s. Similarly, developing country reserves and stock market capitalizations have risen as a share of their GDP, while their loans from BIS-reporting banks have fallen. Developing country participation in derivatives markets, while growing, also remains small. For example, the average daily turnover of reported over-the-counter derivatives trades in emerging markets rose from $162 billion in 2001 to $521 billion in 2007, or from 8.7 percent of turnover to 10.1 percent.[28]

Global current account imbalances are rising

Increased global financial integration is reflected in rising current account imbalances, from 1.8 percent of global GDP in 1983 to 4.2 percent in 2008 (figure 5.8), as investors and savers see greater returns in foreign countries. There is considerable evidence of a "home bias" in portfolio allocation (investors tend to hold a larger share of securities from their own country than the share of their country's securities in the global market), due to capital controls, transactions costs, available information, and risk aversion. For example, one estimate from a couple of decades ago found that U.S. equity traders allocated more than 90 percent of their portfolio to domestic equities, even though the United States

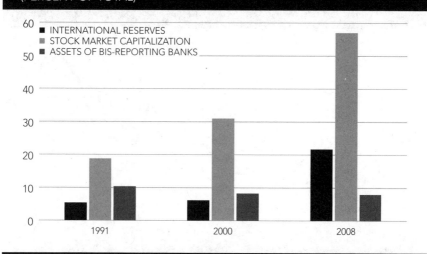

FIGURE 5.7 DEVELOPING COUNTRIES' SHARE IN GLOBAL FINANCE
(PERCENT OF TOTAL)

■ INTERNATIONAL RESERVES
■ STOCK MARKET CAPITALIZATION
■ ASSETS OF BIS-REPORTING BANKS

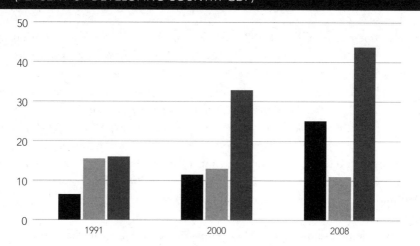

(PERCENT OF DEVELOPING COUNTRY GDP)

Source: World Bank data; IMF data; Bank for International Settlements data.

accounted for less than half of the global market.[29] But it appears that this bias has been falling over time, a reflection of increased financial integration. The home bias in equities declined sharply after the early 1990s in 25 countries, with the most pronounced declines for participants in the European Monetary Union.[30]

By this measure, developing countries have participated in the rise in financial integration. Developing countries' aggregate current account imbalances rose

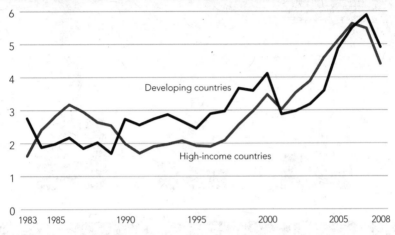

FIGURE 5.8 GLOBAL CURRENT ACCOUNT IMBALANCES NOW UP TO 4.2 PERCENT OF GLOBAL GDP
(PERCENT)

Source: World Bank data; authors' calculations.

from 2.8 percent of GDP in 1983 to 4.9 percent in 2008. The acceleration in developing countries' imbalances after 2001 reflects about equally the increasing surplus in China and in other developing countries. Developing countries' share of global imbalances more than doubled in the boom that preceded the Great Recession, rising from 22 percent in 2002 to 44 percent in 2008.

The rise in developing countries' current account surplus has not yet been reflected in a rise in their share of global external assets, even among the largest emerging markets. The developing country members of the G20 (excluding Russia) accounted for about 10 percent of total G20 external assets in 1981, declining to about 6 percent (including Russia) in the mid-1990s, and then rising to 9 percent by 2007.

But there is reason to expect this share to increase sharply in the future. First, after the Great Recession it is likely that financial sector growth in the advanced countries will be restrained, particularly compared with the boom years of the last decade. Second, since 1981 (the first year that data are available) China has had the fastest growth in external assets of any of the G20 countries (16 percent a year on average). Since China also has the largest stock of external assets among the developing G20, a continuing, rapid growth rate will tend to drive the aggregate growth rate up. Third, and most important, the larger, faster-growing developing countries have been undergoing a slow process of financial liberalization that, along with their rapid growth in output and trade, has fueled the growth in external assets. Barring any great mishap, this process, and thus the rise in financial assets, should continue and perhaps even accelerate in the years to come.

If each country's external assets increase at the same rate as GDP over the next few decades (based on the forecasts in chapter 3), developing countries' share of G20 external assets would reach 30 percent by 2050 (figure 5.9). But it is likely that rising incomes and a gradual loosening of restraints on external financial transactions in China and India will lead to much faster growth than this mechanical forecast. In short, developing countries are set to become much more important actors in international financial markets, though they are unlikely to entirely overcome the lead of rich countries within the forecast period.

The benefits of financial integration for developing countries are limited

Opening to external capital can contribute to development, but it is particularly dangerous for countries with weak institutions.

Financial integration can accelerate financial development

Opening domestic financial markets to foreign competition can accelerate financial development. Residents can enjoy lower borrowing costs, higher returns

FIGURE 5.9 DEVELOPING COUNTRIES' SHARE OF G20 EXTERNAL ASSETS SET TO HIT 30 PERCENT BY 2050
(EXTERNAL ASSETS OF THE G20 COUNTRIES, PERCENT)

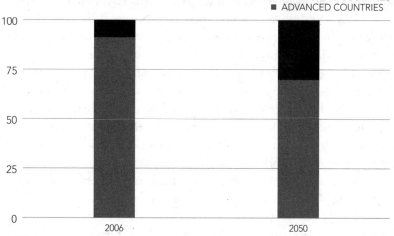

Source: IMF data.

on savings, and the benefits of portfolio diversification. Countries can gain access to international capital markets to help in the face of domestic shocks, and the highly volatile macroeconomic conditions in developing countries probably means that they can benefit disproportionately from this "consumption smoothing."[31]

Better access to foreign capital can increase domestic investment in credit-constrained economies and improve the global allocation of investment. Open capital accounts can strengthen domestic financial systems through stronger competition. Foreign direct investment can be particularly beneficial—improving domestic competition, facilitating participation in international trade,[32] and enabling access to technology. And the potential for capital to leave the country as financial integration advances can have a healthy effect on economic policies.[33]

But developing countries often do not realize the benefits of financial integration

Financial integration does not always reallocate global savings toward developing countries, which in aggregate exported capital (ran a current account surplus) from 1999–2008. At first glance, this is puzzling: capital is more scarce in developing countries than in the advanced economies, so all else equal, capital should earn a higher return in developing countries and should flow there from the advanced economies (which should run current account deficits). But this simple framework omits three forces that drive capital exports from developing countries.

First, despite capital's relative scarcity, it may not earn higher returns in developing countries because corruption, inadequate legal systems, or an insufficient supply of public goods (such as infrastructure) prevent entrepreneurs from reaping the full benefits of their investments.[34] Second, developing countries also have incentives to export capital—including the desire to diversify portfolios, particularly given the small size and poor diversification of many developing economies, and to hold relatively "safe" investments and reserves as a precaution—an important motive for many countries following the East Asian crisis of the late 1990s. Third, most of the 32 developing countries that had a cumulative current account surplus from 1999–2008 are either commodity exporters, which were not in a position to absorb the huge windfall profits from the rise in commodity prices prior to the global recession, or countries that, despite capital exports, maintained investment rates in excess of 25 percent of GDP. In neither of these cases is it obvious that they should have increased domestic investment.

More spectacularly, the relaxation of controls on financial transactions has led to crises with severe implications for growth and welfare (box 5.3). Financial

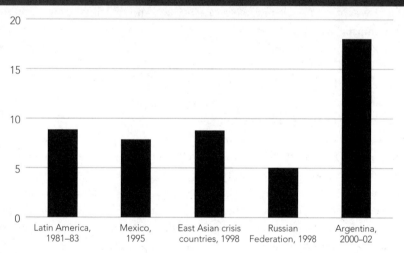

Note: In constant dollars.
Source: World Bank data.

integration appears to have boosted volatility in many countries, rather than serving as a means of smoothing consumption. The costs of volatility are likely to be largest where economies are small and information is relatively scarce (so that capital movements unrelated to fundamental economic developments—in response to rumor or concern over problems in similar economies—can have a large impact) and where governments have less ability to undertake countercyclical policy to support demand or address insolvent financial institutions. Thus the net benefits of removing restrictions on external financial transactions tend to be largest in the more developed economies, and small or negative in the poorest economies.

Financial crises in high-income countries tend be less costly relative to output, though obviously not in absolute terms. The recent crisis—the most severe shock driven by financial instability since the 1930s—reduced GDP in the United States by "only" 2.5 percent (in 2009) and in the Euro area by 3.9 percent, far less than the impact in most of the developing-country crises cited above. The less severe impact of crises on high-income countries is due to their more diversified economies, greater availability of automatic stabilizers (welfare, unemployment insurance), and limited capital flight (safer, alternative investments are often not available). The U.S. role as a safe haven during crises also limits the impact there.

Empirical studies generally find that the benefits for developing countries of opening to foreign capital are on average small or even negative.[35] Studies that focus on portfolio equity flows do tend to find a positive impact on growth.[36] Debt flows appear to generate the greatest risk from financial openness. Studies of the impact of FDI on growth have been mixed: the growth benefits of FDI appear to be subject to initial conditions—higher education levels may increase absorption of FDI—and to sectoral composition—FDI in manufacturing may be more beneficial to growth than FDI in mining, for example.

Implications for the global economy

Developing countries' increasing participation in financial markets has implications for other countries as well. Just as in goods markets, the increasing role of developing countries in global finance can provide substantial opportunities to firms in high-income countries. U.S., European, and Japanese banks can diversify their risks by increasing the share of their assets in developing countries. And because modern financial markets rely on sophisticated products that require substantial knowledge, experience, and technology, high-income country financial conglomerates can reap large profits by providing these services to developing country firms beginning to enter these markets. For example, despite the substantial participation by developing countries in project finance, these often-complex transactions are largely managed by firms from high-income countries (though even here the share of developing-country managers has increased).[37] Similarly, developing countries are important consumers of international bond placements, but firms in high-income countries continue to account for most of the lead managers in such transactions.

But the rise of developing countries also presents challenges for efforts to limit financial risk taking and to cope with global crises.

Developing countries' weak institutions underline the need for coordinating financial regulation

By 2050 six of the eight largest countries will be developing countries with lower incomes and likely with weaker regulatory frameworks than today's advanced economies. Efforts to strengthen these frameworks should thus rank high on the global agenda for economic cooperation. The rapid growth of developing countries makes this particularly difficult. After all, the major industrial economies had two centuries to develop appropriate regulatory frameworks for the financial sector, and they remain works in progress. Some developing countries have telescoped the same economic progress into several decades, leaving precious little time for the development of institutions to manage the financial sector.

The global reach of many financial institutions and the potential for regulatory arbitrage mean that policy coordination must help strengthen supervision and regulation. Tighter controls over risk taking can drive investors to jurisdictions where disclosure and capital requirements are less onerous. Hence the need for agreement among the major financial centers on the degree of disclosure and capital required—and for cooperation in supervising global financial institutions. Just as the reaction to the crisis involved intensive collaboration of policy responses by the major industrial countries,[38] effective regulation of the financial sector will require more intensive collaboration going forward. At the same time, the discrediting of G7 financial policies (particularly those of the United States and the United Kingdom) has spurred the development of regional approaches to financial regulation, in both Europe and Asia. It is not yet clear whether the emerging financial order will strengthen financial integration or fragment financial markets into regional centers.

Different approaches to financial regulation have mixed implications for successful policy coordination

To the extent that a global approach to regulation is pursued, the rise of developing countries will have implications for achieving consensus on, and implementing, stricter financial regulations. Differences among developing country financial systems, and between those of developing countries and rich countries, have mixed, and to some extent contradictory, implications for the prospects of improved policy coordination.

While the crisis was generated by weaknesses in high-income country financial markets, the fact remains that countries with weaker institutions are more prone to crises, and have less ability to monitor the exposure of sophisticated financial institutions that operate in their jurisdictions. Although developing countries are improving their financial institutions as their wealth rises, their growing importance in financial markets has outstripped their early improvements in financial supervision. For example, China's banks have reduced nonperforming loans (from 17.4 percent of assets at the end of 2003 to 1.8 percent in mid-2009) and strengthened capital positions (by 2008 banks holding nearly all commercial bank assets had met the BIS minimum capital adequacy standard).[39]

Even so, political connections continue to channel a substantial amount of lending, and the internal controls of Chinese financial institutions remain weak.[40] Poor governance in other major developing countries (such as Russia) also may limit the effectiveness of financial regulation. Weak financial regulation in countries that by 2030 will be among the world's largest economies dramatically underlines the potential risks to the global economy going forward. A financial collapse in China in 20 years could have even larger repercussions than the recent U.S. housing bust. So encouraging strong regulation in China and other large emerging economies should be everyone's concern.

Weak institutions are one reason the capital requirements agreed to under the first Basel accord (and implemented in many developing countries) were not very successful in improving the soundness of developing country banking systems, as seen in the rise of measured equity capital that preceded many banking crises.[41] Capital requirements were ineffective in developing countries due to weaknesses in accounting, reporting, and judicial systems, as well as the shallow capital markets and often highly concentrated bank ownership that made validating the real value of bank capital difficult. Moreover, even the more advanced emerging markets have relatively low compliance with the uniform financial standards and codes articulated by the Financial Stability Forum.[42] The coming years are likely to feature a further shift in financial weight to countries where financial regulation is weakest, increasing the potential for financial markets to generate major disruptions in global economic activity.

Even though regulatory capabilities may be weaker in developing countries, the regulatory *policies* in some are more restrictive than in many rich countries. For example, China's restrictions on capital transactions, strict control of derivatives transactions, and heavy participation by state institutions in domestic finance may limit the efficiency of financial markets, but these restrictions also limit the potential for instability. And China's economic success may encourage other countries to limit their financial openness as well. An open financial system is likely to be more efficient over the long run, and indeed it may be impossible to reap the benefits of continuing domestic financial development and openness to trade while insulating an economy from international financial flows.[43] The past two decades have seen a gradual increase in flexibility in China's regulatory policies, and it is likely that this trend will continue. But to the extent that China's influence on global financial sector policies increases, these policies are likely to be more restrictive than if they reflected rich-country practices alone.

Developing countries may in other respects have a contradictory influence on global financial sector policies. As discussed in the chapters on trade and global public goods, simply increasing the number of negotiating parties can impede agreement on joint policies, particularly when the new participants have very different incomes and historical experiences. Current arrangements for sharing information among supervisors, through informal contacts and non-binding memoranda of understanding,[44] may not be a sufficient basis for cooperation between countries with widely divergent living standards and institutions. And there is little agreement on how much forbearance regulators should show toward banks on burden-sharing during financial rescues of global institutions.[45] Prudential regulations differ even in Europe's single market,[46] so achieving uniform standards across developing and rich countries is likely to be problematic.

Some developing countries may be less willing to adopt tight controls on risk taking. Stricter regulation that raises the cost of financial intermediation may be viewed as a reasonable price to pay for stability in rich countries with deep financial markets[47] or in developing countries enjoying rapid growth. But some poor countries growing less rapidly, with a large part of the population lacking access to formal financial services, may prefer lower capital requirements, despite the higher risk.[48] So, less restrictive regulatory policies in some developing countries will leave open the potential for regulatory arbitrage in a more global financial system.

This problem could be even greater in regulating derivatives. The notional value of global credit derivatives (such as asset-backed securities and credit default swaps) have grown exponentially, rising from about $1 trillion at the beginning of the 2000s to $62 trillion in 2007, before declining to $31 trillion in the first half of 2009.[49] After accounting for offsetting contracts, the global value of credit derivatives is about 10 percent of this, with the "true" credit risk somewhere in between.[50] It is unlikely that developing countries would avoid the temptation of establishing their own clearinghouses for derivatives as these become established in the advanced countries, with the potential for competition through reducing collateral standards and insurance fund charges. Even in the absence of competing clearinghouses, investors could move derivatives trades to over-the-counter markets in developing countries to circumvent transparency requirements. Developing countries also have an interest in avoiding excessive risk taking, and during the recent crisis developing-country firms suffered huge losses (some of them eventually socialized) through bets on the derivatives markets. So reaching agreement on derivatives regulation by all major participating countries, while difficult, may not be impossible.

But it is impossible to predict how these conflicting forces will play out over the medium term. If the focus remains on simply mandating (strengthened) requirements based on practice in the G7 countries, increasing reporting requirements may overload weak public institutions in developing countries. One possibility is that regulatory policies will be more restrictive and less sophisticated (based, say, on less complicated reports from financial sector institutions and requiring less investment in information processing) than if policy design were solely up to the more advanced countries. The resulting rules could be much less efficient than those designed by the club of rich country bank supervisors, but they also may result in a more stable financial system. Another possibility is that different regulatory approaches will be encouraged for countries at different levels of development (just as the more sophisticated commercial banks had more flexibility in determining capital adequacy than other banks in the transition to Basel II), with some jurisdictions enjoying a competitive advantage.

Given the severe weaknesses that the recent crisis exposed in advanced country regulatory frameworks, developing countries may not wish to copy advanced country financial policies. But they could benefit from assistance from the advanced countries to improve the technical training of supervisors and policymakers, and to adopt more sophisticated information processing in monitoring financial reporting requirements.

The rise of developing countries will increase the resources required for an international lender of last resort

A lender of last resort's provision of liquidity during a crisis is important to financial stability.[51] The IMF and national governments (Europe for Eastern Europe and the United States for Latin America) have often provided such support to emerging market governments in crisis (which banking crises then had the wherewithal to support local banks). Similarly, U.S. and European governments rescued illiquid financial institutions during the recent crisis, measures essential to avoid a second Great Depression, although they entailed huge fiscal costs and raised the specter of moral hazard boosting future financial transactions.

Approaches to the rescue operations varied. In the emerging market crises, coordination among the creditor governments could be effected through the IMF and bilateral consultations. For the recent crisis, bailouts of rich country financial institutions were largely by individual governments. But some involved not-always-successful agreements on burden sharing (such as the European efforts to resolve Dexia and Fortis), while in general the individual actions were heavily conditioned by similar emergency measures in other countries.[52] The U.S. Federal Reserve also expanded swap lines with foreign central banks to enable them to provide temporary dollar support to their financial institutions. Expectations were that, in a crisis, each government should deal with financial institutions headquartered in its country, and the steps taken were ultimately sufficient to restore stability, though it was a close-run thing. This ad hoc approach to cooperation in addressing insolvent institutions was assisted by the long tradition of cooperation and close network of intergovernmental institutions among advanced countries.

How will the rise of developing countries affect emergency support in future crises? As developing countries grow in importance, the resources required to assist them and the incentives for the rich countries to avoid instability that will affect their own prospects will also rise. The crisis has spurred increases in resources to the IMF (lending resources have tripled in the crisis), but whether these resources will be sufficient to address future crises is uncertain. Already questioned is whether IMF resources have to be increased following the large commitments to Greece.[53] And as individual developing countries become equal or greater in size than most advanced countries, and the developing countries become more open to international financial transactions, the potential for crises affecting very large countries will rise, raising the level of resources required to deal with them.

Any further substantial increase in IMF lending resources could increase moral hazard, in the sense that banks and other lenders might be more willing to provide loans if, in the event of an adverse shock, a lender of last resort was reliably available (the argument that governments borrow recklessly for the same reason is not credible, given the adverse consequences of crises for the political leaders responsible). So greater resources might have to be accompanied by strict conditionality, and the possibility of debt restructuring to complement assistance would need to be maintained. The recently approved increase in resources to the IMF could usefully be supplemented by workout procedures for insolvent sovereign debtors—to limit moral hazard and to ensure that poor-country taxpayers must not always cover the losses incurred by their banks and governments.

While there appears to be little appetite for creating new international institutions to integrate developing countries into global financial governance, steps have been taken to change the responsibilities and governance structures of existing institutions.[54] Reliance on the G20 as the major international forum to discuss financial issues, the inclusion of all G20 members in the Financial Stability Board, and the inclusion of Brazil, China, India, Korea, Mexico, and Russia in the Basel Banking Committee were useful preliminary steps toward integrating the rapidly growing developing countries into global financial governance.[55] Further work can ensure that developing countries gain greater representation in the IMF and the World Bank.

Conclusion: A vision for global finance

Global authorities previously tried to reconcile financial development with financial stability by relying heavily on private rating agencies and the self-interest of private firms to contain risks and in a sense self-regulate. The Great Recession revealed that, in the context of expansive monetary policies, reliance on self-assessments and private rating agencies to monitor risk taking is a recipe for disaster. Today there appears to be little alternative but to accept some reduction in the pace of financial innovation as the price for stability. It is thus hoped that the global financial system emerging from the Great Recession will provide for higher capital ratios, stronger controls over risk taking, greater transparency of financial accounts, tighter supervision of non-bank financial institutions, and more attention to systemic risk. The implementation of such initiatives is by no means certain, and progress has so far been inadequate. Nevertheless, our perspective here is to assume that international authorities make good faith efforts to achieve stronger regulation, and that such efforts will require greater international coordination. The question then becomes, how will the rise of developing countries affect these efforts?

The answer is complex. Weak institutions in developing countries could mean that they become a more important source of financial instability, an encouragement to regulatory arbitrage, and an impediment to achieving rough consistency in the treatment of global financial institutions across jurisdictions. But the more controlled financial systems in some of the more successful developing countries could emerge as a source of stability, by encouraging the general adoption of tighter controls on risk taking than in many advanced countries, even if this reduces efficiency.

Notes

1. A good example is the 25 percent decline in New York securities prices during the Panic of 1792, set off by the near failure of the Bank of New York before it was rescued by the U.S. Treasury (Cowen and others 2006).
2. See "A Brief History of Banking" http://people.brandeis.edu/~cecchett/Textbook%20inserts/A%20Brief%20History%20of%20Banking.htm

3. See "A History of British Clearing Banks." www.banking-history.co.uk/history.html

4. Udovitch 1975.

5. McAndrews and Roberds 1999.

6. Kindleberger and Aliber 2005.

7. Hoppit 1986.

8. Kindleberger and Aliber 2005.

9. Bordo 1998.

10. Rajan and Zingales 2001.

11. Bernanke 1983.

12. See several articles at www.nytimes.com/krugman.

13. Reinhart and Rogoff 2009.

14. Acharya and others 2009.

15. Aizenman 2009.

16. Helleiner 2009.

17. World Bank 2010.

18. See, for example, Roubini and Sala-i-Martin 1992.

19. Chinn and Ito 2007.

20. Given the myriad regulations that affect external financial transactions and uncertainty over their effectiveness, defining the degree of openness is difficult. Other attempts tend to concur that developing country policies have become more open to external finance since the early 1990s (Obstfeld 2009).

21. The data on Treasury securities held by foreigners can be found at www.ustreas.gov/tic/mfh.txt.

22. The data are from the IMF COFER database. The estimate is subject to considerable uncertainty, as some 60 percent of developing country reserves have no data on currency composition. We assume that these reserves have the same currency composition as the reserves with data.

23. World Bank 2010.

24. Kar and Cartwright-Smith 2008.

25. World Bank 2009.

26. This is a rough indicator because it also includes errors and omissions in the balance of payments and capital transfers.

27. Alberola and Serena 2008.

28. The data are from the BIS Triennial Central Bank Survey. Emerging markets include the developing countries (as defined by the World Bank), plus a few Central European, Middle Eastern, and Asian countries that only recently achieved high incomes. The bulk of these trades were in Hong Kong and

Singapore; excluding these countries, emerging market over-the-counter turnover rose from $37 billion a day in 2001 to $151 billion in 2007.

29. French and Poterba 1991.
30. Baele and others 2007.
31. Pallage and Robe 2003.
32. See chapter 4 for a discussion of how FDI has boosted components trade.
33. Kaminsky and Schmukler 2002.
34. Rodrik and Subramanian 2008.
35. Kose and others (2006) summarize empirical studies of the relationship between financial integration and growth in developing countries.
36. For example, Gupta and Yuan (2005) find that following equity market liberalizations, industries that depend on external finance grow faster than industries dependent on finance internal to the firm. Similarly, Vanassche (2004) finds that financial openness has a positive effect on growth of industrial sectors generally, and that this impact is greatest in industries that rely more on external finance. Eichengreen and others (2009) find that capital account openness has a positive impact on the growth of financially dependent industries only in high-income countries, and this effect disappears during periods of crisis.
37. The dollar value of project finance transactions managed by developing-country institutions rose from about 0.5 percent of the total in 1997 to 9 percent in 2008 (Project Finance International, www.pfie.com).
38. Pauly 2009.
39. OECD 2010.
40. Cai and Wheale 2007. Moreover, uncertainty remains over the potential for increases in nonperforming loans with the rapid expansion of lending in response to the crisis.
41. Rojas-Suarez 2005.
42. Mosley 2009.
43. Obstfeld 2009.
44. Flamee and Windels 2009.
45. Acharya and others 2009.
46. Cihak and Podpiera 2006.
47. Benassy-Quere and others 2009.
48. Developing countries do not necessarily adopt lower capital requirements than rich countries, and as mentioned above, some developing countries have more restrictive financial regulations than the United States. Overall, as of early in the last decade, only 17 of 110 countries surveyed had minimum capital requirements that did not conform to the Basel guidelines (Barth

and others 2001). But if rich countries aim to raise capital requirements after the crisis (as we believe they should), it is uncertain whether all developing countries will follow.

49. Kiff and others 2009.

50. Global credit risk represented by derivatives may exceed the value of derivatives contracts after netting offsetting transactions because the failure of counterparties can endanger even firms whose net exposure to derivatives risk is zero.

51. See, for example, Hughson and Weidenmier (2009) for an analysis of how the establishment of the Federal Reserve in the United States reduced financial instability.

52. Note the failure of efforts to limit extensions of deposit insurance to foreigners' holdings and the rejection of proposals in the United States to make taxpayer funds available only to banks headquartered in the United States.

53. See, for example, *Economic Times*, June 4, 2010.

54. Porter 2009.

55. Griffith-Jones and Ocampo 2009.

References

Acharya, Viral V., Thomas Philippon, Matthew Richardson, and Nouriel Roubini. "Prologue: A Bird's Eye View: The Financial Crisis of 2007–2009: Causes and Remedies." In *Restoring Financial Stability: How to Repair a Failed System*, eds. Viral V. Acharya and Matthew Richardson. Hoboken, NJ: John Wiley & Sons, 2009.

Aizenman, Joshua. *On the paradox of prudential regulations in the globalized economy: international reserves and the crisis: a reassessment.* NBER Working Paper 14779. Cambridge, MA: National Bureau of Economic Research, 2009.

Alberola, Enrique, and Jose Maria Serena. "Sovereign External Assets and the Resilience of Global Imbalances." Banco de Espana Documentos de Trabajo 0834. Madrid, 2008.

Baele, Lieven, Crina Pungulescu, and Jenke Ter Horst. "Model Uncertainty, Financial Market Integration and the Home Bias Puzzle." *Journal of International Money and Finance*, 26 (2007): 606–30.

Barth, James, Gerard Caprio, and Ross Levine. "Bank Regulation and Supervision: What Works Best?" Policy Research Working Paper 2725. World Bank, Washington, DC, 2001.

Benassy-Quere, Agnes, Rajiv Kumar, and Jean Pisani-Ferry. "The G20 is not just a G7 with extra chairs." Bruegel Policy Contribution Issue 10. Paris: Centre d'études prospectives et d'informations internationals, September, 2009.

Bernanke, Ben. "Nonmonetary Effects of the Financial Crisis in the Propagation of the Great Depression." *American Economic Review*, 73(1983): 257–76.

Bordo, Michael. "Commentary." *Federal Reserve Bank of St. Louis Review*, May/June 1998. http://research.stlouisfed.org/publications/review/98/05/9805mb.pdf.

Bowles, Paul, and Baotai Wang. "The Rocky Road Ahead: China, the US and the Future of the Dollar." *Review of International Political Economy*, 15(2008): 335–53.

Cai, Zhuang, and Peter Wheale. "The New Capital Accord and the Chinese Banking Industry." *Journal of Banking Regulation*, 8 (2007): 262–89.

Carbaugh, Robert J. and David W. Hedrick. "Will the Dollar be Dethroned as the Main Reserve Currency?" *Global Economy Journal*, 9 (2009): Article 1.

Chinn, Menzie D. and Hiro Ito. "A New Measure of Financial Openness." *Journal of Comparative Policy Analysis*, 10 (2008): 309–22.

Cihak, Martin, and Richard Podpiera. "Is One Watchdog Better than Three? International Experience with Integrated Financial Sector Supervision." IMF Working Paper 06/57. International Monetary Fund, Washington, DC, 2006.

Cohen, Benjamin J. "Toward a Leaderless Currency System." In *The Future of the Dollar*, eds. Eric Helleiner and Jonathan Kirshner, 142–63. Ithaca, NY: Cornell University Press, 2008.

Cowen, David J., Richard Sylla, and Robert E. Wright. "The U.S. Panic of 1792: Financial Crisis Management and the Lender of Last Resort." Prepared for NBER DAE Summer Institute, July 2006, and XIV International Economic History Congress, Session 20, "Capital Market Anomalies in Economic History," Helsinki, August 2006, www.helsinki.fi/iehc2006/papers1/Sylla.pdf.

Eichengreen, Barry. "The Financial Crisis and Global Policy Reforms." Paper prepared for the Federal Reserve Bank of San Francisco's conference on Asia and the Financial Crisis in Santa Barbara, California, October 19–21, 2009.

Flamee, Michel, and Paul Windels. "Restructuring Financial Sector Supervision: Creating a Level Playing Field." *Geneva Papers*, 34 (2009): 9–23.

French, Kenneth R., and James M. Poterba. "Investor Diversification and International Equity Markets." *American Economic Review*, 81 (1991): 222–6.

Galati, Gabriele, and Philip Wooldridge. "The Euro as a Reserve Currency: a Challenge to the Pre-eminence of the US Dollar?" *International Journal of Finance and Economics*, 14 (2009): 1–23.

Galbraith, John Kenneth. *Money: Whence It Came, Where It Went*. Boston, Houghlon Mifflin, 1975.

Goldberg, Linda. "Is the International Role of the Dollar Changing?" *Current Issues in Economics and Finance*, 16 (2010): 1–8.

Griffith-Jones, Stephany, and Jose Antonio Ocampo. "Global Governance for Financial Stability and Development." Development Dimensions of Global Economic Governance. Initiative for Policy Dialogue and Colombia University and the United Nations Development Program, 2009, www.brookings.edu/events/2010/1008_global_development.aspx.

Hughson, Eric, and Marc Weidenmier. 2008. "Financial markets and a lender of last resort." In *The first global financial crisis of the 21st century: Part II, June-December, 2008*, eds. Carmen M. Reinhart and Andrew Felton. London: Centre for Economic Policy Research, 2009, http://mpra.ub.uni-muenchen.de/13604/.

Helleiner, Eric. "Reregulation and Fragmentation in International Governance." *Global Governance*, 15 (2009): 16–21.

Hoppit, Julian. "Financial Crises in Eighteenth Century England." *Economic History Review*, 39 (1986): 39–58.

Kaminsky, Graciela and Sergio L. Schmukler. "Emerging Market Instability: Do Sovereign Ratings Affect Country Risk and Stock Returns?" *World Bank Economic Review*, 16 (2002): 171–95.

Kar, Dev, and Devon Cartwright-Smith. *Illicit Financial Flows from Developing Countries: 2002–2006.* Washington, DC: Center for International Policy, 2008.

Kiff, John, Jennifer Elliott, Elias Kazarian, Jodi Scarlata, and Carolyne Spackman. "Credit Derivatives: Systemic Risks and Policy Options.?" IMF Working Paper 09/254. International Monetary Fund, Washington, DC, 2009.

Kindleberger, Charles P., and Robert Z. Aliber. *Manias, Panics and Crashes. A History of Financial Crises.* 5th ed. Basingstoke, United Kingdom: Palgrave MacMillan, 2005.

McAndrews, James, and William Roberds. "Payment Intermediation and the Origins of Banking." Federal Reserve Bank of New York Staff Report 85. New York, 1999.

Mosley, Layna. "An End to Global Standards and Codes?" *Global Governance*, 15 (2009): 10–15.

Obstfeld, Maurice. *International Finance and Growth in Developing Countries: What Have We Learned?* NBER Working Paper 14691. Cambridge, MA: National Bureau of Economic Research, 2009.

OECD (Organisation for Economic Co-operation and Development). *OECD Economic Surveys: China 2010.* Paris, 2010.

Pallage, Stéphane, and Michel A. Robe. "Leland & Pyle Meet Foreign Aid? Adverse Selection and the Procyclicality of Financial Aid Flows." Research Papers 0327. Centre interuniversitaire sur le risque, les politiques économiques et l'emploi, University of Quebec, Montreal, 2003, http://ideas.repec.org/p/lvl/lacicr/0327.html.

Pauly, Louis W. "Managing Financial Emergencies in an Integrating World." Paper prepared for the Duke University Seminar on Global Governance and Democracy, John Hope Franklin Center, Duke University, Durham, NC, April 16, 2009.

Porter, Tony. "Introduction to Special Forum: Crisis and the Future of Global Financial Governance." *Global Governance*, 15 (2009): 1–8.

Rajan, Raghuram G., and Luigi Zingales. "The Great Reversals: The Politics of Financial Development in the 20th Century." *Journal of Financial Economics*, 2001, jfe.rochester.edu/02104.pdf.

Reinhart, Carmen M., and Kenneth S. Rogoff. *This Time is Different: Eight Centuries of Financial Folly.* Princeton, NJ: Princeton University Press, 2009.

Rodrik, Dani and Arvind Subramanian. "Why Did Financial Globalization Disappoint?" *IMF Staff Papers*, 56 (2009): 112–138.

Rojas-Suarez, Liliana. "Financial Regulations in Developing Countries: Can they Effectively Limit the Impact of Capital Account Volatility?" Center for Global Development Working Paper 59. Washington, DC, 2005, http://ssrn.com/abstract=1114148.

Roubini, Nouriel, and Xavier Sala-i-Martin. "Financial repression and economic growth." *Journal of Development Economics*, 39 (1992): 5–30.

Udovitch, Abraham L. "Reflections on the Institutions of Credits and Banking in the Medieval Islamic Near East." *Studia Islamica*, 41 (1975): 5–21.

Williamson, John. "Why SDRs Could Rival the Dollar." Peterson Institute for International Economics Policy Brief PB09-20. Washington, DC, 2009.

World Bank. *Global Development Finance.* Washington, DC, 2009.

CHAPTER 6

MIGRATION

International migration can generate huge economic benefits for sending countries, receiving countries, and migrants. But ineffective restrictions on immigration have severely limited the gains while creating an enormous social problem in illegal immigration.

The tensions surrounding immigration restrictions in rich countries are set to rise, as rapid population growth and rising incomes in developing countries increase the number of potential migrants while the aging of industrial country populations increases the demand for migrant services.

International agreements have been marginal in shaping policies toward migration.

The ineffectiveness of immigration restrictions in the rich destination countries stems from competing views and interests. Opposition to immigration in the receiving countries reflects native workers fearing competing with migrants, concerns over the social impact of a growing foreign presence, and pure bigotry.[1] Yet, employer groups often support easing immigration restrictions, important sectors of destination countries' economies depend on immigrants, and there is reluctance to impose the general limits on civil liberties that would shut out all illegals.

The rise of developing countries, demographic trends, and other factors imply that these dilemmas are likely to sharpen in the coming years. Aging in the industrial countries will boost the demand for migrants. The surge in the working-age population, coupled with rising incomes that increase the ability to emigrate, will increase the potential supply of low-skilled emigrants from developing countries. And the growth of networks and technological progress in transportation and communications will continue to reduce the cost of migration. As the supply of low-skilled migrants increases, the policies to control immigration will become more expensive and intrusive—but will remain only partially effective.

Worse, immigration restrictions motivated largely by social concerns create a huge social problem of illegal immigration and increase the risks migrants face. But destination country policies vary: for example, the United States, a nation of immigrants with relatively flexible labor markets, has been more successful than European countries in integrating immigrants into its economy and society— and less successful in keeping out illegal immigrants (in part due to geography).

While international agreements are unlikely to help much in managing international migration, it is possible to raise the benefits of migration through international codes of conduct for source and destination countries, bilateral agreements to increase legal temporary migration, efforts to fight human trafficking, and programs to disseminate information on the risks and benefits of migration.

Migration can yield large economic gains

The benefits of moving even a limited number of workers (in comparison to the available pool) from low-wage developing countries to high-wage industrial countries are huge. The median wage in industrial countries is about two and a half times the wage of workers (in similar skill groups) in the most advanced developing countries, and five times that of workers in low-income countries.[2] While other means exist to exploit income differences among countries (such as trade, temporary movement of workers, capital flows, and outsourcing), migration is the principal means of doing so in construction, hotels, restaurants, and home help.

By some estimates the global gains from doubling the migrant stock would be greater than those that could come from eliminating all residual barriers to trade in goods.[3] Model-based calculations generally find that migration generates gains for migrants, origin countries, and destination countries (box 6.1). The bulk of the benefits accrue to migrants, who earn higher incomes. But destination countries enjoy an increased supply of nontraded services and a more efficient use of inputs to production. Origin countries gain access to foreign exchange: developing countries' recorded remittances rose from $31 billion in 1990 (0.8 percent of GDP) to an estimated $317 billion (1.9 percent of GDP) in 2009, and including unrecorded remittances (those through informal channels or to countries that do not report remittance receipts) would perhaps double this figure.[4]

BOX 6.1 ESTIMATES OF THE GAINS FROM MIGRATION

A global, computable general equilibrium model finds that a 5 percent rise in the labor force of high-income countries owing to immigration from 2010 to 2025 would increase natives' incomes in these countries by $190 billion, including the effect of rising remittances, and global income by about $1 trillion.[1] Another study estimates that in the short term, a 1 percent increase in the destination countries' population due to immigration would increase GDP by 1 percent, without affecting average wages or labor productivity.[2]

It is also possible to measure the gains from migration through studies of historical events. One example: in 2004 the EU was enlarged to include countries in Eastern Europe. A rush of immigrants came to the United Kingdom and Ireland, and GDP there is expected to be 0.5 to 1.5 percent larger after 10 years.[3]

Notes
1. van der Mensbrugghe and Roland-Holst 2009.
2. Ortega and Per 2009.
3. UNDP 2009.

These model-based calculations understate the economic gains from migration. The models cannot reflect dynamic gains from high-skilled migration to receiving countries. For example, the huge influx of scientists following World War II (particularly from Britain, Canada, and Germany) contributed much to technological progress in the United States.[5] Since many college graduate immigrants have science and engineering degrees, they contribute twice as many patents as do native graduates (Hunt and Gauthier-Loiselle 2009). Nor do the models measure intangible benefits, such as (for sending countries) improved market contacts, technology transfer, and the return of workers with improved skills.

On the other hand, the model-based calculations do not adequately reflect the economic and social costs of migration. Migrants face travel and relocation expenses, the potential for bad decisions due to uncertainty and unreliable information, and, in the case of illegal migration, physical dangers. Workers in receiving countries must deal with transitory unemployment and a reduced return on prior investments in skills, though evidence that immigration has a substantial impact on native workers' wages is limited.[6] Origin countries may lose from large outflows of highly skilled workers who provide essential (and substantially nontradable) services such as education and health care, and generate external benefits from interactions with colleagues. But highly skilled émigrés may have been underemployed in their country of origin due to poor policies or small economic scales that limit specialization.[7]

Immigration may also impose costs on receiving countries through congestion effects and the burden on public spending. Examples include increased traffic, the bidding up of land prices, and a decline in the productivity of public services due to increasing numbers of residents,[8] or higher costs of integrating immigrants as their number increases.[9] But it is difficult to measure congestion effects, and immigrants may also offer opportunities for economies of scale, thus reducing the unit costs of services. Immigrants' net contribution to the government budget will depend on the rules governing taxes and expenditures; the immigrants' age, earnings, and eligibility for, and use of, government services; and the implications of immigration for natives' use of government services, for example, the impact on earnings of the poor. On balance, most empirical studies find that immigrants have little net impact on the government budget in advanced economies.[10]

The benefits of immigration also depend on the policies and social attitudes of the receiving country. Countries with relatively flexible labor markets and a long tradition of immigration, such as the United States, have been more successful in integrating immigrants into the economy and community, which likely increases the economic benefits. By contrast, several European countries with more rigid rules governing the labor market and lower general acceptance of immigrants have had less success with integration and are probably enjoying fewer economic benefits.[11]

The social costs and benefits of migration are impossible to measure, but may in some cases be more significant than the economic implications. Migrants may suffer from the distance from family, friends, and a familiar culture, or may benefit from the excitement of new experiences. Receiving countries may see a reduced consensus on important social issues, as well as religious and racial tensions, but may benefit from the influx of new ideas and greater diversity (as in fashion and food choices).

A lot depends on the attitudes and institutions in the receiving countries, the numbers of migrants, and their economic and social differences from natives. A small, relatively homogeneous country like the Netherlands may feel that its way of life is dramatically changed by increasing diversity (the share of the population with ethnic ties to developing countries is now about 12 percent). By contrast, a large diverse country with a history of absorbing immigrants like the United States may take in additional Hispanic migrants with little impact on natives.

International migration is increasing

If migration is beneficial, the increase in migration over the past 40 years is good news. According to the United Nations Population Division, the number of international migrants rose from 77 million in 1965 to 195 million in 2005, or somewhat faster than the 1.7 percent annual increase in world population over this period.

In the high-income countries migration is increasing relative to population. Since 1960 immigrants have more than doubled as a share of population in the industrial countries, reaching 10 percent in 2005 (figure 6.1). Even so, levels of immigration remain comparable to those reached by the major countries of destination during the open immigration before World War I. The share of immigrants in the U.S. population reached 15 percent in 1890,[12] about 3 percentage points higher than today. But some high-income countries now have much higher shares, including Switzerland (immigrants are 22 percent of the population), Singapore (43 percent), and several Middle Eastern oil exporters (78 percent in Qatar, 71 percent in the United Arab Emirates, and 62 percent in Kuwait).

Rising immigration shares in some countries have strained relationships between immigrants and natives, fueling calls for tighter restrictions, particularly on immigrants from developing countries (in the United States and Europe).

Tensions surrounding immigration are related not only to the size of the immigrant population. For example, the high rates of immigration in Australia and New Zealand (figure 6.2) partly reflect people moving between the two countries, who face little trouble integrating into their new homeland. By contrast, the share of immigrants in France is about the average of industrial countries, but immigration is difficult there because the children and grandchildren of immigrants still face significant barriers to integration. And

FIGURE 6.1 MORE IMMIGRANTS IN INDUSTRIAL COUNTRIES
(PERCENT OF POPULATION)

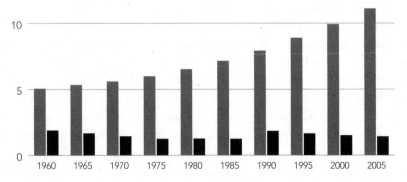

Source: United Nations Population Division data; World Bank data.

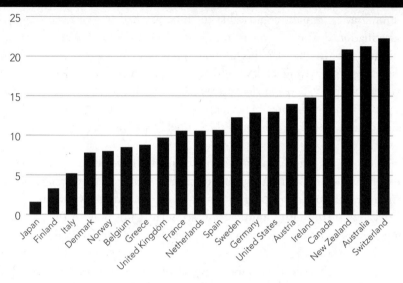

FIGURE 6.2 IMMIGRANTS IN INDUSTRIAL COUNTRIES, 2005
(PERCENT OF POPULATION)

Source: United Nations Population Division data.

Italy, with one of the lowest immigrant shares in industrial countries, passed the most draconian law, threatening jail terms for illegal migrants and those who harbor them.[13]

Industrial country immigration restrictions have perverse effects
Increasing immigration into industrial countries has been accompanied by a tightening of immigration controls, which are only partly effective.

Controls on immigration have a long history
Passports were required for entry into many towns in medieval Europe, and passport controls and visa requirements were common in the early nineteenth century. But the European passport system then broke down with the proliferation of railways, as the speed of travel and numbers of passengers made passport controls difficult to enforce.[14] Passport controls were continued, however, in the Ottoman and Russian empires. Immigration to the major countries of destination (the United States, Canada, Australia, and Argentina) was permitted virtually without restriction, the main exceptions being criminals and persons with infectious diseases. In the United States, immigration peaked with the huge inflows at the end of the nineteenth century and the first decade of the twentieth.

Passport requirements were instituted at the beginning of World War I, and after the war rising anti-immigrant sentiment led to progressively tighter restrictions in many countries. The U.S. Immigration Act of 1924, which remained in force until 1952, set nationality quotas and banned most Asian immigrants. Canada limited immigration to persons of European descent until the 1960s. In England, entry was permitted for citizens of the former British Empire until 1971. France had a fairly open immigration policy until the 1970s.

More recently, the focus has been on limiting illegal immigration, tightening restrictions on low-skilled immigration, and in some countries encouraging high-skilled immigration. The United States adopted a worldwide cap on immigration in the late 1970s, sought to regularize some illegal immigrants while (unsuccessfully) improving the enforcement of immigration laws in the 1980s and 1990s, and created some preferences for the admissions of high-skilled workers.[15] Immigration policies in the United Kingdom limited admission and access to citizenship from the 1960s to early in this decade, when efforts were made to attract low-skilled temporary workers and high-skilled migrants.[16] French policy, while shifting from government to government, has attempted to achieve zero new immigration, curtailed the right to asylum, and facilitated the deportation of immigrants.[17] Almost all governments now restrict entry and eligibility for citizenship, and the ability to determine who is entitled to the benefits of citizenship is seen as essential to maintaining national identity.

But immigration controls are only partly effective

A midrange estimate placed the stock of illegal immigrants at just under 4 million in 12 European countries, plus 12 million in the United States (table 6.1). Another source puts the global stock of illegal immigrants at 30–40 million.[18] The estimated stock of illegal migrants is small relative to population—less than 2 percent in 10 of the 15 countries in table 6.1. Illegal migrants do, however, make up a significant portion of total migrants for many countries—more than 10 percent in 10 of the 15 countries.

Illegal immigration is undesirable in several respects, compared with a situation where controls were 100 percent effective and permitted the existing number of immigrants.[19] They face much higher risks than legal immigrants. For example, deaths while crossing the Mexican-U.S. border averaged more than 300 a year from 1998–2004,[20] and as many as 2,000 Africans drown in the Mediterranean every year trying to cross to Europe.[21] Illegal immigrants may earn lower wages than legal immigrants performing the same work, thus intensifying competition for jobs.[22] A large number of illegal migrants fuels the informal economy. Restrictions that are only partially effective generally encourage

TABLE 6.1 ILLEGAL IMMIGRATION IN THE POPULATION

	ILLEGAL MIGRANTS			
	NUMBER (THOUSANDS)	PERCENT OF POPULATION	PERCENT OF TOTAL MIGRANTS	YEAR
AUSTRIA	50	0.6	4.3	2003
BELGIUM	150	1.4	17.0	2003
BRAZIL	180	0.1	26.2	2008
CANADA	80	0.2	1.3	2007
FRANCE	400	0.7	6.2	2003
GERMANY	1,000	1.2	9.4	2005
GREECE	375	3.4	38.5	2003
ITALY	500	0.9	16.3	2003
MALAYSIA	800	3.0	39.4	2006
NETHERLANDS	100	0.6	5.8	2003
PORTUGAL	80	0.8	10.5	2003
RUSSIAN FEDERATION	11,000	7.7	91.1	2007
SWITZERLAND	190	2.6	11.4	2003
UNITED KINGDOM	1,000	1.7	17.1	2003
UNITED STATES	12,000	3.9	30.6	2008

Note: Data refer to last available estimate. Where a range is given, the midpoint of the range is reported. Data on total migrants are for 2005, the last year of comparable statistics.
Source: For European countries except Germany, Jandl (2003); for Germany, reported in Deutsche Welle (2005); for Brazil, the official estimate reported in Rede Globo (2008); for Canada, reported in CanWest News Service (2007); for Malaysia, reported in *Times of India* (2006); for Russia, reported in *International Herald Tribune* (2007); and for the United States, Passel (2009).

contempt for seemingly impotent governments. Restrictive policies tend to have perverse effects, making it more difficult to control migration and limiting the willingness of migrants to return (for fear of not being able to migrate again). More important, ineffective restrictions encourage inequities and opportunities for exploitation repugnant to Western values. Many decades-long residents in some industrial countries remain illegal and ineligible for government benefits and legal protections. And it is difficult to countenance rules that abet forced prostitution and slave labor.

But eliminating illegal migration is difficult. While partly effective immigration restrictions are obviously undesirable, illegal immigration is difficult to control—thanks to the enormous increases in income possible through successful migration, the severe resource and technical challenges in policing long land borders and coastal areas, the competing interests and values in rich countries that limit support for enforcement, and the networks that support immigration. The draconian measures required for effective limits on illegal immigration would infringe on civil liberties and criminalize the daily activities of a large portion of (upper income) citizens in many industrial countries. Even steps viewed as extreme in many receiving countries are not always effective. For example, illegal migration has been significant in the Persian Gulf, despite the imposition of jail sentences for the violation of immigration laws.[23]

On the other hand, efforts to reduce the population of illegals by regularizing their status may encourage further inflows of illegal workers. For example, some observers claim that expectations of future amnesties in the United States (after the legalization of some immigrants through the 1986 Immigration Reform and Control Act) have encouraged illegal migration.[24]

Evaluating the impact of immigration controls is difficult

Immigration restrictions clearly deter some workers from emigrating, and generally raise the cost of emigration. Witness the high fees illegal immigrants are charged for assistance in crossing the U.S.-Mexico border—estimated at almost $3,000 in 2008.[25] But the impact of restrictions on the total number of immigrants is difficult to measure. One (incomplete) perspective is to view restrictions as a tax on immigration, so that restrictions raise the cost, and reduce the number, of immigrants. However, the level and changes in the number of immigrants due to restrictions depend on the shape of the demand and supply curves for migrant workers and changes in economic conditions that shift these curves. The more inelastic the supply and demand for migrants, the less effective the tax on immigration in controlling immigration. Changes in labor market conditions due to the business cycle may be the most important determinant of the flow of migrants, even in the face of tough restrictions—implying, for example, that a tighter labor market in the receiving country would lead to a surge in illegal migrants.

An extreme example illustrates this point. If the demand for migrants in high-income countries were perfectly inelastic (employers were willing to pay any wage necessary within the relevant range to attract migrants), the tax imposed by restrictions would simply be reflected in higher wages, with no impact on the quantity of immigrants. But changes in economic activity, by changing the demand for potential migrants in both origin and destination countries, would affect the quantity of migrants. The level of restrictions would determine the share of illegals in total immigrants, not the number of immigrants.

This perspective, while illuminating, is incomplete because immigration restrictions affect the risks of immigration as well as the cost. If migrants have to contend with a small probability of injury or death in the course of migration—and a substantial number of potential migrants are unwilling to run these risks regardless of the wage offered—restrictions may impose a larger impediment to migration than indicated by the average tax. Restrictions also affect the likelihood of obtaining a job. Highly skilled workers may have difficulty in obtaining employment in their professions because of the special qualifications required to practice in their field and because the firms and institutions that employ them may be unwilling to flout the law. Moreover, highly skilled workers who have good options in their home country may be less willing to live illegally than unskilled workers. So, immigration restrictions are more likely to reduce the inflow of highly skilled migrants, who "have more to lose," than that of unskilled migrants.

The conflicts inherent in many economies' dependence on high levels of illegal immigration, the adverse implications for migrants and society, the difficulties in enforcement, and the incentive implications of regularization greatly complicate efforts to establish a rational immigration regime. Thus, policies adopted to address illegal immigration are inevitably unsatisfactory compromises between enforcing the law and recognizing the economic and social implications of immigration reform.

This compromise has different forms. Individual industrial countries rely on different mixes of border restrictions, internal identification requirements, and employer verification to enforce immigration rules. For example, while Germany has pursued tighter border controls, interior controls on residence and employment are the primary means of controlling unauthorized immigration.[26] The United Kingdom has traditionally relied on policing the country's sea boundaries, rather than internal controls, to limit unauthorized immigration.[27] And in the United States, immigration control has focused on (largely impotent) border enforcement,[28] while efforts at sanctioning employers have been pitiful.[29,30] One can imagine unambiguous improvements in policies that would, for example, deliver the same level of restrictiveness at lower cost to resources and civil liberties. To the extent that demographic factors and rapid economic growth in developing countries are set to increase pressures for migration (as argued below), such improvements in policies are a high priority in industrial countries.

Pressures for migration will rise

The conflict between rising pressures for migration and tighter immigration restrictions in destination countries is likely to intensify in the coming years.[31]

Increased pressures for migration will be driven by demographic trends, advances in technology, networks, and climate change.

Demographic trends will increase the pressures for migration. With important exceptions, the populations of developing countries (which supply the bulk of international migrants) are younger and growing faster than those in industrial countries. The old-age dependency ratio (of people over 65 to the working-age population) is 24 percent in industrial countries (figure 6.3), and forecasts envision a continued rise in the ratio for the foreseeable future.[32] The aging of industrial country populations will increase the demand for migrants, at a minimum to provide services to the aged.[33] Conversely, children under 15 account for 29 percent of developing countries' populations (figure 6.4). Many countries in Sub-Saharan Africa (where children under 15 make up 43 percent of the population) and the Middle East and North Africa (32 percent) are unlikely to achieve the growth rates needed to absorb the very large numbers of new entrants to the workforce expected in coming years.

Advances in technology will also promote migration. Technological progress that reduces the cost of transportation (the real cost of U.S. air travel has fallen

FIGURE 6.3 OLD AGE DEPENDENCY RATIOS ARE HIGH IN THE INDUSTRIAL COUNTRIES AND IN EASTERN EUROPE AND CENTRAL ASIA
(PERCENT OF POPULATION OVER 65 RELATIVE TO WORKING AGE POPULATION)

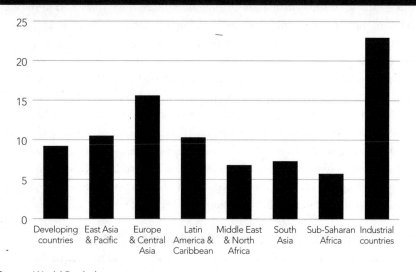

Source: World Bank data.

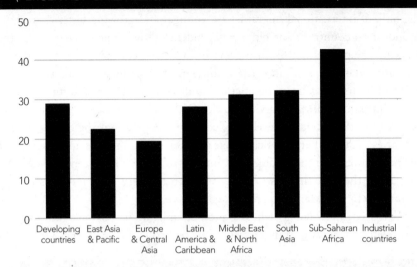

FIGURE 6.4 SHARES OF CHILDREN IN THE TOTAL POPULATION ARE HIGH FOR MOST DEVELOPING REGIONS
(PERCENT OF CHILDREN UNDER 15 IN TOTAL POPULATION)

Source: World Bank data.

by 41 percent since 1980 and 71 percent since 1960)[34] and communication (witness the growing availability of cell phones and falling international phone rates that help reduce immigrants' isolation) also reduces the cost of migration. And greater access to information through the Internet has improved knowledge about migration opportunities, reducing the uncertainty involved in emigration.

Migration networks also help future migrants. Migrants from countries with considerable past emigration gain from networks that can provide information on job opportunities and conditions, help with transitional expenses, and generally reduce the risks in migration.[35] So migration can, in a sense, be self-perpetuating.

Climate change is another significant pressure on migration. Soil erosion, the flooding of low-lying areas, and the degradation of agricultural productivity that accompany climate change will greatly increase the number of people who will have to move to higher ground and more productive farmland. One estimate puts that number at 200 million (about equal to the UN estimate of total international migrants in 2005), though not all of those displaced will move to other countries.[36]

Rising incomes in developing countries will boost migration

Economic progress in developing countries is likely to add further to the rise in migration pressures. Although rising incomes may encourage some who might otherwise leave to stay at home, they will also create vast new opportunities for others in lower-income locales to migrate.

Rapid growth will reduce incentives for some workers to migrate

Rapid growth in incomes will increase the attractiveness of staying at home, reducing incentives for developing country workers to leave (and also the benefits of migration to receiving countries) and indeed attracting former migrants back home. The past half century has shown how dramatic shifts in net emigration can accompany sustained economic progress. Several rapidly growing economies that were once labor exporters with minimal numbers of immigrants (Greece, Ireland, Italy, Korea, Portugal, and Spain) have had immigration surge as their incomes have converged with those in the most advanced economies (table 6.2). In Greece, for example, immigrants' share of the population increased from less than 1 percent in 1960 to almost 9 percent in 2005, while per capita incomes rose from less than one-fifth of that of the United States to more than half. And data on immigrants reflect only residents born in another country; these countries also benefited from the return of former emigrants, but there are no data to measure this.

Even so, industrial countries are expected to remain much richer than developing countries for a long period of time. For example, U.S. per capita income is expected to remain almost three times larger than China's in 2050 (see chapter 3). Thus, workers in developing countries will continue to enjoy considerable potential for increasing their incomes through international migration.

TABLE 6.2 IMMIGRANTS AS PERCENT OF THE POPULATION, 1960–2005

	IMMIGRANTS (PERCENT OF POPULATION)		PER CAPITA INCOME (PERCENT OF U.S. PER CAPITA INCOME)	
	1960	2005	1960	2005
GREECE	0.6	8.8	18.5	53.1
IRELAND	2.6	14.8	23.8	115.3
ITALY	0.9	5.2	27.9	72.4
KOREA, REP.	0.5	1.1	5.4	41.9
PORTUGAL	0.4	7.2	12.4	42.0
SPAIN	0.7	10.6	13.8	62.2

Source: World Bank data.

But growth may still increase migration, for several reasons

Economic development may increase emigration, particularly of the poor, who often lack opportunities to migrate to industrial countries due to limited skills, language and cultural barriers, and inadequate resources to finance the costs of travel and transitional expenses. As incomes (and education) rise, the ability to migrate will increase while the difference in wages between the home country and potential receiving countries, though narrowing, remains substantial. In addition, the displacement of workers in conjunction with economic growth will increase the supply of migrants (as in Mexico following NAFTA[37]).

Whether migration generally tends to rise with incomes at low levels of economic development is a matter of some controversy (box 6.2). But the potential supply of emigration from India and China is huge: according to the World Bank, 46.7 percent of China's population (more than 600 million people) and 52.4 percent of India's (more than 560 million people) live on less than $2.00 a day. Vast rural areas have large numbers of people who have failed to participate in the modernization evidenced in the urban centers of Shanghai and Mumbai. Increases in rural incomes and the disruptions of modernization will increase the ability to migrate while having only a marginal impact on the income gains enjoyed by migrants. This shift toward greater migration of the poor in developing countries will add to the policy challenges of rich destination countries, which are primarily concerned with excluding low-skilled workers.

Rising incomes in the developing world will likely also increase urbanization with links to migration. As in the past, they will likely be reflected in rural-urban migration and the growth of cities. Migrants in cities are in a better position than they would be in their rural homelands to understand international opportunities, link with networks that serve international migrants, and save the funds required for international migration. In the past, international migration has been connected to urbanization. For example, the development of maquiladoras along the Mexico-U.S. border has increased both internal migration and international migration.[38]

Rapid growth may also attract migrants from other developing countries, and international migration may rise because of larger South–South migration. Already, the number of international migrants within the developing world is approaching the number of international migrants from developing to high-income countries (table 6.3). About 80 percent of identified migration within the developing world is with neighboring countries,[39] and to the extent that growth prospects within a region are similar across countries, migration across borders is unlikely to accelerate sharply.[40] But the rapid growth of developing economies in East and South Asia is increasing income disparities with Sub-Saharan Africa, perhaps encouraging even larger flows of migrants.

BOX 6.2 THE ARGUMENT OVER THE MIGRATION HUMP

The term "migration hump" reflects the possible shape of a curve describing migration in rapidly growing economies over time: migration initially increases with an increased ability to migrate, but eventually declines as incomes in source countries converge with those in receiving countries. A migration hump may reflect rising population growth rates with higher incomes, disruptions that accompany economic development, greater ability to finance the initial costs of migration, or greater incentives to gain remittances as higher incomes improve local financial institutions and hence the return on savings.[1] But Lucas finds little empirical support for a migration hump. Net migration rates from 1995–2000 were a declining function of per capita income. Lundgren and Zaiceva and Zimmerman find no evidence for a migration hump in European migration data,[2] and Naude reaches a similar conclusion for emigration from Sub-Saharan Africa from 1965 to 2005.[3]

By contrast, other analysts see indications of a migration hump in data for rapidly growing countries that have shifted from net exporters to net importers of labor,[4] in one Mexican region,[5] in southern Europe and Turkey,[6] and in migration to Germany,[7] though Lucas remarks on the last three that the turning point (the income where migration begins to decline with further increases in income) is "so low as to be practically irrelevant."

The paucity of empirical tests of the migration hump hypothesis despite frequent references to it in the policy debate reflects the difficulties in modeling the determinants of migration flows. The supply of migrants may to a large extent be a market phenomenon, but actual migration also reflects the impact of legal prohibitions and attendant costs, which are difficult to estimate.

Notes
1. Lucas 2004.
2. Lundgren 2009; Zaiceva and Zimmerman 2008.
3. Naude 2008.
4. de Haas 2005.
5. Stark and Taylor 1991.
6. Faini and Venturini 1993.
7. Volger and Rotte 2000.

TABLE 6.3 SOUTH–SOUTH MIGRATION RIVALING SOUTH–NORTH
(MILLIONS)

	MIGRANTS TO		
MIGRATION FROM	DEVELOPING COUNTRIES	HIGH-INCOME COUNTRIES	TOTAL
DEVELOPING COUNTRIES	73.9	81.9	155.8
HIGH-INCOME COUNTRIES	4.2	30.6	34.8
TOTAL	78.1	112.5	190.6

Note: Data are for 2000.
Source: Ratha and Shaw 2007.

Rapidly growing developing countries may also attract émigrés to return home, reaping the benefits of their return. The expectation of continuing rising incomes may persuade highly skilled emigrants that opportunities are improving in their home country. Thus, for example, the BRICs could reap dynamic gains from expanding their pool of highly educated workers. Indeed, survey data indicate that only 6 percent of students from India and 10 percent of students from China wish to stay in the United States.[41] By contrast, countries where growth is not expected to be as robust may see continuing outflows of highly skilled emigrants to both high-income countries and faster-growing developing countries. But most major developing countries expected to achieve high growth rates over the next 40 years (see chapter 3) have only a small share of their college graduates abroad (table 6.4). While the potential number of returning high-skilled workers may not be large, it is possible that the more specialized and prominent high-skilled workers are the most likely to emigrate, so that returnees could have a greater impact than the number might indicate.

The rise of developing countries will affect the migration experience

The rise of developing countries could improve the migration experience for their nationals, as richer developing countries' governments provide more information on migration to industrial countries. Some countries aggressively encourage emigration, in part through providing information on job opportunities. For example, the government of the Philippines has explicit targets for emigration

TABLE 6.4 RAPIDLY GROWING ECONOMIES HAVE MOST OF THEIR COLLEGE GRADUATES AT HOME

	PROJECTED GDP GROWTH, 2009–50 (ANNUAL AVERAGE)	TERTIARY-EDUCATED EMIGRÉS, 2000 (PERCENT OF WORKERS)
ARGENTINA	4.1	2.8
BRAZIL	4.2	2.0
CHINA	5.6	3.8
INDIA	6.2	4.3
INDONESIA	5.0	2.9
MEXICO	4.3	15.5
RUSSIAN FEDERATION	3.3	1.4
SOUTH AFRICA	4.3	7.4
TURKEY	4.3	5.8

Source: Authors' forecasts; Docquier and Marfouk 2004.

and provides help with document processing, licensing recruitment agencies, and offering courses to departing emigrants.[42]

Similarly, having more administrative resources may enable developing countries to improve the migration experience. Strengthening the regulation of recruitment agencies could reduce the provision of misleading information and improve competition in the market. In some countries, recruitment agencies have amassed considerable market power through their access to information and ties to employers in destination countries, enabling them to capture rents generated by industrial country immigration restrictions.[43] In addition, increasing resources and a rising importance in global affairs will enable developing countries to protect émigrés subject to abuse or exploitation in foreign countries.

Both sending and receiving countries can benefit from circular migration. While high-skilled migration from rapidly growing developing countries may decline, technical exchanges may increase due to falling transport costs and advances in communication. For example, Indian expatriates working in Silicon Valley have had a major impact on the development of the high-tech corridor in Bangalore through investments, consultant services, and entrepreneurship.[44] The growth of an international pool of technical workers and academics (which workers from developing countries are increasingly joining) is beginning to erode sharp distinctions between migrants and native workers, and opening new opportunities for generating gains from collaboration for both developing and industrial countries.

Finally, rising incomes in developing countries will have an ambiguous impact on the criminal gangs, such as the Russian mafia and El Salvador's MS-13, that have extended their reach through international networks of migrants (box 6.3). Increased resources for law enforcement will facilitate more effective crackdowns, and higher incomes may provide more alternative livelihoods to potential gang members. But rising access to technology—gangs are using the Internet to advertise and communicate with members at a distance[45]—is likely to make the more entrenched gangs more powerful. And criminal activity will be encouraged by tighter immigration restrictions and rising pressures for low-skilled migration.

International cooperation in migration is limited

International agreements have little impact on migration, particularly in comparison to the extensive cooperation governing trade and financial flows. Why? Mainly because of the social implications.

Migration differs from trade and financial integration

While migration can have economic implications similar to trade in goods and financial assets, the social and political implications of absorbing new citizens

BOX 6.3 EXPORTING CRIMINALITY—EMIGRATION AND GANGS

The influx of illegal migrants has been associated with the growth of criminal gangs—particularly those in drug distribution, but including a wide variety of fraudulent and violent activities. Ethnic and national ties have historically been a key means of cementing solidarity among gang members. Gangs in receiving countries are often supported by their origin-country counterparts as useful conduits for drugs. For example, ties exist between Chinese and Vietnamese drug organizations and Asian gangs operating in Canada, while U.S.-based gangs are strengthening their links with foreign-based drug trafficking organizations to gain direct access to illegal drugs.[1] As gang presence has increased—the National Youth Gang Center estimates youth gang members in the United States rose from about 100,000 in 1980 to 731,000 in 2002—the role of immigrant gangs has increased as well.[2] The most prominent of them are extensions of gangs from Latin America, such as MS-13, which the FBI estimates has 10,000 members in the United States[3] and Eastern European gangs active in Western Europe.

　　The spread of the Russian mafia is probably the most dramatic example of how increased immigration can contribute to criminality. Russian criminals came to the United States in the 1970s and 1980s under the guise of refugees fleeing religious persecution,[4] but the major infusion of Russian gangsters—as in Brighton Beach, New York; Israel, Paris, and London[5]—dates back to the collapse of the Soviet Union. Indeed, the collapse of communism, the rise of globalization, and the opportunism of organized crime fueled the exponential growth in the global shadow economy, to perhaps nearly one-fifth of global GDP.[6]

Notes
1. FBI 2009.
2. National Alliance of Gang Investigators Association 2005.
3. Feere and Vaughan 2008.
4. California Department of Justice 1996.
5. BBC 1998.
6. Glenny 2008.

differ substantially from importing goods or accepting foreign investment. Thus governments have been reluctant to cede to international agreements any responsibility for determining who can immigrate. It would be unrealistic, for example, to expect that an international agreement could be reached on rules governing international migration similar to those established under the WTO for trade (box 6.4).

Indeed, the basic framework for negotiating trade agreements, where governments reduce barriers on imports in exchange for similar concessions from their trading partners, would have little applicability to international agreements on migration. The main destination countries have only limited outmigration, so origin countries would lack the leverage often afforded in international trade. Also note that many origin countries are ambivalent about

BOX 6.4 APPLYING GLOBAL TRADE PRINCIPLES TO INTERNATIONAL MIGRATION

The principles generally accepted for trade would have striking implications if applied to migration. Limits on immigration would have to be replaced by taxes on entry. Given the huge wage gains from migration, such taxes would have to be very large to deter migrants. (Note that such taxes would represent substantial government revenue gains that now accrue to workers and employers.) Even if quantitative limits on immigration were retained, countries could not discriminate based on country of origin. Once in a country, foreigners could not be subject to limits on employment or access to government benefits that are not imposed on natives. Countries could not arbitrarily change limits on immigration in response to cyclical conditions or foreign policy concerns. Country decisions on whether to admit immigrants would be subject to review by a foreign court (countries could not be forced to adopt particular rules or change decisions, but could be subject to sanctions, such as higher limits on potential migrants from the country). And all countries would have to agree to abide by these rules for them to become effective.

Such rules would not gain general acceptance if applied to migration. Few governments would agree to manage migration through taxes, permit entry to immigrants likely to become welfare recipients, or eschew changes in immigration restrictions. Indeed, the only trade provision that could gain widespread acceptance for immigration is dispute settlement, and that only because the penalty (limits on emigration from countries found in violation) is unlikely to be seen as a severe sanction by high-income countries.

supporting outmigration, so their interest in negotiating increased access is unclear.

The political economy of migration agreements also tends to impede international agreements. As with international trade, powerful domestic interests push opposing views on immigration. With trade, it is possible to craft compromises that balance the interests of firms and workers in export industries with those in industries that compete with imports. For example, import-competing firms might accept a reduction in tariffs on some goods in the interest of protecting other goods, and exporters might support a general trade agreement even if the concessions granted were not everything they hoped to achieve. Such compromises are more difficult for migration, where it can be hard to define the benefits to specific industries. However, some scope does exist for favoring some groups by granting concessions for particular classes of workers (such as the highly skilled) or particular sectors (such as agricultural workers).

More important, migration tends to touch groups with little economic interest in the outcome, and to touch on issues traditionally viewed as not subject to foreign influence. So, the ability of governments to sell agreements on migration to their citizenry is more limited than for trade.

Most international agreements do not allow for unrestricted migration
The European Union, which includes free movement of workers as a principle of integration, is an important exception to the general irrelevance of international agreements on migration. To some extent the willingness to open borders reflects the common historical heritage of these countries. Moreover, the EU countries either enjoy very similar incomes, or their entry to the EU was expected to lead to rapid convergence with incomes of the existing members. Thus the economic incentives for migration were expected to be small, or to attenuate over time. Even for the relatively low-income Eastern European countries, the stock of their immigrants in Western Europe only doubled following accession to the EU (from 2003 to 2009)[46]—not enough to greatly disrupt labor markets. Still, even among EU members the acceptance of migrants with low incomes and different cultural norms is not automatic; witness France's and Italy's recent treatment of Roma from Romania and Bulgaria.

But limited opportunities do exist for improving the migration experience through bilateral, regional, and international agreements. One can envision some progress in expanding the scope and importance of these agreements.

A large number of countries have entered bilateral agreements to support temporary or seasonal migration programs (box 6.5). But many recent agreements cover so few workers as to be irrelevant to migration flows between signing countries. For example, Morocco's agreement with Spain allowed for the movement of only 700 workers at a time when there were more than 200,000 Moroccan workers in Spain.[47] Moreover, the commitments by destination countries are limited to the number of migrants explicitly allowed under the agreement, and destination countries generally retain the right to determine eligibility.

Bilateral labor agreements can marginally expand legal migration opportunities for the sending country, and help returning migrants retain the social security benefits they earned while working abroad. And recruitment through bilateral migration treaties has resulted in the movement of workers from irregular to regular status. For example, a survey of French and German employers found that seasonal agreements with Poland helped limit irregular migration.[48] But these agreements were designed specifically to deal with the surge in Polish immigrants after the lifting of emigration restrictions with the collapse of the Soviet bloc. Bilateral labor agreements are likely to have less of an impact on illegal immigration in countries with a large pre-existing stock of irregular migrants and long-standing migrant networks.

By contrast, industrial countries enter bilateral agreements with developing countries largely to restrict migration, either by eliciting the cooperation of

BOX 6.5 BILATERAL AGREEMENTS TO ENCOURAGE LOW-SKILLED MIGRATION

Bilateral labor agreements have a long history in some countries.[1] They were frequently used to address labor shortages by European governments following World War II through the 1970s, and by Asian oil exporters in the 1970s and 1980s. The number of agreements mushroomed in the 1990s,[2] though the programs tended to be smaller than in the first few decades after World War II.[3]

More than 176 bilateral agreements and other forms of labor recruitment are in force in OECD countries. Of the 92 countries responding to a survey by the ILO, 57 reported bilateral migration agreements covering the rights of workers, recruitment, services, and return.[4] The bulk of the agreements entered by European high-income countries is with other European countries (both intra-EU and with Eastern Europe). The most common types of bilateral agreements in support of temporary migration are for seasonal workers (typically limited to sectors where employment varies over the course of the year—such as hospitality, catering, agriculture, construction); contract and project-linked workers; workers who come for training; and young adults who seek incidental employment when traveling for vacation.[5]

Notes
1. Germany and Switzerland signed the first agreement governing labor migration in 1890 (Durand 2004), though treaties between the United States and Spain in 1795 provided for the establishment and residence of nationals of the two states (Geronimi 2004).
2. Geronimi 2004.
3. Koehler and Laczko 2006.
4. This count excludes agreements limited to social security payments and the exchange of trainees.
5. Bobeva and Garson 2004.

the sending country in stemming illegal immigration (Italy has signed 28 readmission agreements to facilitate the repatriation of irregular migrants)[49] or to contain migration to specific channels with time limitations in order to facilitate enforcement of return (such as several U.S.-Mexico agreements governing farm laborers).[50] But evidence suggests that return programs attract only a few migrants, likely only those who were planning to return in any event.[51] And while some agreements have resulted in very few overstays (such as the Canadian Seasonal Workers Agricultural Program[52] and the UK seasonal agricultural workers program[53]), this has been due to the small size of these programs and the substantial administrative resources devoted to them.[54]

Agreements that cover larger numbers of migrants have been less successful in avoiding greater permanent migration. For example, in the German Guestworker program, procedures that facilitated longer-term residency, coupled with immigration for family unification, resulted in rising immigration after the program's termination. In the United States, programs that restricted migrants to specific employers or types of jobs led to growing domination of job categories by immigrants, and thus opportunities for continuing employment after the expiration of temporary visas.[55]

Most regional agreements and international institutions have had little impact. Regional migration agreements, with the important exception of the European Union, have done little to facilitate migration. Regional integration agreements in Africa, Latin America, and Asia have called for the free movement of persons among participating states, but these provisions have not been fully implemented. For example, ASEAN established a plan to achieve a free flow of skilled workers within the region,[56] but there has been little progress since then beyond agreements to combat trafficking and loosen visa requirements for temporary visits. African regional organizations have taken steps to facilitate short-term stays in member countries, but large economic unions in which citizens can move and work freely remain a longer-term goal.[57]

The International Organization of Migration, the International Labour Organization, the United Nations, the OECD, and the World Bank have devoted some resources to conduct research, manage small migration programs, and protect migrants. But in all, international cooperation has contributed little toward facilitating migration or, with the important exception of efforts to protect refugees, making migration safer. And the prospects for increasing the role of international agreements in migration management are poor. One potential area of compromise is for receiving countries to admit a larger number of immigrants in return for assistance from sending countries in controlling illegal immigration. But sending countries generally have less control over their borders than receiving countries have over theirs. And as developing countries become more important in the global economy, they may be less likely to accept concessions (such as assistance with preventing illegal migration) as a condition of enhancing legal migration opportunities.

Even so, international coordination can help in issues where general consensus exists on appropriate policies. Progress could be made in facilitating temporary migration through the General Agreements on Trade in Services. Countries agree on the need to control trafficking, both to limit illegal immigration and to protect the migrant victims. As incomes rise in developing countries, they will have more resources to enforce laws against trafficking, and perhaps a more informed and vocal citizenry willing to focus on the issue. In addition, international agreements under the United Nations and the International Labour Organization already provide standards for the treatment of migrants—such as equal protection under the law, nondiscrimination in employment and remuneration, eligibility for social security benefits, access to education (for children), and access to social services.[58] While such standards may not be binding, they can be useful in shaming democratic governments into treating immigrants fairly, helping to bolster the case advocates make for immigrants, and providing guidance to unilateral efforts to improve the migration experience. Future efforts to improve the welfare of migrants could focus on ensuring that agreed standards are respected by receiving countries.

Conclusion

The marginal contribution of international coordination in migration places the burden for improving migration policies squarely on the destination countries. Existing immigration restrictions have heightened social problems and failed to capitalize on substantial opportunities to increase incomes. These perverse effects will intensify as the pressures for low-skilled migration rise. The advanced countries need to turn from the increasingly popular choice of relying on police action to control immigration and focus on improving the integration of their immigrant populations, and their descendants, into their societies.

The failure of international policy coordination to protect migrants and improve the gains from migration is regrettable, with grave implications for many migrants. But this failure has not prevented migration from generating substantial benefits for destination countries, origin countries, and particularly migrants. In this sense migration, as well as trade and finance, differ from efforts to preserve the global commons, where policy coordination is essential for progress—a more difficult subject to which we now turn.

Notes

1. On other economic issues often raised concerning migration, there is little evidence that migrants contribute significantly to congestion effects (for example, increased traffic and demand for housing) or represent a net burden on government expenditures (see below).
2. Freeman and Oostendorp 2000.
3. World Bank 2006.
4. See World Bank 2006 for a discussion of the benefits and costs of migration.
5. In 1961 the foreign-born made up about 5 percent of the American population but 24 percent of the members of the National Academy of Sciences. Of the 71 American holders of Nobel Prizes in physics, chemistry, medicine, and physiology, 24 were foreign born (Dinnerstein and Reimers 1999).
6. Dadush and Falcao 2009.
7. World Bank 2006.
8. Clemente, Pueyo, and Sanz 2008.

9. Giordani and Ruta 2009.
10. See, for example, Rowthorn 2008.
11. This generalization does not apply to the sparsely populated, rich oil exporters with very high immigration rates.
12. Gibson and Lennon 1991.
13. See BBC 2009.
14. See www.passport.gc.ca/pptc/hist.aspx?lang=eng.
15. CBO 2006.
16. Boswell 2008.
17. Cluver 2007.
18. Papademetriou 2005. Part of the difference between Papademetriou (2005) and the individual estimates in table 6.1 is that the former assumes relatively large illegal immigration in developing countries (he mentions Mexico and South Africa explicitly). But he also appears to estimate about twice the size of illegal immigration in Europe, for reasons not clear.
19. Effective controls based on the existing number of immigrants would also change the composition of immigrants, as more highly skilled (and preferred) workers would seek entry, limiting the number of unskilled workers.
20. GAO 2006.
21. Perelman 2005.
22. Massey (1987) finds that wage differentials between legal and illegal Mexican immigrants in the United States were explained by lower skills, not their legal status. But Rivera-Batiz (1999) concludes that legal Mexican immigrants in the United States earned about 40 percent more than illegal Mexican immigrants, with only about half this difference explained by characteristics such as skills and length of residence. Moreover, immigrants who regularized their status following the 1986 U.S. immigration reform enjoyed substantial wage gains not explained by changes in such characteristics as experience and education.
23. Lucas 2004.
24. This seems logical, but is difficult to analyze. White and others (1990) conclude that apprehensions fell along the U.S.-Mexican border in the 23-month period following enactment of the 1986 Immigration Reform and Control Act, indicating (according to their estimates) a decline in illegal border crossings of up to 2 million.
25. See mmp.opr.princeton.edu/results/001costs-en.aspx.
26. Martin 2004.
27. Jordan and Duvell 2002.
28. Hanson 2006.

29. Cornelius 2005.

30. Employer sanctions investigations in the United States dropped precipitously in the late 1990s and first few years of the 2000s (Brownwell 2005). The use of electronic databases to check on the immigration status of employees holds some promise for improving enforcement, although errors in the data and concerns over civil rights infringement still limit their application (Legomsky 2007).

31. We refer to "pressures for migration" rather than levels of migration, which also will be influenced by the nature and effectiveness of immigration restrictions.

32. Gaurilov and Heuveline 2003.

33. Whether aging will increase the demand for workers in general is uncertain. Aging may also reduce national savings and thus the capital stock, which could reduce the demand for labor, so the net impact on labor demand is indeterminate. However, to the extent that natural resources are important in production and are not also declining, labor demand may rise. Aging also increases the need for young immigrant workers to support failing social security systems (though this is only a medium-term solution, since immigrants also age), which could encourage more liberal immigration policies.

34. See www.airlines.org/economics/finance/PaPricesYield.htm.

35. Empirical evidence of the role of networks in facilitating migration include, for the United States, Bartel (1989) and Munshi (2003); for Mexico, Mora and Taylor (2005) and McKenzie and Rapoport (2007); and for Asia, Massey and others (1998). By contrast, Krissman (2006) argues that networks cannot explain large-scale, cross-border migration.

36. Brown 2008.

37. Martin 2005.

38. Natali 2009.

39. Ratha and Shaw 2007.

40. A major reason for short-term migration across borders is to take advantage of differences in seasons or for commerce, but the migration statistics are supposed to reflect only stays of more than one year.

41. Wadhwa and others 2009.

42. Castles and Miller 2008.

43. Lucas 2004.

44. See Grimes and Solomon (2004) and Lacy (2003).

45. FBI 2009.

46. European Commission 2009.

47. Collyer 2004.
48. Bobeva and Garson 2004.
49. Bobeva and Garson 2004.
50. Some bilateral migration agreements also reflect other goals, such as improving relations in general or contributing to development in the sending countries.
51. Sorensen and others 2002.
52. Omelaniuk 2006.
53. Abella 2006.
54. Basok (2000) attributes the performance of the Canadian program in part to recruitment policies and procedures that provided the opportunity for workers to return, effective enforcement by the Canadian government of employment and housing-related standards for workers, and the relatively small program size that facilitated monitoring. The low level of overstays in the Canadian program was also due to the small size of Canadian farms (which encouraged personal relationships that reduced the likelihood of desertion) and the lack of social networks and economic infrastructure supportive of illegal migrants.
55. Martin 2003.
56. ASEAN 2009.
57. The Economic Community of West African States (ECOWAS) provided for travel between member countries without visa for up to 90 days (Pizarro 2006), but has since only affirmed its commitment to continuing efforts to improve mobility within the region. Citizens of the East African Community and the Common Market for East and Southern Africa enjoy visa-free entry in member countries (Oucho 2006), but little progress has been made in the past few years (see www.eac.int/component/content/article/46-eaceconomy.html?start=6). And the Southern African Development Community (SADC) agreement in 2005 on visa-free entry up to 90 days per year of nationals from other member states has not been fully implemented, but South Africa and Zimbabwe have agreed to waive bilateral visa requirements for stays of up to 90 days (Muleya 2009).
58. See www.migrantsrights.org/convention.htm#part8 and www.ilo.org/public/english/protection/migrant/areas/standards.htm.

References

Abella, Manolo. "Policies and Best Practices for Management of Temporary Migration." International Symposium on International Migration and Development. United Nations Department of Economic and Social Affairs, Population Division, Turin, Italy, 2006.

ASEAN (Association of Southeast Asian Nations). "ASEAN Plan of Action for Cooperation on Immigration Matters." Jakarta, 2009, www.aseansec.org/16572.htm.

Bartel, Ann P. "Where Do the New US immigrants Live?" *Journal of Labor Economics*, 7 (1989): 371–91.

Basok, Tanya. 2000. "He Came, He Saw, He . . . Stayed. Guest Worker Programmes and the Issue of Non-Return." *International Migration*, 38 (2): 216–38.

BBC. "The rise and rise of the Russian mafia." British Broadcasting Company News, November 21, 1998.

———. "Italy adopts law to curb migrants." British Broadcasting Company News, July 3, 2009, http://news.bbc.co.uk/2/hi/8132084.stm.

Bobeva, Daniela, and Jean-Pierre Garson. "Overview of Bilateral Agreements and Other Forms of Labour Recruitment." In *Migration for Employment: Bilateral Agreements at the Crossroads*, ed. Organisation for Economic Co-operation and Development. Paris, 2004.

Boswell, Christina. "UK Labour Migration Policy: Permanent Revolution." Centro Studi di Politica Internazionale. Rome, 2008, www.cespi.it.

Brown, Oli. "Migration and Climate Change." International Organization for Migration Research Series 31. Geneva, 2008, www.iisd.org/pdf/2008/migration_climate.pdf.

Brownwell, Peter. "The Declining Enforcement of Employer Sanctions." Migration Policy Institute, Washington, DC, 2005, www.migrationinformation.org/Feature/display.cfm?ID=332.

California Department of Justice. *Organized Crime in California: Annual Report to the California Legislature*. Sacramento, CA, 1996. www.fas.org/irp/world/para/docs/orgcrm96.pdf.

CanWest News Service. "Canadians want illegal immigrants deported: poll." October 27, 2007, www.canada.com/globaltv/national/story.html?id=22dc364c-0bc8-44fa-ad5c-cbb68368f903.

Castles, Stephen, and Mark J. Miller. *The Age of Migration*. 4th ed. Hampshire, United Kingdom, Palgrave MacMillan, 2008.

CBO (Congressional Budget Office). "Immigration Policy in the United States." Washington, DC, 2006.

Clemente, Jesus, Fernando Pueyo, and Fernando Sanz. "A Migration Model with Congestion Costs: Does the Size of Government Matter?" *Economic Modeling*, 25 (2008): 300–11.

Cluver, Cathryn. "French Immigration Policy: History Repeated?" Migration: The World Affairs Blog Network, April 11, 2007, http://migration.foreignpolicyblogs.com/2007/04/11/french-immigration-policy-history-repeated.

Collyer, Michael. "The Development Impact of Temporary International Labour Migration on Southern Mediterranean Sending Countries: Contrasting Examples of Morocco and Egypt." Development Research Centre on Migration, Globalisation and Poverty Working Paper T6. Sussex, United Kingdom, 2004.

Cornelius, Wayne. "Controlling 'Unwanted' Immigration: Lessons from the United States, 1993–2004." *Journal of Ethnic and Migration Studies*, 31 (2005): 775–94.

Dadush, Uri, and Lauren Falcao. "Migrants and the Global Financial Crisis." Carnegie Endowment for International Peace Policy Brief 83. Washington, DC, 2009, www.carnegieendowment.org/files/migrants_financial_crisis.pdf.

Deutsche Welle. "A German Amnesty for Illegal Immigrants?" October 3, 2005, www.dw-world.de/dw/article/0,,1513837,00.html.

Dinnerstein, Leonard, and David M. Reimers. *Ethnic Americans: A History of Immigration*. New York: Columbia University Press, 1999, www.ciaonet.org/book/dil01/index.html.

Docquier, Frederic, and Abdeslam Marfouk. "Measuring the International Mobility of Skilled Workers (1990–2000): Release 1.0." Policy Research Working Paper 3381. World Bank, Washington, DC, 2004.

Durand, Martine. "Conclusions." In *Migration for Employment: Bilateral Agreements at the Crossroads*, ed. Organisation for Economic Co-operation and Development. Paris, 2004.

European Commission. "Five years of an Enlarged EU: Economic Achievements and Challenges." Directorate-General for Economic and Financial Affairs, Brussels, 2009.

Faini, Riccardo, and Alessandra Venturini. "Trade, aid and migrations: Some basic policy issues." *European Economic Review*, 37 (1993): 435–42.

FBI (U.S. Federal Bureau of Investigation). "National Gang Threat Assessment 2009." National Gang Intelligence Center, Washington, DC, 2009.

Feere, Jon, and Jessica Vaughan. "Taking Back the Streets: ICE and Local Law Enforcement Target Immigrant Gangs." Center for Immigration Studies, Washington, DC, 2008, http://cis.org/ImmigrantGangs.

Freeman, Richard B., and Remco H. Oostendorp. *Wages Around the World: Pay across Occupations and Countries*. NBER Working Paper 8058. Cambridge, MA: National Bureau of Economic Research, 2000.

GAO (U.S. Government Accountability Office). "Illegal Immigration." Washington, DC, 2006, www.gao.gov/new.items/d06770.pdf.

Gavrilov, Leonid A. and Patrick Heuveline. "Aging of Population." in *The Encyclopedia of Aging*, eds. Paul Demeny and Geoffrey McNicoll. New York: Macmillan Reference, 2003.

Geronimi, Eduardo. 2004. "Acuerdos bilaterales de migration de mano de obra: Modo de empleo." International Labour Organization Working Paper 65. Geneva, 2004.

Gibson, Campbell J., and Emily Lennon. "Historical Census Statistics on the Foreign-born Population of the United States: 1850–1990." Population Division Working Paper 29. U.S. Census Bureau, Washington, DC, 1991, www.census.gov/population/www/documentation/twps0029/twps0029.html.

Giordani, Paolo E., and Michele Ruta. "The Immigration Policy Puzzle." CELEG Working Paper 0905. LUISS Guido Carli, Rome, 2009, www.eui.eu/Personal/ Fellows/PaoloGiordani/papers/immigration-puzzle.pdf.

Glenny, Misha. *McMafia: A Journey through the Global Criminal Underworld.* New York: Random House, 2008.

Grimes, Ann, and Jay Solomon. "Venture capitalists book a passage to India." *Wall Street Journal*, October 14, 2004.

Hanson, Gordon. *Illegal Migration from Mexico to the United States.* NBER Working Papers 12141. Cambridge, MA: National Bureau of Economic Research, 2006.

de Haas, Hein. "International Migration, Remittances, and Development: Myths and Facts." *Third World Quarterly*, 26 (2005): 1269–84.

de Haas, Hein. "Morocco's Migration Transition: Trends, Determinants and Future Scenarios." Global Migration Perspectives 28. Global Commission on International Migration, Geneva, 2005.

Hunt, Jennifer, and Marjolaine Gauthier-Loiselle. "How Much Does Immigration Boost Innovation?" Montreal: McGill University. IZA Discussion Paper no. 3921, 2009.

International Herald Tribune. "Russia cracking down on illegal immigrants." January 15, 2007, www.nytimes.com/2007/01/15/world/europe/15iht -migrate.4211072.html.

Jandl, Michael. "Estimates of the Numbers of Illegal and Smuggled Immigrants in Europe." International Centre for Migration Policy Development. Presentation at Workshop 1.6, International Metropolis Conference, September 17, 2003.

Jordan, Bill, and Franck Duvell. *Irregular Migration: The Dilemmas of Transnational Mobility.* Cheltenham, UK: Edward Elgar, 2002.

Koehler, J., and F. Laczko. "'Development-Friendly' Migration Policies: A Selected Review of the Literature." International Organization of Migration Research and Publications Division, Geneva, 2006.

Krissman, Fred. "Sin Coyote Ni Patrón: Why the 'Migrant Network' Fails to Explain International Migration." *International Migration Review*, 39 (2006): 4–44.

Lacy, Sarah. "Silicon Valley VCs 'blown away' by market opportunities in India." *Business Journal*, December 12, 2003.

Legomsky, Stephen. 2007. Testimony before the United States House of Representatives Committee on the Judiciary Subcommittee on Immigration, Citizenship, Refugees, Border Security, and International Law.

Lucas, Robert B. "International Migration Regimes and Economic Development." Report from the seminar of the Executive Group on Development Issues on International Migration Regimes and Economic Development, Stockholm, May 13, 2004, www.egdi.gov.se/seminars6.htm.

Lundgren, Ted. "Labour Migration Under Market Conditions." Thesis at the Free International University of Moldova, Chisinau, 2009, www.cnaa.md/en/thesis/14501/.

Martin, Philip. "Managing Labor Migration: Temporary Worker Programs for the 21st Century." International Institute for Labor Studies, Geneva, 2003.

———. "Germany: Managing Migration in the Twenty-First Century." In *Controlling Immigration: A Global Perspective*, eds. Wayne A. Cornelius, Takeyuki Tsuda, Philip L. Martin, and James F. Hollifield, 221–53. Stanford University Press, 2004.

———. "Mexico-US Migration." In *NAFTA Revisited: Achievements and Challenges*, eds. Gary C. Hufbauer and Jeffrey J. Schott, 441–66. Washington, DC: Institute for International Economics, 2005.

Massey, Douglas S. "Do Undocumented Migrants Earn Lower Wages than Legal Immigrants? New Evidence from Mexico." *International Migration Review*, 21 (1987): 236–74, www.jstor.org/stable/pdfplus/2546315.pdf.

Massey, Douglas S., Joaquin Arango, Graeme Hugo, Ali Kouaouci, Adella Pellegrino, and J. Edward Taylor. "Theories of International Migration: A Review and Appraisal." *Population and Development Review*, 19 (1993): 431–66.

McKenzie, David, and Hillel Rapoport. "Self-selection patterns in Mexico-U.S. migration: the role of migration networks." Policy Research Working Paper 4118. Washington, DC: World Bank, 2007.

Mora, Jorge, and J. Edward Taylor. "Determinants of Migration, Destination and Sector Choice: Disentangling Individual, Household, and Community Effects." In *International Migration, Remittances and Development*, eds. Caglar Ozden and Maurice Schiff. New York: Palgrave MacMillan, 2005.

Muleya, Tupeyo. "Zimbabwe: Govt, SA Sign Labour Migration Agreement." AllAfrica Global Media, August 28, 2009, http://allafrica.com/stories/200908280072.html.

Munshi, Kaivan. "Networks in the Modern Economy: Mexican Migrants in the U.S. Labor Market." *Quarterly Journal of Economics*, 118 (2003): 549–99.

Natali, Claudia. "Linkages between Internal and International Migrations: Policy Implications for Development." Paper presented at the Conference on Urban-Rural Linkages and Migration. International Organization for Migration, Dortmund, Germany, September 16, 2009.

National Alliance of Gang Investigators Association. *2005 National Gang Threat Assessment.* Washington, DC: Bureau of Justice Assistance, U.S. Department of Justice, 2005, www.ojp.usdoj.gov/BJA/what/2005_threat_assesment.pdf.

Naude, Wim. "Conflict, Disaster and No Jobs: Reasons for Migration from Sub-Saharan Africa." WIDER Research Paper 2008/85. World Institute for Development Economics Research, New York, 2008.

Omelaniuk, Irena. "Canada." Draft prepared for the World Bank Knowledge for Change Program, 2006.

Ortega, Francesc, and Giovanni Per. "The Causes and Effects of International Labor Mobility: Evidence From OECD Countries 1980–2005." Human Development Research Paper 6. United Nations Development Programme, Human Development Report Office, New York, 2009, http://hdr.undp.org/en/reports/global/hdr2009/papers/HDRP_2009_06.pdf.

Oucho, John O. "Migration and refugees in Eastern Africa: A challenge for the East African Community." In *Views on Migration in Sub-Saharan Africa*, eds. Catherine Cross, Derik Gelderblom, Niel Roux, and Jonathan Mafukidze. Pretoria: HSRC Press, 2006.

Papademetriou, Demetrious G. "The Global Struggle with Illegal Immigration: No End in Sight." Migration Policy Institute, Washington, DC, 2005, www.migrationinformation.org/Feature/display.cfm?ID=336.

Passel, Jeffrey S. "A Portrait of Unauthorized Immigrants in the United States." Pew Research Center, Washington, DC, 2009.

Perelman, Marc. "African Deaths Spark Debate in Europe over Immigration." *Jewish Daily Forward*, October 14, 2005.

Pizarro, Gabriela Rodriguez. "Specific Groups and Individuals: Migrant Workers." E/CN.4/2006/73/Add.2. UN Economic and Social Council, Commission on Human Rights, New York, 2006.

Ratha, Dilip, and William Shaw. "South-South Migration and Remittances." Policy Research Working Paper 102. World Bank, Washington, DC, 2007.

Rede Globo. "Brazil has 600 thousand illegal immigrants, says body." March 27, 2008, http://g1.globo.com/Noticias/Brasil/0,,MUL365307-5598,00.html.

Rivera-Batiz, Francisco L. "Undocumented Workers in the Labor Market: An Analysis of the Earnings of Legal and Illegal Immigrants in the U.S." *Journal of Population Economics*, February 1999, 91–116, http://faculty.tc.columbia.edu/upload/flr9/MexicanundocumentedImmigrants1999.pdf.

Rotte, Ralph, and Michael Vogler. "The effects of development on migration: Theoretical issues and new empirical evidence." *Journal of Population Economics*, 13 (2000): 485–508.

Rowthorn, Robert. "The fiscal impact of immigration on the advanced economies." *Oxford Review of Economic Policy*, 24 (2008): 560–80.

Sorensen, Ninna Nyberg, Nicholas Van Hear, and Poul Engberg-Pedersen. "The Migration-Development Nexus: Evidence and Policy Options." Centre for Development Research Working Paper 2.6. Copenhagen, 2002.

Stark, Oded, and J. Edward Taylor. "Migration Incentives, Migration Types: The Role of Relative Deprivation." *Economic Journal*, 101 (1991): 1163–78.

Times of India. "Indians among illegal immigrants rounded up in Malaysia." July 31, 2006, http://articles.timesofindia.indiatimes.com/2006-07-31/rest-of-world/27812349_1_illegal-immigrants-foreign-workers-malaysia.

UNDP (United Nation Development Programme). *Human Development Report 2009: Overcoming barriers: Human mobility and development*. New York: Palgrave Macmillan, 2009.

van der Mensbrugghe, Dominique, and David Roland-Holst. "Global Economic Prospects for Increasing Developing Country Migration into Developed Countries." Human Development Research Paper 50. United Nations Development Programme, Human Development Report Office, New York, 2009, http://hdr.undp.org/en/reports/global/hdr2009/papers/HDRP_2009_50.pdf.

Wadhwa, Vivek, Anna Lee Saxenian, Robert B. Freeman, and Alex Salkever. "Losing the World's Best and Brightest: America's New Immigrant Entrepreneurs, Part V." 2009, http://ssrn.com/abstract=1362012.

White, Michael J., Frank D. Bean, and Thomas J. Espenshade. "The US 1986 Immigration Reform and Control Act and undocumented migration to the United States." *Population Research and Policy Review*, 9 (1990): 93–116.

World Bank. *Global Economic Prospects 2006: Economic Implications of Remittances and Migration*. Washington, DC, 2006.

Zaiceva, Anzelika, and Klaus F. Zimmermann. "Scale, Diversity and Determinants of Labour Migration in Europe." *Oxford Review of Economic Policy*, 24 (2008): 427–51.

CHAPTER 7

THE GLOBAL COMMONS

A TWENTY-FIRST CENTURY TRAGEDY?

Global cooperation is necessary to avoid exhausting essential resources, to prevent global pandemics, and to restrain climate change. Markets cannot solve these problems on their own.

The participation of developing countries is essential to arrive at workable and efficient solutions. But the differences in incomes, technologies, political systems, and social values—between the advanced and developing countries, as well as among the developing countries—will complicate reaching agreements on many issues related to preserving the global commons.

Agreements are easier to reach where there is a broad consensus on the importance of the problem, only a few countries are major polluters, and the costs of environmental degradation are borne largely by the countries that are the major source of the problem. This perspective helps explain why global efforts to control pandemics, for example, have had more success than efforts to prevent climate change.

Climate change represents the great threat to global prosperity and to the continuing rise of developing countries. Dealing with it effectively requires agreement among the United States, Europe, and China—with technology playing a big role.

The rise of developing countries may lead to environmental catastrophe. Without a concerted international response and radical change in domestic policy, climate change over the coming decades may cause the inundation of coastal areas, the transformation of vast tracks of arable land into desert, increasing destruction by storms, the massive extinctions of species, and the further deterioration of human health.

Averting such disasters, and making progress on other global public goods, requires policy coordination among governments. Intergovernmental coordination is also important for trade, finance, and migration—the channels of integration discussed in previous chapters—but policies can be improved through autonomous decisions. Still, even the largest country can contribute little to preserving the global commons by itself, so individual countries have few incentives to make the required sacrifices. Policy coordination is essential.

The rise of developing countries greatly raises the stakes for, and the urgency of, policy coordination to protect the global commons.[1] Policymakers in both developing and advanced countries have to gain a better understanding of the effect of their rapidly increasing economic activity on the climate and on the environment more generally—and of the objective constraints that each country faces in taking remedial action. And climate change is only the most spectacular example of how developing countries need to be more fully integrated into efforts to supply public goods. They will become more important in global measures to contain infectious diseases, reap the benefits of technological progress in telecommunications, and preserve environmental resources such as the oceans and Antarctica, even outer space.

A historical perspective on the global commons

Environmental degradation has threatened human welfare since the dawn of history. Ancient farmers had to discover that periodically leaving land fallow prevented soil depletion. Theories explaining the collapse of the Mayan civilization include (among others) a 200-year drought[2] and the exhaustion of agricultural potential and sources of meat.[3] Cholera ravaged urban centers until concerted efforts were made to supply clean water. But these challenges, while difficult, were all essentially local.[4]

By the late twentieth century, however, growth and technological progress transformed many environmental challenges into global problems. Since Roman times, the earth's population has grown from 231 million to 6.8 billion, or 29-fold in 2,000 years (figure 7.1). Average incomes increased nearly 13-fold over this period, so world output increased 377 times (13 × 29). This burgeoning population and improved standard of living have been supported by an astronomical rise in the ability to exploit scarce resources. Unfortunately, the earth itself has not changed much over the past two millennia. Rapacious twenty-first century economies are on a collision course with a fixed supply of natural resources.

This may sound like the discredited Malthusian arguments such as the Club of Rome's "Limits to Growth," but it is not. The potential exhaustion of resources

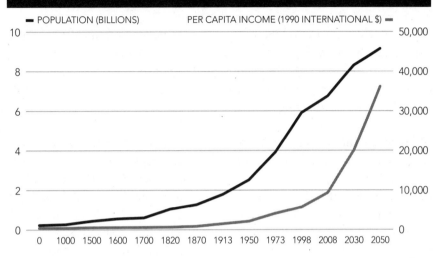

FIGURE 7.1 POPULATION AND INCOME GROWTH OVER TWO MILLENNIA

- POPULATION (BILLIONS)   PER CAPITA INCOME (1990 INTERNATIONAL $) -

Source: Maddison 2001; authors' calculations.

is not dangerous where market signals can be relied on to cope with scarcity. For example, though for practical purposes the earth has a fixed supply of copper, the annual extraction of copper has increased 2.5 times since 1970.[5] The dwindling availability of easily extracted copper has raised its price, spurring efforts to use substitutes and to search deeper within the earth and in more inhospitable regions for new deposits. As a result, available reserves of copper increased from 280 million tons in 1970 to 480 million in 2006, and there is little need for global coordination to avoid a scarcity of copper. Because the market for copper works, it can be safely predicted that we will never "run out" of copper, only that its price will rise to a point where other materials will take its place.

Unfortunately, market prices fail massively in preventing the depletion of the global commons where there are no clear property rights. For clean air, many fish species, and numerous other resources, no incentives exist to preserve them or invest in their reproduction (even where that is possible). More generally, market prices fail to reflect externalities, where the decision to produce or consume significantly affects others not involved in the transaction. The effect of externalities on global welfare can be mild, as in ancient times when economic activity was tiny—or horrendous, when economic activity is very intense and market prices fail to capture the cost to society by a large margin, as with carbon emissions today.

In these cases, government efforts to regulate use are essential to avoid exhaustion and limit damage. In addition, government policies (for example, subsidies provided through the tax system to oil companies and directly to fishers) can contribute to environmental damage.

Where the resource, or the impact of using it, is not limited to a single nation or region, global cooperation is required to limit exploitation and eliminate distorting policies. Without major technological breakthroughs, or the colonization of other planets, global coordination is the only hope for limiting the strain on earth's carrying capacity.

Developing countries are increasing the burden on the global commons

Responsibility for the looming environmental catastrophe can—in most areas—be placed squarely on the industrial countries. They generated most of the carbon emissions that drive global warming, are responsible for the bulk of the chlorofluorocarbons that threaten the ozone layer, and consume a large percentage of the dwindling annual fish harvest from the oceans.[6] But today's industrial countries were once developing countries, and today's developing countries look like they are set with a vengeance on the same path as industrial countries.

As their living standards rise, consumers in developing countries become more like those in rich countries: people drive cars rather than ride bicycles; homes rely on fossil fuels for heat and air conditioning; and consumers demand greater variety. Producers also use more fossil fuels, as farmers rely more on fertilizers and as energy-dependent factories replace artisans.

Moreover, developing country firms tend to use technology that is older and less efficient, and more wasteful in energy and other natural resources, than the technology industrial country firms use. For example, according to China's State Energy Research Institute, each dollar of GDP in China requires 2.5 times more energy to produce than in the United States, 5 times more than in the European Union, and nearly 9 times more than in Japan. Part of this difference reflects the very different kinds of products made and consumed in China. However, developing countries' per capita consumption of energy (measured as kilograms of oil equivalent) is approximately one-fifth of that in industrial countries, because poorer countries are in production sectors that use less energy (subsistence agriculture) or use production processes that are less energy-intensive. People with lower incomes also use fewer products that require energy (for example, hot tubs) and tend to be more conscious of wasting energy (for example, they leave lights on only when necessary).

So, rising incomes can have contrasting implications for the environment. Technological progress can both reduce reliance on natural resources (substituting man-made for natural fibers and improving automobile engines to increase gas mileage) and increase the use of natural resources (for example, the invention of the automobile boosted demand for gasoline). Similarly, rich countries tend to make greater efforts than poor countries to control air pollution, but richer people can afford to be more wasteful than poor people.

The bottom line is that developing countries are increasing their competition for scarce environmental resources and boosting their carbon emissions. And developing countries are getting rich much faster than today's rich countries did (it took the United States 50 years to double its per capita income from about $1,300 in 1820, while China doubled its GDP per capita from 2001 to 2009, and increased it almost 20 times over the past 40 years). And their populations are five times larger than those of industrial countries. Thus their call on environmental resources promises to be enormous (chapter 3). Here are four instances where the rise of the developing countries calls for greater coordination to protect the global commons, starting from the most important, climate change, then moving to forest cover, the ozone layer, and telecommunications networks.

Climate change

Climate change demonstrates the potentially catastrophic implications of current trends in production and consumption, as well as the growing importance of developing countries. Global temperatures are rising: since 1900, temperatures have risen by 0.7 degrees Celsius,[7] with a 0.15 degree Celsius increase registered between 1990 and 2005 alone.[8] Since 1957 extremely high sea levels, heavy rains, and heat waves have grown more common.[9] As a result, heat-related deaths have risen, and infectious disease vectors have changed in Europe.[10]

According to the Stern Report, as extreme climate events grow increasingly common and temperatures rise 2–3 degrees Celsius by 2099—the most likely climate change scenario[11]—the equivalent of a 5 percent reduction in per capita consumption, now and forever, will hit the global economy, with reductions as high as 20 percent possible. And the impact of climate change will be calamitous for some groups and countries. Damage costs from storms could double (if temperatures increase 3 degrees Celsius by 2099). Malaria and dengue fever will strike many more people, potentially impairing overall growth.[12] Food will become more scarce in developing regions as water supplies dwindle in drier regions and floods increase in wetter regions. And low-lying areas will be inundated (for example, urban centers like Jakarta, Shanghai, Tokyo, Manila, Bangkok, Mumbai; small island states; the Gangetic plain in Bangladesh; and Egypt's Nile Delta).[13]

Simple calculations[14] based on the forecasts in chapter 3 illustrate the need for policy action to be taken to mitigate climate change. Assuming that each G20 country's ratio of PPP output to CO_2 and CO_2-equivalent emissions continues on its current gradual decline from its 2005 level, global temperatures increases would be expected to exceed 4 degrees Celsius by 2050. Such an increase would likely be catastrophic for many developing countries. Even if each country meets the (nonbinding) commitments they put forward at the 2009 Conference of the Parties in Copenhagen by 2020, and then holds emission *levels* (not the ratio of output to emissions) constant from 2020 through 2050—an extraordinarily optimistic scenario—a temperature increase slightly higher than 2 degrees Celsius is still expected, and some of the consequences outlined above will be realized.[15]

As time goes on, developing countries will become a more important source of carbon emissions. Rich countries generated 65 percent of total carbon emissions from 1965 to 2004, and developing countries only 35 percent.[16] But by 2004 developing countries accounted for almost half of total emissions (figure 7.2). With the major developing country emitters (such as Brazil, China, India, and Russia) likely to grow faster than most industrial countries, developing countries' share of global carbon emissions is likely to rise further (to 73 percent of global emissions under the optimistic scenario in the preceding paragraph). That is why ensuring participation by the major developing country emitters is so critical for limiting climate change.

Developing countries are contributing more to climate change, but the average person in developing countries makes a far smaller contribution to climate change than the average person in rich countries (see figure 7.2). While China is now the largest source of carbon emissions, per capita emissions in China are less than one-fourth those in the United States. With energy efficiency in China likely to improve, even if China continues to grow much faster than the United States indefinitely (chapter 3 explains why this is unlikely), it would take several decades for per capita emissions in China to reach those in the United States.

Forest cover

The potential conversion over the next 50 years of one billion hectares of natural ecosystems (an area larger than the United States) to agricultural land in developing countries will further degrade the global environment.[17] Global tropical forest cover fell by 8 percent from 1990–2005 (figure 7.3). With less forest cover, carbon emissions will be absorbed slower and global warming will accelerate. Tropical forests are estimated to sequester carbon at about the same rate that the European Union emitted carbon in January 2004,[18] though recent data suggest that the ability of tropical forests to sequester carbon is declining rapidly.[19]

The loss and fragmentation of the Amazon's forests could significantly alter rainfall patterns across the globe. For example, rainfall in the U.S. Midwest may

(PERCENT OF EMISSIONS)

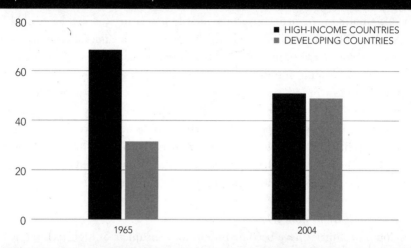

(TONS PER CAPITA)

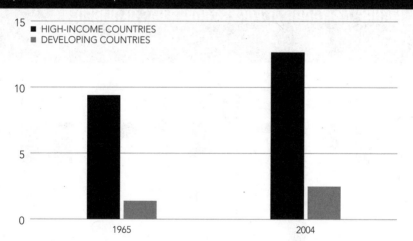

Source: www.earthtrends.wri.org.

be substantially reduced.[20] And the reduction of natural habitats, along with the greater use of agrochemicals, is driving species to extinction at a rate 100 to 1,000 times more rapidly than in prehuman times.[21] This reduced biodiversity could forever prevent the discovery of life-saving medicines and valuable raw materials.

The ozone layer

Developing countries produce other resources that threaten global sustainability. For example, by the 1980s, it was clear that the use of aerosol cans and air conditioning that released chlorofluorocarbons (CFCs) into the atmosphere was punching holes in the ozone layer, potentially increasing the incidence of skin cancer. The 1987 Montreal Protocol, which agreed to phase out CFCs, was one of the notable global environmental successes in recent years. But CFC production increased in developing countries in the late 1990s, because they were not slated to eliminate most production and consumption of the major ozone-depleting chemicals until 2010 (some countries are on schedule).[22] They also sold CFCs illegally to consumers in industrial countries who wished to avoid switching to CFC-free technology (mainly in air conditioners). Although this trade may be declining as the older machines that used CFCs are being phased out, the illegal CFC trade a few years ago was estimated at 7–14,000 tons.[23]

Telecommunications networks

Developing countries have become important consumers of high-tech services. For example, developing countries' share of global Internet connections rose from

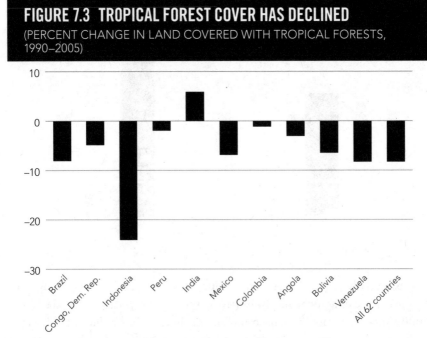

FIGURE 7.3 TROPICAL FOREST COVER HAS DECLINED
(PERCENT CHANGE IN LAND COVERED WITH TROPICAL FORESTS, 1990–2005)

Note: Includes 62 countries with some type of wet tropical forest.
Source: http://rainforests.mongabay.com/deforestation_alpha.html.

less than 5 percent in 1995 to 50 percent in 2007, though per capita Internet use remains low (developing countries average only 12 Internet users per 100 people, compared with 70 in industrial countries—figure 7.4). Rapid expansion of cell phones and other wireless services in developing countries has also contributed to the growing scarcity of radio spectrum.

FIGURE 7.4 INTERNET USE IN DEVELOPING REMAINS MUCH LOWER THAN IN INDUSTRIAL COUNTRIES, 1995–2007
(INTERNET USERS PER 100 PEOPLE)

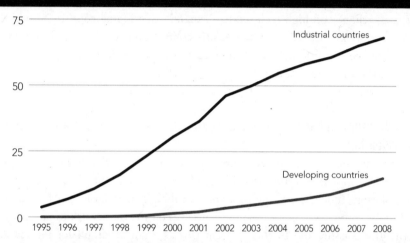

(PERCENT OF GLOBAL INTERNET USERS)

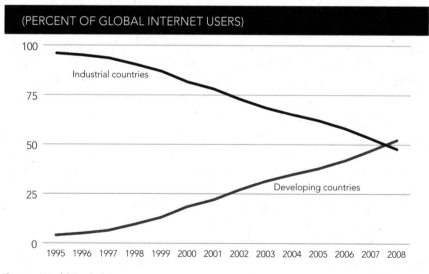

Source: World Bank data.

Developing countries' rising demand for high-tech services can be beneficial to other users. Greater Internet use by developing countries can generate global benefits, because networks tend to increase in value as the number of users rises (though technological upgrades are continually required to accommodate the growing number of users). By contrast, developing countries' increasing demands could increase the burden on scarce radio spectrum.[24]

Despite the increasing role of developing countries, they have had minimal influence on Internet (and radio spectrum) governance,[25] in part because they lack the expertise.[26] For example, developing countries have only limited representation in technical forums that make decisions on Internet governance.[27] As their reliance on high-tech services expands, developing countries are likely to take more aggressive stances to ensure control over services (see below for a discussion of the Internet). For example, the scarce radio frequencies used by low-Earth-orbit and medium-Earth-orbit satellites, and the limited number of geostationary orbits, are likely to intensify competition over access.[28]

How differences between developing and industrial countries affect policy coordination

The growing importance of developing countries requires a change in negotiations to improve global coordination. If developing countries are to participate in the solution, they must be given a voice in design. It is no longer feasible for industrial countries to agree among themselves on the framework for addressing some global issue, and to then present this as a fait accompli for ratification by the rest of the world. The emergence of the G20 as the primary forum for global economic consultations (rather than the G8) is a striking example of this evolution.

Developing country involvement can, however, complicate negotiations. Simply increasing the number of participants in negotiations can make it more difficult to reach agreement. For example, developing countries' participation in the United Nations Committee for the Peaceful Uses of Outer Space made it more difficult to reach consensus on major issues.[29] The great differences in incomes, technological capabilities, political structures, and social values between developing and industrial countries (and among developing countries) complicates matters even more.

Even so, when and if agreements can be reached, the participation of developing countries can make outcomes not only more equitable but also more efficient. Developing countries greatly broaden the set of possible interventions in dealing with a problem and, relative to the impact on the global commons, these interventions may be cheaper to effect in developing countries.

Negotiations over mitigating climate change illustrate most clearly how differences among countries affect negotiations, as well as the ethical dilemmas that can arise. Developing countries, home to about a billion chronically hungry people, confront providing for the basic human needs of a large part of their population. Understandably, they are likely to value changes in short-term income at the margin more than countries at much higher incomes. And because they also in a sense have "less to lose," they may be more willing to risk long-term damage than to forgo part of their meager income today.

Thus China (now the largest source of carbon emissions) and India, with per capita incomes only 6 percent and 2 percent of U.S. levels (13 percent and 6 percent if purchasing power parity exchange rates are used), respectively, are likely to resist binding emissions limits on themselves (and certainly argue for much greater reductions in rich countries). Given that the timing and precise effect of climate change on individual locales is still uncertain, poor countries may be willing to risk more climate change in the interest of promoting development.

Moreover, serious ethical issues arise in allocating emissions limits between developing and industrial countries. One could certainly argue that developing countries should not bear a proportionate share of reducing emissions (based on their share of current emissions), since they have contributed a relatively small share of historical emissions and the welfare cost of their meeting emissions targets would be higher (since reductions in income are more painful at lower incomes). One proposal is to lay out a long-term path for carbon emissions for each country, where developing countries would face little reduction in the earlier years, with increasing reductions as their incomes and technologies advance.[30] Unfortunately, long-term commitments by current governments have uncertain credibility.

Despite these practical and ethical issues, the participation of developing countries in limiting carbon emissions is not only essential to reducing climate change (as argued above), but necessary to an efficient solution. The Stern Report's review of climate change defines an efficient reduction in carbon emissions when the marginal cost of the measures taken equals the marginal social cost of carbon emissions.[31] If the discount rate used in these calculations is set too low (reflecting the time preferences of high-income consumers), the policies adopted will not be efficient, since developing country interests will be proportionately greater in the future (due to their faster growth in population and incomes than in industrial countries).[32]

While industrial and some developing countries tend to adopt opposing positions on climate change, there is some potential for coalitions across the two groups, based on the expected impact on the countries. For example, the poorer island nations and tropical countries, bound to suffer disproportionately from climate change, may argue for stricter limits. But the potential for conflict between developing and industrial countries over climate change is enormous. Disputes concerning carbon emissions could endanger the global trading system (as rich countries attempt to impose tariffs on polluting exporters) or conceivably threaten world peace as rich countries take more direct action to suppress emissions in developing countries that seek to achieve rich-country lifestyles.

Differences in technological capacity have also complicated international policy coordination. In the third Law of the Sea Conference (1973–82), developing countries with limited technological capacity and capital argued that deep sea mining should be supervised by an international organization and the revenues distributed among all countries. By contrast, the industrial countries wanted to organize an international claims registry to avoid boundary disputes, but otherwise leave deep sea mining to private exploitation.[33] These differing positions raised an important ethical issue: Are resources not within the geographical border of any country the "common heritage of mankind," and thus all countries should enjoy the benefits? Or do they simply belong to whomever has the technology and finance to get them first?

A compromise on deep sea mining was struck in the mid-1990s. The final treaty recognized the principle that seabed resources were the "common heritage of mankind" and established a regulatory regime to oversee deep sea mining.[34] However, requirements that firms pay high licensing fees to the international regulatory agency and provide technology to developing countries as conditions of undertaking mining operations were dropped. As with any compromise, all major parties (rich-country governments, developing-country governments, and mining companies) disliked parts of this agreement, but it did set up a framework that will allow mining by private firms while recognizing the rights of the global community over seabed resources. Thus while the participation of developing countries may have made reaching agreement more problematic than if only the rich countries had been involved, the outcome could be seen as both more equitable and more conducive to sustainable exploitation than a result that entirely ignored the interests of developing countries.

There are other examples of how differences in technological capacity increase the tensions surrounding efforts to achieve global coordination. Poor and fast-growing countries have complicated the agreements over use of the global commons by laying claims to a larger share of resources than their present capabilities and economic weight suggest they should be entitled to. For example, developing countries near the equator have claimed rights over the location of geostationary telecommunications satellites (the equator is their most efficient location) even though these countries lack the ability to launch satellites; in 1979 developing countries claimed a share of radar frequencies based on their future, not current, needs, for fear that the frequencies would no longer be available when they achieved the ability to use them.[35] While complicating negotiations, these claims can make outcomes both more equitable and more efficient in the future, as a larger share will go to countries that need these resources and will be better placed to use them.

Advances in technology can also create new frictions between industrial and developing countries, as happened in fisheries. "Factory ships" that can harvest and process very large quantities of fish have threatened the sustainability of many traditional fishing areas. Increased overfishing and exhaustion of migratory fish species have intensified the need for agreed limits on fish harvests. (The FAO estimates that almost 30 percent of global fish stocks are overexploited, depleted, or recovering, and that 50 percent are fully exploited.)[36] Setting and enforcing limits that strike a reasonable compromise between the interests of industrial-scale and traditional fishing is problematic, particularly given the limited information on fish stocks and the administrative weaknesses of regional fishery organizations in many developing countries.

Even when the will to act exists, weaknesses in public administration make it difficult for developing countries to deliver. For example, sustainable management of migratory fish species is in the interest of all harvesting and consuming nations, but many developing countries that control offshore fisheries lack the technology and capacity to monitor fish populations or control excessive exploitation.[37] Similarly, limited resources to devote to public administration make it difficult to control land use and deforestation, administer the distribution of condoms and treat AIDS, react quickly and effectively to signs of a possible flu epidemic, and enforce pollution standards. While administrative capacity varies greatly among developing countries, the average value of some indicators of developing countries' administrative capacity (bureaucratic quality and corruption) in the International Country Risk Guide (ICRG) are about half the average value for high-income countries (figure 7.5).

Although the fastest growing and more successful developing countries (such as those likely to have the largest environmental imprint) tend to have better administrative capacity than very poor countries, their capacity may be uneven across the national territory and across sectors—making them reluctant to undertake commitments. Examples include the differences in incomes and public administration between Moscow and rural areas of the Caucasus, Shanghai and western China, and Mumbai and Orissa.

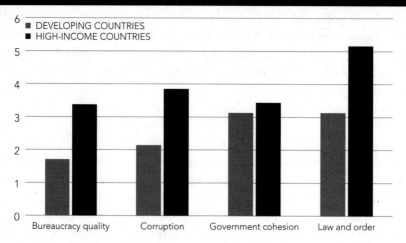

FIGURE 7.5 INDICES OF ADMINISTRATIVE CAPACITY
(GDP, REAL $, TRILLIONS)

- DEVELOPING COUNTRIES
- HIGH-INCOME COUNTRIES

Bureaucracy quality | Corruption | Government cohesion | Law and order

Note: Indices are developed based on survey data. The minimum value for all indices is zero. The maximum value of the bureaucratic quality and government cohesion indices is 4, and the corruption and law and order indices is 6. Data refer to averages as of June 2009. *Source:* ICRG 2009.

Authoritarian and unaccountable governments in developing countries have sometimes made global coordination more difficult. For example, low-cost and widely available air travel has made it critical to respond rapidly to initial outbreaks of infectious diseases. But developing country governments have at times impeded these efforts. For example, during the 1970 cholera epidemic, Iran and Egypt dismissed cholera reports as "summer diarrhea," while Guinea denounced World Health Organization (WHO) findings on the incidence of cholera and withdrew from the organization.[38] More recently, China notified the WHO of the SARS outbreak four and a half months after the first known case.[39] The control of information and the press in some developing countries makes withholding information easier than in the more open societies in rich countries.[40] But economic progress in developing countries has made it more difficult to enforce controls. By 2003 the Internet, e-mail, and mobile phones made it impossible for the Chinese authorities to bottle up information on the disease for long.[41]

To be sure, the elaborate checks and balances in democracies, beginning with the United States, can also make global cooperation difficult. For example, several international treaties, including the Kyoto Protocol, as well as numerous trade agreements have failed or been less well executed because the United States did not ratify them. Many other potential agreements have been slowed or stopped because it was thought unlikely the U.S. Congress would approve them (such as the Doha Round of trade negotiations).

Cultural differences and social norms, as well as disparate political systems, also affect global coordination. The Internet Corporation for Assigned Names and Numbers, which controls the assignment of domain names and Internet Protocol numbers, is a U.S. nonprofit organization that operates under a memorandum of understanding with the U.S. Commerce Department. Other countries (including other rich countries) have long questioned why a critical international communications vehicle should be dominated by a single country, while the United States has maintained that greater official intervention could impair the openness and interoperability of the system. Advocates of an open Internet fear the influence of some developing countries that are particularly concerned over objectionable material (Islamic societies that abhor Internet pornography) or who control Internet access to protect a particular regime (such as China).

In short, although the impact of developing countries on global public goods has grown, differences with industrial countries make it more difficult to reach agreements to improve global coordination. Yet developing country participation can also make outcomes more equitable and efficient. Indeed, ignoring the interests of developing countries is bound to make outcomes not just inequitable by definition, but also inefficient.

Lessons from previous and ongoing efforts at policy coordination

The Kyoto Protocol is a spectacular example of the failure of international coordination on a crucial issue. Efforts to accommodate diverse interests produced unambitious targets to reduce emissions, yet failed to secure the engagement of major emitters, including China, India, and the United States (which failed to ratify). This undermined the legitimacy of the agreement, and the targets were missed.

But there are also examples of cooperation on global issues, such as the Montreal Protocol to protect the ozone layer, some regional agreements to avoid excessive exploitation of migratory fish species, and agreements to apportion telecommunications frequencies. The commonalities and differences among these (relative) success stories can provide some insights into what kinds of issues are most amenable to global cooperation and how to achieve it. These lessons can then be used to evaluate the level of difficulty presented by the major coordination issues that confront us now.

When are agreements most likely to succeed? Success is more likely if:

- There is a broad consensus on the importance and extent of the problem.

- Only a few countries are major contributors to the problem.
- The costs of environmental degradation are borne largely by the countries that are the major source.
- The problem consists of enhancing everyone's economic efficiency rather than avoiding competing overuse of a scarce resource.
- Negotiations start off on the right foot.

Agreement on global coordination generally requires general acceptance that a problem exists, is important, and is amenable to improvements. For many issues, such as climate change and the threat to the ozone layer, this involves some consensus among the scientists studying an issue. Two things helped agreement on the Montreal Protocol. One was the general consensus among scientists of the dire implications of CFC emissions. Without the Protocol and its policy changes, it is estimated that ozone depletion would have resulted in 19 million more cases of non-melanoma skin cancer and 1.5 million cases of melanoma cancer by 2050.[42] The second was the participation by scientists and environmental groups in the negotiations.

Even where scientific analysis is not necessary to detect the problem, scientists often play a role in the solution. For example, experienced fishers may be able to tell when the availability of a particular fish species is declining, but science may be essential for gaining precise measurements of the existing stock and the rate of exhaustion. More dramatically, the obvious threat to welfare posed by the spread of influenza meant that scientific analysis was not essential to galvanize coordination among public agencies to detect and isolate cases. That enabled the WHO to take extraordinary measures (such as publicizing avian flu episodes without the consent of member governments) with only limited protests from affected countries.[43] But analysis is required to design approaches to containing a flu epidemic (such as vaccine production).

Finally, the lack of scientific knowledge may hamper progress in other areas. For example, meager understanding of the impact of mining on the mysterious environment of the seabed makes it difficult to design rules to control deep sea mining.[44]

The smaller the number of countries that participate in negotiations, the easier it is to reach agreement and to monitor compliance. For example, the Montreal Protocol is credited with eliminating 95 percent of ozone-depleting substances in developed countries and between half and three-quarters of such substances in developing countries,[45] leading to predictions that the ozone layer may be healed by 2050.[46] Before the negotiations the industrial countries accounted for more than 80 percent of total CFC emissions,[47] so a limited number of negotiators could achieve real progress in limiting CFCs. It also helped that the major countries had similar incomes, so the tradeoffs they faced between growth and pollution were similar. Moreover, the countries were accustomed to cooperating across a broad spectrum of issues, enhancing the incentives to reach agreement.[48]

Another example is the record of international agreements in limiting overfishing. Effective limitation of fish harvests has been achieved for a few species that migrate through the waters of only a couple of countries, while less progress has been made for migratory species that move through the open seas, where conservation requires the adherence to limitations on harvests by all countries capable of exploitation.[49]

Limiting the number of participants in negotiations can be contrasted with reliance on international forums (for example, the United Nations) that involve as many countries as possible. Some countries often press for UN involvement, or for requiring consensus among many countries for agreement, at times to garner political support from countries that have little stake in the issue. While such tactics can help form coalitions and support tradeoffs among different issues, they can also introduce too many actors and extraneous considerations into negotiations, where agreement can be achieved only by limiting the numbers of countries and focusing on the issues.

But where the issue is sharing a global resource, limiting negotiations to a small "critical mass" of players may be perceived as inequitable and illegitimate by nonparticipants. Thus, developing appropriate protocols for treatment of interested parties that are nonparticipants of agreements is vital (discussed further below).

Global coordination is easier if countries causing the problem also bear the major share of the impact. In the limiting case, global coordination is unnecessary if the source and impact of pollution are limited to a single political jurisdiction. For the Montreal Protocol, leadership by a limited number of countries that were the major polluters (Canada, Germany, Norway, and the United States) was encouraged because the location of these countries made residents particularly vulnerable to ozone depletion over the Arctic. International coordination in controlling infectious diseases is made easier because the country where disease is found is likely to suffer first from an epidemic.

Some issues lend themselves more readily to coordination than others. Agreements to improve the efficiency of a common resource—such as apportioning radio frequencies or ensuring the interoperability of telecommunications facilities such as telephones, postal services, and the Internet—tend to be more successful than agreements to restrict exploitation of a limited resource (such as migratory fish). The former are visibly positive-sum games where coordination enhances efficiency, while the latter, at least in the short run, are zero-sum games that limit profitable economic activities in the interest of future availability of the resource.

The former agreements also lend themselves more to evolution over time as new technologies develop, while the latter may require an attempt at a comprehensive solution based on current circumstances. Note, however, that achieving technical agreements to enhance efficiency can come at the cost of narrowing an issue's scope. For example, global discussions allocated IP (Internet protocol) addresses and preserved the openness and interoperability of the Internet. But there has been much less progress on other important issues affecting Internet governance, such as intellectual property, privacy, policing cyberspace for spam, cybercrime, and child pornography.

So far, we have emphasized how the intrinsic nature of an issue helps determine the difficulties in achieving international coordination. But the approach in setting up the negotiating framework can also affect success. International coordination should be viewed as path-dependent: if it starts down the wrong road, it can be hard to recover. That is, the precedents established in early agreements play a role in determining the context of negotiations over subsequent revisions. For example, the exemptions from emission restraints granted developing countries under the Kyoto Agreement, while justifiable on equity grounds, have made it more difficult to achieve emissions limits in the current climate change negotiations.

More generally, agreements based on principles valid over the long term are more likely than ad hoc compromises to lay the groundwork for success.

Implications for future efforts at policy coordination

The lessons from successful examples of international coordination have somber implications for progress on climate change through a binding global agreement, and argue instead for a less ambitious approach. But they also encourage a more positive view of the likelihood of reaching globally binding agreements to control infectious diseases.

Climate change has all the attributes of a difficult problem. The weight of scientific evidence argues overwhelmingly for immediate action to control carbon emissions, but even within the boundaries of science, the path and incidence of climate change are subject to enormous uncertainty. In many countries the wider public remains skeptical that climate change is the result of human activity. The extremely difficult analysis of historical changes in climate and the predictions for the future are fraught with major controversies, so that opponents of change can point to large areas of disagreement and to scientists who discount the threat of climate change entirely.[50]

The number of countries that are large emitters is growing and is as diverse as can be. Except for perhaps the two or three largest emitters, each country's contribution is largely unrelated to the effect of climate change on that country. So, while most countries may ultimately be affected, the biggest contributors are not necessarily the most affected (for example, the potential damages facing the United States are not as large relative to income as those facing Bangladesh). That impairs the incentives for making the sacrifices required to control emissions. A further complication is that there are big differences between the countries that have historical responsibility for the problem and those that have responsibility at the margin, tending to obscure discussions of equitable burden-sharing.

And significant progress in limiting emissions requires sacrifices and costs to economic growth in the interests of future generations, without the kind of clear gains generated, say, from agreements to manage telecommunications.

Arguably, global climate change negotiations have also started on the wrong foot, by attempting to reach a global deal among close to 200 countries as part of a UN process, even though only about 8 countries account for 85 percent of emissions, including the effect of deforestation. Having included such a large group from the start, it now becomes difficult to change course and exclude them.

In short, climate change is intrinsically a difficult issue to coordinate, particularly given the current universal negotiating framework. Steps to limit the parties to future agreements to a "critical mass" of the largest emitters, initially involving Europe, the United States, and China, are essential to progress. Provisions will be necessary for the inclusion of other countries, with appropriate side-payments to encourage participation, but the big three will have to show the way. Also essential is a renewed push for research in alternative energy. Technological progress will have to generate a large share of future reductions in emissions, and governments will have to recognize that the public interest demands public investment in low-carbon energy sources.

Even in the absence of effective international agreements, progress can be achieved through actions by regional, national, and local jurisdictions. For example, the European Union established a marketplace for trading emissions and in 2007 adopted legislation to set emission standards for new passenger cars. In the United States, the Environmental Protection Agency has undertaken various regulatory actions to limit greenhouse gases.[51]

The implications of these lessons for the control of infectious diseases are somewhat more heartening. All countries with regular access to modern transportation services have to be part of the efforts to avoid epidemics. Modern air transport can spread flu almost instantaneously, and individual countries face considerable difficulties in shutting their borders to potential flu carriers.

Thus effective measures against potential epidemics have to involve virtually all countries, creating a rather unwieldy process for reaching agreements and achieving compliance. But other aspects of infectious diseases make them more amenable to solutions through global coordination. There is little disagreement that pandemics need to be addressed, though controversy remains concerning the relative effectiveness of quarantines and vaccines in stopping the spread of disease. Moreover, all countries could be greatly affected by infectious diseases within their borders, so all have an incentive to cooperate in limiting transmission.

The way forward

As we have emphasized, the rise of developing countries can make global coordination more difficult because of the greater number of countries that need to be involved and because of the many differences between the newcomers and industrial countries. At the same time, their involvement is becoming more and more important to achieving efficient and equitable solutions.

A useful principle is that negotiations should be limited to the minimum number of participants required for adequate progress. For climate change that might involve the major emitters. For fisheries the countries that control the seas where the fish travel (or for high seas migratory fish, the major producers and consumers). For biodiversity the countries with large virgin forests and the rich donors. For seabed mining the countries with the necessary technology (but with veto power by the broader community). For the Internet major users with aggregated representation by smaller users. And for infectious diseases nearly everyone.

Mechanisms are likely to be needed to include more countries as circumstances change, to ensure that agreements are viewed as legitimate, and to accommodate changes in the extent of the problem and the economic relationships among countries.

This is particularly important when participants enjoy technological advantages. The clearest examples are sea mining and the exploitation of Antarctica. Reaching an effective agreement can best be achieved by limiting negotiations to the countries that have the technology to exploit these inhospitable locations. But excluded countries will not see enabling a few countries to exhaust a global resource as equitable. Hence the need for protocols that ensure fair treatment of nonparticipants, including reasonable modalities for excluded countries to participate. For example, in Antarctica, conserving the resource for a few years might give excluded countries a greater opportunity to participate.

A somewhat different problem arises in environmental negotiations to limit exploitation, where technological proficiency is not essential to exploiting the resource. As participation in the agreement involves the cost of forgoing profitable economic activities (the benefits are spread among the world as a whole), countries may not object to being excluded and may continue to exploit the resource as "free riders." Subsidies from the countries party to the agreement could be provided to encourage the excluded countries to limit their pollution and to accede to the agreement reached among the major polluters. In that case, first reaching agreement among the major players and then subsidizing the accession of minor players may be more successful in achieving an effective agreement than initially including all countries in the negotiations.

Dealing with a large number of participants is easiest in agreements to facilitate technical coordination. The benefits of cooperation are clear to all concerned, and the costs of participation are minimal. So reaching an initial agreement among all countries, or providing for the accession of initially excluded countries, is fairly easy. For example, the importance of agreement on the division of radio spectrum for efficient use and the incentives created for incumbents by network externalities facilitated a relatively smooth expansion of the number of countries involved in agreements, from just the major European powers in the early twentieth century to the formation of the International Telecommunications Union as a specialized agency of the United Nations in 1947, with all member countries participating.

In sum, the provisions of such mechanisms should include how to treat both excluded countries and countries that join the agreement subsequent to its ratification. For example, if agreement on limiting carbon emissions can be reached by the major polluters, it could include provisions that nonparticipants would not be penalized by participants (say, through trade sanctions), new countries acceding to the agreement would be subject to similar restrictions on emissions, and developing countries joining the agreement would be eligible for the same subsidies and transfers of technology as the developing countries that joined initially.

Greater efforts are also needed to overcome some of the difficulties that developing countries present to international coordination. One approach is for the rich countries to provide technology and fund part of the cost that developing countries face in complying with environmental agreements. For climate change they would provide technology to improve energy efficiency and pay for projects that reduce emissions. One useful model is the dedicated funding created by the Montreal Protocol to transfer technology on substitutes for CFC emissions, which both encouraged participation by developing countries and boosted compliance with the agreement. For infectious disease control, improving developing countries' infrastructure for monitoring disease outbreaks could have significant global benefits. For fisheries, helping regional fisheries organizations in developing countries improve their ability to monitor stocks and capture rates could help ensure the sustainability of species that the rich countries consume.

Even in the absence of effective agreement, global frameworks can be useful. Even fairly weak limits (such as commitments that do not reflect a reduction in carbon emissions) can help in avoiding backsliding. Agreements can provide an efficient framework for technical assistance and aid to developing countries, an important step toward enhancing their cooperation in protecting the global commons. Global agreements can provide guidelines for the country-driven processes outlined here. And global agreements can set up the necessary framework for gathering information and monitoring progress toward meeting standards.

There is no simple guide to achieving global coordination to protect the global commons, no universal theory or cookie cutter set of rules. With the rise of developing countries, we have elaborated a few useful principles that should be considered in structuring negotiations over global coordination. Implementing these principles for specific issues, and making decisions on the tradeoffs they require, is more complex and idiosyncratic. But meeting this challenge is critical to the welfare of billions of people and to the sustainability of the planet.

Notes

1. The global commons refers to international public goods where the exclusion of beneficiaries through physical and institutional means is especially costly, and exploitation by one user reduces resource availability for others (Ostrom and others 1999). Some of the issues in this chapter, such as infectious diseases and perhaps climate change, do not strictly fit this definition.
2. Gill 2000.
3. Beeland 2007.
4. Plague and other infectious diseases did have near-global reach.
5. ICSG 2007.
6. Of the top 10 importers of all fish products, accounting for more than 80 percent of total imports, all except China are high-income countries (FAO 2008).
7. Stern 2007.
8. Parry et al 2007.
9. Parry and others 2007.
10. Parry and others 2007.
11. The majority of models assume that temperatures will rise 2–3 degrees Celsius from pre-industrial levels within the next 50 years and agree that, at any further increase, the negative impacts will be significantly more extreme. IPCC estimates for likely increases from 1999 range from 1.1 to 6.4 degrees

Celsius by 2099. Even if all emissions are kept at 2000 levels, temperatures will rise by about 0.2 degrees Celsius in the next two decades and then by 0.1 degrees Celsius per decade through 2099.

12. According to Sachs and Gallup, countries with intensive malaria grew by 1.3 percentage points less per person per year between 1965 and 1990 than those without it (Sachs and Gallup 2001). As health outcomes deteriorate, malnutrition will weaken human capital development, and money will increasingly be diverted to health expenditures.

13. UNDP 2007. Currently, $1 trillion of the world's assets lie at less than 1 meter above current sea level (Stern 2007).

14. See annex for details.

15. See annex table A3 for a detailed description of country proposals.

16. Earthtrends (http://earthtrends.wri.org). We begin with 1965 because data are missing for Japan prior to that year. Rich countries are defined as countries viewed as high income by the World Bank.

17. Laurence 2006.

18. Lewis and others 2006.

19. Eilperin 2009.

20. Avissar and others 2006.

21. Naidoo and Adamowicz 2001.

22. China, for example, had by 2007 reduced CFC production to one-tenth the 1998 level (GAIA Movement 2007).

23. www.goodplanet.info/eng/Contenu/Points-de-vues/Illegal-Trade-in-Ozone-Depleting-Substances/(theme)/309.

24. Nevertheless, the scarcity of spectrum is in part dictated by misallocation and inefficient use, which may account for one-half of the total value of available spectrum. Moreover, technological innovation can ease spectrum scarcity (Wellenius and Neto 2006).

25. Sadowsky and others 2004.

26. MacLean and others 2002.

27. Economic Commission for Africa 2005

28. Jakhu 2000.

29. Buck 1998.

30. See "Designing the Post-Kyoto Climate Regime: Lessons from the Harvard Project on International Climate Agreements."

31. www.hm-treasury.gov.uk/stern_review_report.htm

32. The discount rate favored by the faster-growing developing countries that contribute most to climate change is likely to be higher than that of the slower-growing industrial countries. Increments to consumption are more

important at low levels of consumption than at higher levels. If income and consumption are going to be much higher in the future, individuals will place greater value on consumption at the present lower level of consumption than at the expected future level, implying a high discount rate on future consumption.

33. Buck 1998.

34. Browne 2006.

35. Wijkman 1982.

36. FAO 2008.

37. World Bank 2007.

38. Time 1970.

39. Caballero-Anthony 2005.

40. Of course, many developing countries also enjoy a free press and open access to information. But restraints on press freedom are common in more developing than industrial countries.

41. Fidler 2004.

42. UNEP 2008.

43. Fidler 2004.

44. For example, Birney and others (2006) discuss how uncertainty over the environmental impact of a proposed sea mining project (by Placer Dome off the shores of Papua New Guinea) makes it difficult to design safeguards against environmental degradation.

45. www.igsd.org/montreal/index.php.

46. Harrison and Matson 2001.

47. UNEP 2008.

48. It is also possible, of course, that the influence of contentious issues among the parties could impede agreement: for example, negotiators might not want to appear to be "weak" and hence are unwilling to compromise, or countries could insist on concessions in other areas as a condition of agreement.

49. Most of the high-seas bottom-dwelling species are considered unregulated, according to the FAO (2004).

50. Various scientists have disputed most important aspects of the majority findings on climate change. Some claim that the observed increase in Earth's temperature is similar to past cycles and that man's role in fostering climate change is negligible (Brusca 2009, Singer and Avery 2005). Others find no discernible trend in global temperatures, or that it is impossible to predict future changes in climate (Lindzen 2001). Still others argue that temperatures may be rising, but that this will have no discernible impact on welfare (Michaels 2008).

51. See www.epa.gov/climatechange/initiatives/index.html.

References

Avissar, Roni, Renato Ramos da Silva, and David Werth. "Impacts of Tropical Deforestation on Regional and Global Hydroclimatology." In *Emerging Threats to Tropical Forests*, eds. William F. Laurence and Carlos A. Peres, 67–80. University of Chicago Press, 2006.

Beeland, DeLene. "UF study: Maya politics likely played role in ancient large-game decline." *University of Florida News* (Gainesville, FL), November 8, 2007.

Birney, Kristi, Amber Griffin, Jonathan Gwiazda, Johnny Kefauver, Takehiko Nagai, and Douglas Varchol. "Potential Deep-Sea Mining of Seafloor Massive Sulfides: A Case Study in Papua New Guinea." Donald Bren School of Environmental Science & Management, Santa Barbara, CA, 2006.

Buck, Susan J. *The Global Commons: An Introduction*. Washington, DC: Island Press, 1989.

Browne, Marjorie Ann. "The Law of the Sea Convention and U.S. Policy." Congressional Research Service Issue Brief for the U.S. Congress, Washington, DC, 2006.

Brusca, Raymond. "Professor Denies Global Warming Theory." *Daily Princetonian* (Princeton, NJ), January 12, 2005.

Caballero-Anthony, Mely. "SARS in Asia: Crisis, Vulnerabilities, and Regional Responses." *Asian Survey*, 45 (2005): 475–95.

Economic Commission for Africa. "The Internet Governance Space: Exploring the Core Issues from Africa's Perspective." Fourth Meeting of the Committee on Development Information, Addis Ababa. April 23–28, 2005.

Eilperin, Juliet. "As emissions increase, carbon sinks get clogged." *Washington Post*, December 3, 2009.

Erhardt-Martinez, Karen. "Social Determinants of Deforestation in Developing Countries: A Cross-National Study." *Social Forces*, 77 (1998): 567–86.

FAO (Food and Agricultural Organization). "Report of the Expert Consultation on Economic Incentives and Responsible Fisheries." Rome, 2004.

———. *The State of World Fisheries and Aquaculture*. Rome, 2008.

Fidler, David P. "Germs, governance and global public health in the wake of SARS." *Journal of Clinical Investigation*, 113 (2004): 799–804.

GAIA Movement 2007.

Green, Rhys E., Stephen J. Cornell, Jorn P. W. Scharlemann, and Andrew Balmford. "Farming and the Fate of Wild Nature." *Science*, 307 (2005): 550–55.

Harrison, John, and Pamela Matson. "The Atmospheric Commons." In *Protecting the Commons: A Framework for Resource Management in the Americas*, eds. Joanna Burger, Elinor Ostrom, Richard B. Norgaard, David Policansky, and Bernard D. Goldstein. Washington, DC: Island Press, 2001.

The Harvard Project on International Climate Agreements. "Designing the Post-Kyoto Climate Regime: Lessons from the Harvard Project on International Climate Agreements." Poznan, Poland, 2008.

ICRG (International Country Risk Guide). Database. Syracuse, NY, 2009.

ICSG (International Copper Study Group). *World Copper Factbook 2007*. Lisbon, 2007.

Jakhu, Ram S. "International Regulatory Aspects of Radio Spectrum Management (Implications for Developing Countries like India)." Proceedings of the Second Annual Workshop Held at the Indian Institute of Management, 2000, www.ictregulationtoolkit.org/en/Document.3301.pdf.

Laurence, William F. "Introduction: What are Emerging Threats?" In *Emerging Threats to Tropical Forests*, eds. William F. Laurence and Carlos A. Peres. Chicago, IL: University of Chicago Press, 2006.

Lewis, Simon L. Oliver L. Philiips, and Timothy R. Baker. "Impacts of Global Change on the Structure, Dynamics, and Functioning of South American Tropical Forests." In *Emerging Threats to Tropical Forests*, eds. William F. Laurence and Carlos A. Peres. Chicago, IL: University of Chicago Press, 2006.

Lindzen, Richard S. "Scientist's Report doesn't Support the Kyoto Treaty." *Wall Street Journal*, June 11, 2001.

MacLean, Don, David Souter, James Deane, and Sarah Lilley. "Louder Voices: Strengthening Developing Country Participation in International ICT Decision-Making." Commonwealth Telecommunications Organisation, London, 2002, www.cto.int.

Maddison, Angus. *The World Economy: A Millennial Perspective*. Paris: Organisation for Economic Cooperation and Development, Development Centre Studies, 2001.

Michaels, Patrick. "Our Climate Numbers Are a Big Old Mess." *Wall Street Journal*, April 18, 2008.

Naidoo, Robin, and Wiktor L. Adamowicz. "Effects of Economic Prosperity on Numbers of Threatened Species." *Conservation Biology*, 15 (2001): 1021–9.

Ostrom, Elinor, Joanna Burger, Christopher Field, Richard B. Norgaard, and David Policansky. "Revisiting the Commons: Local Lessons, Global Challenges." *Science*, 284 (1999): 278–82.

Parry, Martin, Osvaldo Canziani, Jean Palutikof, Paul van der Linden, and Clair Hanson, eds. *Climate Change 2007: Impacts, Adaptation and Vulnerability*. Cambridge, UK: Cambridge University Press, 2007.

Sachs, J. D., and J. L. Gallup. "The Economic Burden of Malaria." *American Journal of Tropical Medicine and Hygiene*, 64 (2001): 85–96.

Sadowsky, George, Raul Zambrano, and Pierre Dandjijou. "Internet Governance: Discussion Document." Prepared for the United Nations ICT Task Force, New York, 2004.

Singer, S. Fred, and Dennis T. Avery. "The Physical Evidence of Earth's Unstoppable 1500 Year Climate Cycle." National Center for Policy Analysis Report 279. Dallas, TX, 2005.

Stern, Nicholas. *The Stern Review: The Economics of Climate Change*. Cambridge, UK: Cambridge University Press, 2007.

Time. "Disease: Bracing for El Tor." September 14, 1970.

UNDP (United Nations Development Programme). *Human Development Report 2007/2008. Fighting climate change: Human solidarity in a divided world*. New York, 2007.

UNEP (United Nations Environmental Programme). *Deep Sea Biodiversity and Ecosystems: A Scoping Report on their Socio-economy, Management and Governance*. Cambridge, UK: Regional Seas Reports and Studies, 2007.

———. "Backgrounder: Basic Facts and Data on the Science and Politics of Ozone Protection." September 2008. http://ozone.unep.org/Events/ozone_day_2009/press_backgrounder.pdf.

Wellenius, Bjorn, and Isabel Neto. "The radio spectrum: opportunities and challenges for the developing world." *Info*, 8 (2006): 18–33.

Wijkman, Magnus. "Managing the Global Commons." *International Organization*, 36 (1982): 511–36.

World Bank. *Global Economic Prospects: Managing the Next Wave of Globalization*. Washington, DC, 2007.

CHAPTER 8

AFRICA

Growth in Sub-Saharan Africa accelerated in the decade before the recent financial crisis, driven especially by an improved external environment, though better policies and less conflict also helped.

Continuing progress will require overcoming numerous challenges, including low savings and investment rates, insufficient productivity gains, inadequate export diversification, and poor governance. But growing opportunities to export to, and receive investment from, emerging economies will support Africa's development. The emergence of a middle class in Africa will also create more demand. Unless education services improve, however, the opportunities in the huge wave of young people set to enter the labor force over the next few decades will be missed.

This book is about the rapidly growing emerging giants that will rule the world economy in a few decades. The transformation of Brazil, China, India, Indonesia, Mexico, and Russia into global powerhouses will lift hundreds of millions of people out of poverty and enormously improve global welfare. But these countries are not the whole story of development. Sub-Saharan Africa has been left out of the narrative.[1]

The prospects for Sub-Saharan Africa may not have the earth-shaking implications that growth in the BRICs does. No African country is expected to make it among the top 10 economies by 2050. But whether growth continues in Sub-Saharan Africa, or even accelerates, is critical in human terms. Since the disastrous 1980s and early 1990s, poverty in the region has fallen, and growth has improved, but almost half the region's people still lived on less than $1.25 a day in 2005. In this chapter, we leave behind the global story for a moment and ask a question about human welfare: Can Sub-Saharan Africa achieve rising living standards over the coming decades?

First, we ask whether the acceleration of growth since the mid-1990s was due to temporary (or cyclical) factors that could reverse over time, or whether it stemmed from improvements in policies that, if sustained, could generate rising incomes for many years. Second, we consider the main challenges Sub-Saharan Africa faces, highlighting the policy issues critical to growth prospects. This discussion complements the model-based growth forecasts for selected African economies in chapter 3.

Africa's economic growth has accelerated

After stagnating for much of its postcolonial period, economic growth in Africa began accelerating after the mid-1990s. GDP increased by an average of 4.6 percent a year from 1999 to 2008, more than doubling its pace from the previous decade. Lower middle-income countries saw the strongest economic expansion, growing 6 percent a year from 1999 to 2008 as commodity prices boomed in the 2000s. But the acceleration was widespread and included South Africa, an upper middle-income country that accounts for more than a quarter of Sub-Saharan GDP. Seventeen African economies—12 of them low income—grew at an average annual rate of 5 percent or more in the decade leading up to 2008, up from only 7 in the previous decade (figure 8.1). Crucially, the continent's per capita income grew at an average of 2 percent a year in the 2000s, finally ending the continent's long period of decline.

Africa's growth also accelerated more than that of developing economies in other regions, if from a low base. Its GDP growth rate doubled, while growth in East Asia and the Pacific, South Asia, Latin America, and the Middle East and North Africa (MENA) rose by factors of only 0.7 to 1.6.

Despite the marked uptick, the region's 1999–2008 growth rates remained in the bottom half of developing economy growth rates. Countries in Africa grew slower than those at corresponding income levels in East Asia and the Pacific, Europe and Central Asia, and South Asia (figure 8.2).

But absolute poverty persists

Sub-Saharan Africa's growth in part reflected rapid population growth rather than rapid increases in per capita income. For example, per capita income in low-income African economies grew at about one-fourth the pace of those in low-income economies in East Asia and the Pacific, including Laos, Myanmar, and Cambodia.

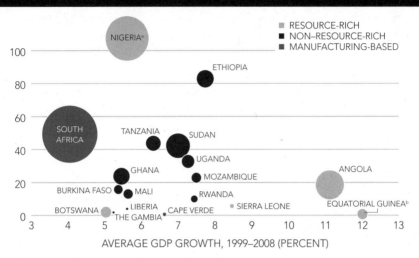

FIGURE 8.1 RAPID GROWTH WAS WIDESPREAD
(TOP PERFORMING AFRICAN ECONOMIES, MILLION POPULATION)

a. Nigeria's population is actually 150 million.
b. Equatorial Guinea's average GDP growth rate over 1999–2008 was 23.2 percent.
Note: Circle size indicates relative total GDP. Except South Africa, these economies grew by an annual average of more than 5 percent over 1999–2008.
Source: World Bank data.

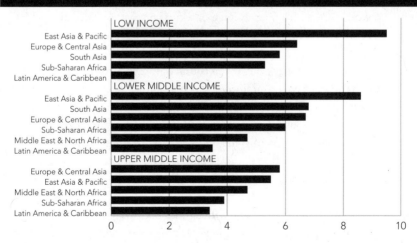

FIGURE 8.2 GROWTH IN SUB-SAHARAN AFRICA WAS SLOWER THAN IN OTHER REGIONS
(AVERAGE GDP GROWTH, 1999–2008, PERCENT)

Source: World Bank data; authors' calculations.

Recall that per capita income in Africa started from an abysmally low level, and that base levels matter. Even if Africa's per capita income continues to grow at 2 percent a year for the coming decade, its per capita income will only gain $460 (in purchasing power parity, or PPP, terms). In contrast, if per capita income in Japan—one of the richest and slowest growing economies in the world—grows by just 1 percent a year over the same period, its absolute gain would be more than seven times that in Africa, and the gain alone would be nearly 70 percent higher than Africa's current per capita income. So, the absolute income gap will widen considerably even if Africa makes proportional gains.

Very low initial incomes and slower growth also explain why Africa continues to lag behind other developing regions in eradicating absolute poverty. Although the share of Africans living on less than $1.25 a day declined from 58 percent of the total population in 1990 to 46 percent in 2005, the number of people living in poverty rose from nearly 300 million to 380 million. Other poor developing regions made much greater strides. East and South Asia, which had poverty rates comparable to Africa's in 1990, respectively reduced their poverty rates by 38 and 11 percentage points by 2005, thanks to decades of sustained, rapid economic growth.

Resources and external developments were not the whole story

Resources were a major part of the growth picture in Sub-Saharan Africa. In resource-rich economies—where rents from resources account for more than 10 percent of government revenue, and which represent nearly one-third of the continent's GDP—output grew 6 percent a year over 1999–2008—about twice the growth over the previous decade and higher than the 4.7 percent growth in the non–resource-rich economies. Oil-exporting economies benefited from the rise in oil prices, which surged from an average of $15 a barrel in 1998 to about $100 a barrel in 2008.[2] As a result, their GDP growth more than doubled to 6.6 percent—2 percentage points higher than that in oil-exporting Middle East and North Africa economies and more than any other major country grouping in Sub-Saharan Africa.

The rise in the price of commodities, which account for more than 70 percent of Sub-Saharan exports, drove an improvement in the region's terms of trade. Oil prices were largely responsible, as oil exporters there and in the Middle East saw the largest advances in terms of trade, compared with a much smaller increase in Latin America and a decline in developing Asia (figure 8.3). Higher prices of other raw materials, such as minerals, also helped Africa.

New sources of external demand and finance also boosted growth

Rising trade with fast-growing developing economies also helped Africa's exports, which more than quadrupled from 1998 to 2008. The share of developing

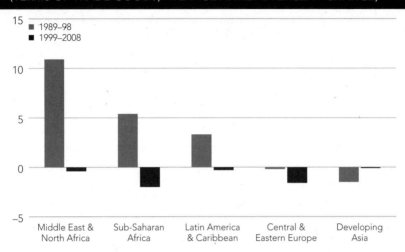

FIGURE 8.3 SUB-SAHARAN AFRICA ENJOYED LARGE TERMS OF TRADE GAINS IN THE PRECRISIS DECADE
(TERMS OF TRADE GOODS, AVERAGE ANNUAL PERCENT CHANGE)

■ 1989–98
■ 1999–2008

Middle East & North Africa | Sub-Saharan Africa | Latin America & Caribbean | Central & Eastern Europe | Developing Asia

Source: IMF data.

economies in Africa's extraregional trade climbed from less than 20 percent in 1995 to 33 percent in 2008. China has become a major player in Africa, more so than in other developing regions. Its share in Africa's exports rose 10 percentage points in 1998–2008, compared with 6 percentage points in Middle East and North Africa's exports and 4 percentage points in Latin America's.

And inward foreign direct investment (FDI) surged with Africa's trade, particularly in oil-exporting economies, which received nearly half the FDI flows into Africa from 1999 to 2008. Net inflows of FDI reached about $35 billion in 2008, after averaging around $17 billion in 1999–2008, a more than fourfold increase from the previous decade's $4 billion average. But even this impressive growth lags behind that of other developing regions—Eastern Europe and Central Asia, Middle East and North Africa, and South Asia—which also started from relatively low levels.

Non–resource-rich economies also grew

Natural resources do not tell the whole story. The region's 36 non–resource-rich countries, though lagging behind the resource-rich, more than doubled their growth rate to nearly 4 percent from the previous decade, mainly due to fast-growing services. Top performers in this group include Ethiopia, Mozambique, and Uganda, which grew by an average of 7 percent or more a year in the decade before the financial crisis.

Non–resource-rich economies also showed substantial improvements in trade and foreign investment, though at much lower rates than the resource-rich and especially oil-rich economies. The exports of non–resource-rich economies gained 4.7 percentage points of GDP between 1989–1998 and 1999–2008. This trailed the 8.1 percentage point rise in resource-rich countries, reflecting the more favorable external environment for resource-related exports. FDI also increased sharply to 2.5 percent of GDP from a low base, still lower than the 2.7 percent for resource-rich economies.

Services have become the new drivers of growth

Growth in non–resource-rich economies occurred broadly across sectors, especially services, the major source of output in non–resource-rich economies, at more than 50 percent of GDP (figure 8.4). The rise of services largely reflects higher public spending in education and health, as well as expanded private activity in real estate, hotels, restaurants, and banking.

Agriculture and manufacturing saw their shares of GDP fall in both groups of countries—worrisome, given their potential for productivity gains. Industry rose in resource-rich economies due to growth in mining and construction, not in manufacturing. In Nigeria, a major resource-rich economy, the decline in manufacturing was accompanied by a sharp rise in services, signaling the "Dutch Disease."[3]

Better policies contributed to faster growth

Better macroeconomic management clearly helped Africa, with good progress in reducing inflation and budget deficits.

Between 1989–1998 and 1999–2008 average inflation fell by two-thirds in lower middle-income economies and by half in most low-income (excluding Zimbabwe) and upper middle-income economies. Africa's two largest economies, South Africa and Nigeria, respectively reduced their inflation rates by 50 and 66 percent. In the 2000s nearly 30 of the 45 Sub-Saharan countries enjoyed single-digit inflation—10 more than in the 1990s. Low-income and lower middle-income economies also saw inflation drop substantially more than in developing countries elsewhere.

Thanks to large fiscal surpluses in oil-exporting economies in the 2000s—averaging 6.3 percent of GDP—Africa's fiscal balance (including grants) turned from a deficit of 2.6 percent of GDP in 1997–2002 to a surplus of 1.3 percent in 2008. In some countries, such as Botswana, funds were established using rents from mineral wealth to provide for public debt service. The continent's average external debt as a percentage of GDP also fell by a quarter between 1989–1998

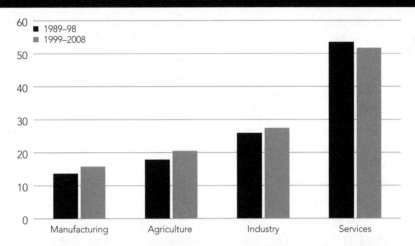

FIGURE 8.4 SERVICES WERE THE ENGINE OF GROWTH
(VALUE-ADDED, PERCENT OF GDP)
NON–RESOURCE-RICH ECONOMIES

- 1989–98
- 1999–2008

Manufacturing Agriculture Industry Services

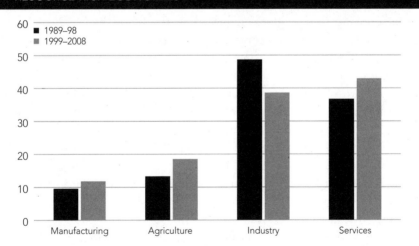

RESOURCE-RICH ECONOMIES

- 1989–98
- 1999–2008

Manufacturing Agriculture Industry Services

Source: World Bank data.

and 1999–2008, due in part to faster economic growth and debt relief under the Heavily Indebted Poor Countries (HIPC) initiative. This reduction was bigger than that in other developing regions.

Africa also made substantial gains in education enrollments. Gross primary school enrollment rose from 78 percent in 1999 to 97 percent in 2008, secondary school enrollment from 24 percent to 33 percent. Those increases were greater than those in other developing regions, but enrollments remain far lower in Africa. Most African economies face a severe shortage of highly educated people, critical to sustaining the current growth momentum.

Trade reform helped Africa integrate further into the global economy, though tariffs have fallen by less than in other developing regions. In the two decades leading up to 2008, tariff rates for manufactured products fell by about 46 percent in Africa, compared with more than 70 percent in all developing economies. But greater openness paid dividends in higher exports: between 1989–1998 and 1999–2008 exports of goods and services as a percentage of GDP increased 5 percentage points to 32 percent in Sub-Saharan Africa—comparable to increases of 5.6 to 7.6 percentage points for Latin America and the Caribbean, Middle East and North Africa, and South Asia.

Despite the improvements, Africa remains hobbled by major policy and institutional weaknesses, greater than those facing other developing regions. At around 46 percent of GDP, foreign debt in Sub-Saharan Africa is still 10 percentage points higher than that in Latin America and Middle East and North Africa. Inflation is still above 10 percent in about 15 African countries.

And even with some recent successes—which placed countries such as Rwanda among the top global reformers in the World Bank's 2010 Doing Business Index—the business climate in Africa remains enormously challenging, particularly for starting a business, obtaining credit, and securing investor protections. Sub-Saharan Africa ranked lower than all other developing regions in all but two of the nine components of the World Bank's index (dealing with construction permits and enforcing contracts). Lower middle-income economies—including large countries like Cameroon and Nigeria—scored particularly poorly, all ranking in the bottom half of the world's 53 lower middle-income economies.

Perhaps the most significant improvement has been the decline in violence. The number of state-based conflicts—which had severely impaired growth in many African countries—fell from 16 in 1999 to 6 in 2005 (figure 8.5). Democracy is also becoming more established across the continent, with a clear shift toward more elections and stronger political institutions, particularly in some of the top performing economies, such as Ghana.

But the region still has work to do. Major conflicts—in Chad, Darfur, and Somalia, for example—remain unresolved. And the region continues to score poorly on World Bank governance indicators—such as political stability, rule of law, and government effectiveness—which could affect its ability to grow. And despite the increase in parliamentary elections, dominant executives persist.

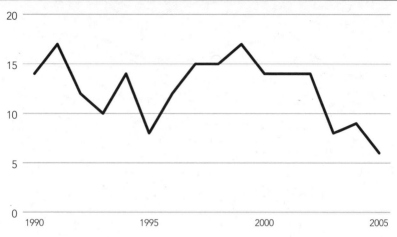

FIGURE 8.5 THE INCIDENCE OF CONFLICT IS FALLING
(NUMBER OF STATE-BASED ARMED CONFLICTS IN SUB-SAHARAN AFRICA)

Source: Human Security Gateway database.

African development faces severe challenges and promising opportunities over the long term

Higher oil and mineral prices, new sources of demand, and improved policies drove Africa's recent acceleration in growth. Whether prices will stay high over the medium term is an open question, but African policymakers can control at least some drivers of growth. Here we take a forward-looking view of the challenges and opportunities that confront African development over the long term, highlighting the policy implications.

Low investment and savings

Africa's investment rate, stagnant since the 1990s at less than 20 percent of GDP, is much smaller than the 30–35 percent in the most successful developing regions (figure 8.6). In large economies such as Ethiopia, Nigeria, and South Africa investment rates averaged around 19 percent of GDP in each of the past two decades, more than 10 percentage points below rapidly growing Asian countries such as Thailand and Vietnam.

Encouragingly, FDI accounted for a larger share of this investment, having more than doubled from a small base (see chapter 6 for a discussion of the benefits of FDI). But FDI tends to flow to traditional sectors, such as mining and petroleum, and African economies need to raise domestic investment to support agriculture and manufacturing. But underdeveloped financial intermediaries

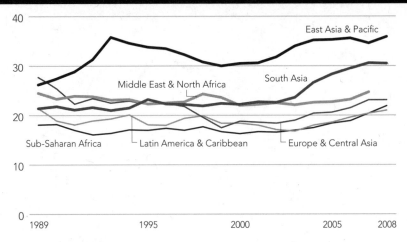

FIGURE 8.6 INVESTMENT REMAINS LOW IN SUB-SAHARAN AFRICA
(PERCENT OF GDP)

Source: World Bank data.

and other institutional weaknesses, such as inadequate infrastructure and lack of political stability, reduce the capacity to mobilize savings, while incomes are often too close to subsistence to allow for substantial savings. Africa's domestic savings rates of around 16 percent of GDP are much lower than developing Asia's 25–40 percent, keeping Africa dependent on foreign sources of capital, such as aid and loans, to finance investment.

Inadequate productivity gains
Characterizing Africa's slow growth is little or no improvement in total factor productivity (TFP). Future growth will depend on higher TFP—through advances in technological capabilities, for example—and not just on labor and fixed investment.

Looking at an index that measures a country's capacity to absorb foreign technology—which reflects education, infrastructure, governance, business climate, and openness to trade—can help evaluate Africa's capacity to increase its TFP.[4] Of the 30 developing countries evaluated, which represent the five largest economies from each of the six developing regions listed by the World Bank, four large African economies—Angola, Ethiopia, Kenya, and Nigeria—fall in the bottom quarter of the sample, due mainly to low scores for governance, education, and infrastructure. The other African economy in the sample, South Africa—with its relatively high scores on business climate and governance indicators—is ranked in the top 10 countries and offers better prospects for accelerating productivity growth.

The average infrastructure and education index—which includes paved roads, Internet use, and secondary education enrollment—for the five largest African economies lags more than 20 percentage points behind the 30-country average. Despite recent advances in Internet and mobile phone access, investment in Africa's infrastructure remains limited. In contrast, improved infrastructure in Central Europe and East Asia has positioned countries such as Poland and Thailand to improve productivity further.

Disappointing export performance and dependence on commodities

Although rising exports contributed to Africa's improved growth, most of the rise came from prices rather than volumes. The volume of exports grew 4.7 percent a year on average over 1999–2008—considerably lower than the 16 percent increase in the value of exports and slower than the 5.7 percent in the previous decade.

Most countries in the region remain exporters of primary products, such as oil and agricultural commodities, with manufactures accounting for the majority of exports in only a few economies, including South Africa and Mauritius. Primary products accounted for 75 percent of Africa's exports to non-African developing economies in 2008, up from 55 percent in 1995.

Commodity dependence, if not properly managed, can impair the prospects for development. While the surge in commodity prices since 2002 has improved Africa's terms of trade, commodity prices have tended to fall over the long term relative to those of manufactured goods.[5] That trend may well continue as increased investment and technological progress increase the supply of commodities and slowing global population growth hits demand.[6] Dependence on volatile commodity prices also makes the region more vulnerable to external shocks. Commodity dependence can support a successful development strategy, but only if windfall profits are saved in anticipation of eventual price declines, if government control of commodity rents does not result in corruption and excessive rent-seeking, and if commodity revenues are put back into the economy to generate productivity gains.[7] Three big ifs.

Mushrooming economic ties with emerging economies

While Africa has a long history of trade with Europe and other advanced economies, it now sends about half its exports to other developing countries, driven mainly by its rapidly rising trade with Asian economies. Asia's share of Africa's trade doubled to 28 percent over 1990–2008, and its rising demand for commodities will help Africa's economy. By mid-century China and India are expected to be among the top three export destinations for Africa, accounting for one-third of its exports.[8] The EU and the United States, by contrast, will account for only a quarter of Africa's exports by 2050, down from more than 50 percent in 2006 (see chapter 4). This reorientation will reduce Africa's vulnerability to a slowdown in advanced economies.

Emergence of middle-class consumers in Africa and elsewhere

The emergence of middle-class consumers will also support Africa's economic growth in the long term. Much of this increase will come from Africa itself. The size of the global middle and rich (GMR) class in six large African economies[9]— which account for two-thirds of the continent's GDP and more than one-third of its population—already rose 60 percent in just 10 years, from about 40 million people in 1998 to 61 million in 2007. And under plausible income distribution assumptions, a large proportion of the citizens in many African economies are projected to join the GMR by 2050. Specifically, 40–50 percent of the populations in Ghana, Kenya, and South Africa—which represent about 35 percent of the continent's GDP—will be in the GMR class. As more African households enjoy more disposable income, they will likely spend a large share of it on household and personal products, durable goods, and services, presenting a potential boon for African suppliers and supporting economic growth through domestic demand.

The increase in the GMR class in other large emerging economies will open space for Africa's exports as well. In China the GMR class is expected to grow from about 120 million people in 2009 to 780 million in 2030 and 1.1 billion in 2050. As wages and capital–labor ratios rise in the most successful developing economies, new markets will open for Africa. This may also open a door for low-wage countries in Africa to boost their exports of low-wage manufacturers.

Lagging demographic transition

The coming rise in Africa's labor force presents both challenges and opportunities.[10] Population growth is high, with a fertility rate of 5 births per woman—more than twice the rate in most other developing regions. The age-dependency ratio—around 85 dependents for every 100 workers—is also high, 25–40 percentage points above that of other developing regions. Together, these factors are expected to boost Sub-Saharan Africa's labor force (now about 500 million people) by 50 percent over the next 15 years.

This enormous infusion of labor will likely induce high output growth in Africa. But whether it translates into high per capita income growth will depend on governments' ability to invest in education and, most important, on the quality of that education. Without substantial and efficient increases in resources devoted to education (and health), the rise in the labor force could lead to massive increases in unemployment, low wages, declining productivity, and social unrest. But if governments can provide the new generation with the nutrition, health care, and education to become productive workers, income growth in Sub-Saharan Africa could accelerate sharply over the next few decades.

There is little time to lose to capitalize on the demographic transition, as fertility rates and the age-dependency ratio will decline over the long term. According to UN projections the fertility rate in Africa could fall to 3 births per woman by 2030 and to fewer than 2.5 births by 2050, as female education improves and family planning services become more readily available.

Conclusion

Widening gaps between the governance and business climate indicators of Africa and other developing regions suggest that the productivity gains in Africa will continue to be relatively slow, and some of the recent optimism about the region may not be fully warranted. Commodity prices may decline as supply responds to high prices in coming years. And both domestic savings and investment rates in Africa remain much lower than those in the emerging economies that have seen large growth accelerations in the past. Prospects for sluggish growth in industrial countries—still Africa's main export destination—and the likelihood that commodity prices remain highly volatile also argue for caution.

But there clearly is new hope for Africa, grounded in the region's greater stability, the rise of an African middle class, and the opportunities presented by stronger links with fast-growing emerging markets. In the long term, as wages rise in these countries, Africa's comparative advantage could shift toward manufactures, and new export growth opportunities may open up, allowing the world's poorest continent to make real sustained economic progress.

A critical policy challenge will be to ensure that the coming increase in young workers becomes an asset rather than a liability by providing them with health and education services. Africa's future depends on its policymakers' ability to establish rules that allow markets to function and private investment to thrive, as well as to provide the public services essential for human welfare. Africa has made genuine progress on first-generation reforms over the last decade, notably macroeconomic stability and openness to the world. If it is to catch up with other, more dynamic developing regions, it must make more progress in governance and in improving the quality of its public institutions.

Notes

1. This chapter is adapted from Ali and Dadush 2011.
2. According to the IMF's definition of oil-exporting economies, oil exports account for 30 percent or more of merchandise exports in such countries. This group includes Angola, Cameroon, Chad, Republic of Congo, Equatorial Guinea, Nigeria, and Sudan.
3. The "Dutch Disease" refers to the negative consequences of a resource boom, including declines in manufacturing and competitiveness, as the exchange rate appreciates and wages rise.
4. For a detailed explanation of the methodology behind the computation of the index, see Dadush and Stancil 2010.
5. Primary commodity prices have historically declined relative to those of manufactured goods, with estimates of the long-term decline ranging from −0.6 to −2.3 percent a year (Grynberg and Newton 2007).
6. For example, food production can increase greatly. Recent Food and Agriculture Organization and Organisation for Economic Co-operation and Development estimates show that an additional 1.6 billion hectares could be cultivated, more than doubling the 1.4 billion hectares now used.
7. See Sinnott, Nash, and de la Torre 2010.
8. See Dadush and Ali 2010.
9. These include Angola, Cameroon, Côte d'Ivoire, Kenya, Nigeria, and South Africa.
10. A delayed demographic transition refers to the population change when a country moves from high to low fertility and mortality rates as part of economic development.

References

Ali, Shimelse, and Uri Dadush."Whither Africa?" Policy Outlook, Carnegie Endowment for International Peace, Washington, DC, 2011.

Ali, Shimelse, and Uri Dadush. "The Transformation of World Trade." Policy Outlook, Carnegie Endowment for International Peace, Washington, DC, 2010.

Dadush, Uri, and Bennett Stancil. "The World Order in 2050." Policy Outlook, Carnegie Endowment for International Peace, Washington, DC, 2010.

Grynberg, Roman, and Samantha Newton. *Commodity Prices and Development.* Oxford, UK: Oxford University Press, 2007.

Sinnott, Emily, John Nash, and Augusto de la Torre. *Natural Resources in Latin America and the Caribbean: Beyond Booms and Busts.* Washington, DC: World Bank, 2010.

CHAPTER 9

CONFRONTING CHANGE

THE NEED FOR A GLOBAL CONSCIENCE

Grasping the opportunity in the rise of developing countries will require major changes to domestic policy and greatly enhanced international cooperation.

Certain principles can help make international cooperation more effective. A key principle is to build consensus for action at the country level, where the power to drive change is concentrated. Another is to co-opt a critical mass of countries in dealing with problems.

The world is most advanced on domestic policies and international collaboration in trade. It is far from controlling the risks in financial integration. It is failing dismally to deal with migration pressures and derive gains from migration. Its progress in mitigating climate change has also been deeply disappointing.

The new G20 summit of developing and advanced countries has clear weaknesses but is the most promising vehicle for making progress on many of these issues.

Building a "global conscience" is a work in progress, but it offers hope that a way forward can be found to deal with the challenges.

The preceding chapters have reviewed the challenges that lie ahead in each of the main channels of globalization—trade, finance, migration, and the global commons. The picture we have painted is necessarily fragmented and incomplete, reflecting reality on the ground. In this concluding chapter, we first try to bring together the different strands to propose some principles for how international cooperation can maximize the gains from the rise of the developing countries. We then assess how policies and international coordination in each of the channels of globalization stack up against these principles. Finally, we discuss the possible role of the G20 in dealing with some of these issues. The goal is simply to draw out some broad lessons from the preceding chapters; spelling out a detailed roadmap for dealing with such a complex and broad agenda would be impossible.

The principles outlined here reflect the evolution of the global economy, already discussed at length. While the next 40 years will see developing countries transform the global economy, taking advantage of the opportunities and avoiding the risks presented by their rise will continue to depend primarily on country-driven reforms, not international agreements. For better or worse, countries forge their own future. They alone have the sovereign capacity to implement real change, and they alone can determine how to interact with the global community in ways that consolidate the gains and mitigate the risks. International agreements play a secondary, though sometimes crucial, role.

Two principles

The first principle follows directly from the primacy of national policies: building awareness and understanding at the country level of the need to promote integration, as well as effective international coordination, is essential. Building a global conscience requires understanding (through analysis and research), civil society activism, education, and continuous engagement in international economic and political dialogue. In this the G20, the United Nations, the governing bodies of the Bretton Woods Institutions, and the General Council of the WTO make one of their biggest contributions. Even in areas where effective international agreements cannot be reached, independent national approaches, which may differ in detail but are based on common principles, can make much progress.

At the same time, international institutions—and the commentators who watch them—must recognize the limitations that stem from this principle and set their expectations accordingly. They must differentiate issues that multilateral institutions can influence significantly and those that have to rely predominantly on domestic political processes. Much as the world's most powerful economies may need to accelerate their fiscal and structural reforms, for example, no creative monetary arrangement or system of indicators that diagnoses imbalances will compel them to do what they need to do but do not want to do. While this distinction may seem clear, some important, essentially domestic, problems have recently been branded as "global" and therefore supposedly in need of international intervention—global rebalancing and "currency wars" chief among them. These issues are the root of much frustration with inaction by multilateral institutions—particularly the G20—but they have more to do with the fall-out from the financial crisis and unsound fiscal policies in the core of the system, the United States and Europe, and deficiencies in China's development model than with any "systemic" shortcoming. One has to distinguish between the need to improve the rules of the game and the need for key players to raise their game—too often, the latter is confused with the former.

The second principle is to tailor the selection of participants in international negotiations to the issues under negotiation. While international agreements must strive for legitimacy—the ideal would be to bring all countries to the table and only enact decisions reached unanimously—they must balance that goal with the equally important goal of efficacy. As a result, we reject as unrealistic and ultimately ineffectual the ambition to achieve universal consensus on the issues, as the UN Framework Convention on Climate Change and the WTO aim to do. Those organizations have little more than a growing list of failed initiatives and lowest-common-denominator declarations to show for their effort, such as the Copenhagen Accord and the stagnating Doha trade negotiations. The lack of realism in this approach has nothing to do with the international dimension—it is impossible to imagine any domestic assembly carrying out its mandate on the basis of unanimous decisionmaking. At the same time, agreements among a very small and select group of countries—the other side of the spectrum—not only lack the legitimacy to be adopted broadly, but also engage too few actors to make a dent in global problems, and fail to achieve the efficiency possible through dividing labor among a large group.

For many global issues, agreement by a critical mass of players, with provisions to extend the agreement to nonparticipants on reasonable terms, are therefore most likely to be effective. And as globalization progresses, negotiations will focus increasingly on deeper integration (such as deals on services trade and financial regulation), where agreement among a limited number of regional partners may be feasible but universal agreement is doomed to failure. This approach includes bilateral or regional agreements that cover a broad range of issues (NAFTA is an example), as well as narrower agreements by a critical mass of countries around a specific issue (such as the transfer of green technology). The recent G20 summits as the main forum for deliberations on economic issues is a good example of this "plurilateral" approach.

In selecting the critical mass of players, it is essential on both legitimacy and effectiveness grounds to include developing countries as full participants. However, some commentators suggest that doing so will prove extremely challenging and may limit the reach and effectiveness of the international forums. They argue that, as the emerging powers demand more voice in international organizations, they may resist taking on the associated responsibilities: because many of their citizens remain poor, they will be less willing to commit to international standards that may limit growth. Furthermore, the argument goes, even as these countries look to increase their role in global governance, they do not want global governance to grow: because they place national sovereignty above international consensus, international agreements will inevitably become more limited.[1]

But such critiques overlook today's reality. The same criticisms could be leveled against the advanced countries, which have traditionally dominated international decisions. They, too, can fail to take on the responsibilities associated with international agreements—the United States and the Kyoto Protocol being one clear example. And they often adopt policies, such as agricultural protection, that clearly respond to special interests and ignore broader welfare. Since the recent disastrous financial crisis originated in the United States and other advanced countries, and was the result of inappropriate macroeconomic and regulatory policies, there is also a strong case that advanced countries have much to do before they can be held up as examples of "responsible stakeholders." Indeed, by diffusing decisionmaking power, the emerging countries could limit the most egregious excesses.

International organizations must thus include developing countries, and this participation should evolve to reflect the diversity among the developing country group. The per capita income in the richest advanced country is perhaps three times that in the poorest advanced country, while the per capita income of the richest developing country is more than 50 times that of the poorest developing country. All developing countries must be prepared to undertake commitments, but different levels of obligation should apply. The largest and most advanced developing countries should take on commitments close to those of advanced countries, while the poorest developing countries should take on less onerous commitments and receive more help. It is also in the interest of advanced countries to assist developing countries in meeting commitments under international agreements, through transfers of technology and support to strengthen administrative capabilities.

The two overriding principles—building awareness in countries, and relying on a critical mass of countries—do not mean that multilateral processes (those involving essentially all countries) cannot still play a significant role. On the contrary, to support the progress by countries independently or in regional or issue groups, they can provide a global forum for discussion, analysis, and advocacy, and for agreeing on general principles. They can also, in some instances, provide a mechanism where progress already achieved can be extended and consolidated—that is, made legally binding and applied broadly to the whole membership, as in the WTO. But it is unrealistic to expect these multilateral processes to force the pace of change. Indeed, relying mainly on them can delay progress by absolving countries or country groups of the responsibility to move forward.

To work, international agreements, whether regional, plurilateral, or multilateral, should include well-specified mechanisms for enforcement and amendment. Enforcement may include sanctions (as in WTO dispute settlement provisions) or, at a minimum, monitoring and peer review (such as the IMF Article IV). The ability to amend agreements will become more important as technological progress continues to change what is feasible and efficient. And large divergences in growth rates between the more successful developing countries and the advanced countries will continue to change global power relationships.

How does today's international coordination stack up?

Measured against these criteria, the international community receives low marks in all four channels of globalization, except possibly in trade. In several respects, country policies, as well as the international mechanisms for integrating the developing countries into the global economy, are wholly inadequate.

Trade is in the best shape

Progress, however deficient, has been greatest in international trade. Trade liberalization has been driven primarily by unilateral policies, as countries have come to see that it is in their own interest to open, encouraged to a degree by the international institutions. Regional and bilateral agreements, which increasingly involve developing countries, have been important in recent years. Some agreements to achieve deeper integration—as between the EU and North African countries—have included substantial commitments to provide technical assistance and support to developing country parties, A small number of plurilateral agreements—such as the Information Technology Agreement and the Government Procurement Agreement—have also contributed to opening trade in selected areas. Reasonably effective dispute settlement mechanisms operate in the WTO and in the better established regional agreements, and the WTO monitors trade policies and provides a forum for peer-review among members.

But consolidating existing liberalization through multilateral negotiations has stalled for a long time, reflecting the complex agenda, the number and diversity of players, and a negotiation mechanism that requires virtual unanimity on everything. The principle of special and differential treatment is well established, allowing developing countries to undertake less onerous obligations. But it tends to lump most developing countries together, even though a handful are already among the largest traders. Future progress will likely rely even more on autonomous policies and regional agreements. A drastic change in approach will be required to make genuine progress multilaterally.

Some progress in finance

There has been some progress in promoting and regulating international finance. International policy coordination has contained financial crises by improving macroeconomic policy responses and discouraging the most egregious kinds of trade and financial protectionism. But the framework for international coordination of financial markets and for containing risks remains weak and fragmented.

The dangers in unbridled finance were strikingly apparent during the Great Recession, which spurred considerable research and discussions over regulatory approaches and some examples of implicit policy coordination (such as the rescue packages at the height of the crisis). Discussions over financial arrangements have generally avoided the trap of attempting universal consensus. The Basel process has provided a common framework for setting capital requirements. The provision of emergency assistance and the coordinating role of the IMF have been essential in containing crises. Relying on the G20 for macroeconomic discussions and involving developing countries in the expanded Financial Stability Board are useful steps toward recognizing the growing importance of developing countries. And the beginnings of a peer-review process with the G20, along with moves by the IMF to undertake Financial Structural Adjustment Programs for the 25 most important countries systematically, should at least establish the knowledge base to bring pressure to bear on countries that are acting irresponsibly.

However, the Basel process has failed to impose adequate capital requirements and disciplines to restrain risk taking. The Basel III agreement does not go far enough in strengthening financial regulation (owing particularly to the lack of provisions for nonbank financial institutions). And different approaches among countries continue to encourage regulatory arbitrage. No enforcement mechanism exists to limit bad financial policies with potentially systemic implications, other than the painful and often-too-late reliance on markets to limit access to finance. Crisis resolution relies excessively on ad hoc decisions rather than well-established international mechanisms—such as orderly restructuring mechanisms for sovereign debt owed to the private sector. The "too big to fail" problem remains unaddressed in all the major financial centers.

The international financial institutions fail to recognize the growing weight of developing countries (for example, in voting rights in the IMF and the World Bank). They are not well placed to deal with the destructive crises likely to arise as developing countries with weak financial systems become even more important in the global economy.

Migration remains a missed opportunity

Both domestic and international policies have failed to establish a useful framework for international migration. Destination country policies are almost entirely formed by domestic social and economic concerns, with little regard to common principles or even broad domestic economic benefits. Even in some areas of general agreement (such as preventing trafficking), enforcement has been weak. While multilateral institutions have been involved in efforts to reach international understanding on policies, they have had little effect on either opening the door for, or protecting, migrants, with the important exception of refugees. Even the WTO's Mode IV, while covering temporary work rather than migration, has had little success in easing restrictions. Recent bilateral agreements to increase legal migration cover only a miniscule number of potential migrants. With the exception of the EU, agreements to open borders within regions have had little impact, either because their coverage is limited or they lack effective enforcement provisions. The voice of developing countries has been almost entirely ignored by the advanced countries in formulating policies on immigration. International coordination thus receives a failing grade on nearly all issues involving migration, and there is no reason to expect any improvement in the near future—if anything, domestic migration policies are becoming even more restrictive and counterproductive.

What could change this sorry state of affairs? Increased demand for migrants in the advanced countries, and the increased supply from developing countries, as well as their rising influence. That could encourage the largest destination countries to learn from each other and to adopt more rational frameworks based on best practices. A core set of approaches and principles could form the base for an international code, even if it remains voluntary and general.

Global commons—where the biggest dangers lie

The failure of international coordination to control climate change presents the most serious threat to global prosperity. As everyone is affected by other countries' contribution to global carbon emissions, a reforming country does not benefit as significantly from autonomous policy change as it would from policy changes in trade, finance, and migration. Thus, greater reliance must be placed on international coordination to address climate change, as well as other threats to the global commons.

So far, however, international coordination has focused on attempts to achieve universal acceptance of limits on carbon emissions, with little success. While the importance of developing countries has been recognized, they have so far been unwilling to bear much responsibility for limiting carbon emissions. Without effective enforcement, many parties do not observe even the limited agreements (and countries of the former Soviet Union are meeting the Kyoto targets thanks to their economic collapse in the early 1990s, not to effective policies).

While the current framework for controlling emissions has failed, it is not yet time for despair. Global cooperation has disseminated scientific findings and established some principles to guide country policies. Some countries, as well as administrative subdivisions within countries, have pursued limits on emissions. Further progress is possible through agreements that first involve the largest emitters and can then be broadened to include others. What could create a more propitious environment for less carbon-intensive growth strategies? A combination of technological innovations, technology transfer, and the rising price of nonrenewable energy. For this, global norms and some sense of global community are essential. Unless citizens of the major countries believe that other countries are willing and able to make substantial reductions in emissions, progress is impossible.

Can the G20 make the difference?

The G20 meeting of heads of state, a creature born of the financial crisis, has recently appointed itself as the preeminent forum for economic policymaking. Comprising 10 developing countries, 9 advanced countries, and the EU, the group reflects the reality of a world economy, where developing and advanced countries have roughly equal weight. It has the potential to fill a large gap in global economic governance that its predecessors—the G7 club of rich countries and the G8, which also included Russia—could not bridge. The G7 helped the liberal democracies prevail in the Cold War and the G8 brought Russia into the mainstream. But with the rise of the developing countries, both groups are outdated, post–World War and post–Cold War creatures.

The G20 has started the kind of international conversation that is now necessary—one that engages developing and advanced countries as equals and aims to bridge the large gaps in perceptions and interests between the two groups. As argued previously, these frictions are inevitable—not only because of the economic power shift toward developing countries, but also because of the vast divergence between them and advanced countries in expectations, priorities, governance, and capacity. These differences reflect economic structures, living standards, and different priorities, hence interests. Far from being capricious or artificial, the differences are real, rooted in economic circumstances and history.

By placing advanced and developing countries on an equal footing, the G20 recognizes this reality and can help mediate the differences. As Stewart Patrick recently argued in *Foreign Affairs*, the G20 also creates the possibility of shifting coalitions that cut across developing and advanced country lines. The G20's working groups illustrate the possibilities: each is co-chaired by representatives of an advanced and a developing country, and each aims to tackle a potentially divisive issue, such as imbalances, climate change, and food security. This gives both sets of countries the opportunity to develop big reform ideas and achieve buy-in among their respective constituencies. Moreover, the G20 has pushed other international institutions in the direction of increasing the representation of developing countries. Thus, the Financial Stability Forum, which included only G7 countries, has been replaced by the Financial Stability Board, which includes developing countries as well. And the IMF—which the G20 also helped infuse with more resources—saw its shareholding and board rebalanced in favor of developing countries.

The G20 is clearly a step in the right direction, but is it enough? Will it succeed in transforming itself from a crisis-fighter to a forum for global economic governance and reform of the international institutions in the long run?

A gathering of heads of state of economies accounting for some 80 percent of world GDP, the G20 seems well positioned to fill this role, but it has come to be criticized on many fronts. Some argue that it is too large to be effective, while others question the legitimacy of a self-appointed preeminent forum of only 20 economies. To play its strategic role in global economic policy, the G20 must strike the balance between having too many countries and institutions around the table and being too small to be representative. Paralysis from the former poses the bigger risk. The G20 has already become too big and unwieldy, wading too deeply into details. And it is taking on too many issues, some of which are inherently domestic and thus simply create alibis for domestic policy failures.

On the broad economic issues, the G20 may already be too large: though its 20 members together represent nearly 80 percent of world GDP, the five smallest members, which include Argentina, for example, account for only 5 percent of world GDP. And Europe is overrepresented. It accounts for about one-quarter of world GDP, but holds four individual country seats—France, Germany, Italy, and the United Kingdom—and an EU seat, plus Spain and the Netherlands have observer status. By contrast, the United States, which also accounts for about one-quarter of world GDP, holds only one seat. The G20's composition could certainly use some revision, particularly to correct the overrepresentation of Europe. Establishing a constitutency structure with rotating chairs, as in the governing bodies of the World Bank and the IMF, could also help to better balance geography and economic size.

To improve continuity and build institutional memory and capacity, proposals have been aired to establish a G20 secretariat and a more permanent presidency. The current set-up—a rotating secretariat and rolling presidency (including a "troika" arrangement whereby the previous and successive year's president countries help set the agenda)—is not ideal, but it is not clear that any alternative would be preferable. For example, the 12-month presidency is better than the EU's six-month presidency, while a longer term would risk giving one nation too much weight. And while a permanent secretariat would lead to more continuity and involve a more professional cadre, it would also, once established, increase the risk of mission-creep and competition with other institutions. In addition, it would sacrifice the benefits of a rolling secretariat, such as limited bureaucracy and the annual injection of new teams eager to make a mark. It is not clear, therefore, that the G20 needs to alter its approach to institutional organization.

For both efficiency and legitimacy, the G20 must above all recognize its own limitations and comparative advantage. It is not designed to be a decisionmaking body: its deliberations are not ratified by parliaments and therefore are not binding. Nor can it, as described above, deal with domestic problems, even when they are branded as "global." The G20 is well positioned, however, to function like an international board of nonexecutive directors, or steering committee. It can aim to develop broad consensus on the approach to take on global issues, nudge the executive in individual countries in certain directions, and provide political cover for policy change at home.

Because of this, the G20 should not attempt to engage at the granular level. The farther it ventures into the weeds, the greater the risk that it wades into the territory of established institutions, such as the IMF or World Bank, and the greater the risk of paralysis as it loses both efficacy and legitimacy. Instead, the G20 countries, which together dominate the ownership and voting power of the major financial institutions, should look to those institutions for explicit decisions, as well as execution and enforcement of the G20's vision. The G20 should provide broad guidance for the international financial institutions without stepping on their toes. And it must continue to carve out its own role as steering committee. The G20 has already successfully used this approach, calling on the IMF to aid its mutual assessment process, the World Bank to develop a template for a new development agenda, and the OECD, UNCTAD, and WTO to systematically monitor and report on protectionism. Similarly, its plan for combating corruption builds on an existing UN agreement.

The G20 has already helped the world avoid descent into a second Great Depression. It has marshaled all large economies to coordinate their stimulus packages, carry out financial rescues, and avoid egregious protectionism. On that alone, the institution's balance sheet is positive, and at a minimum it will continue to provide insurance against the next financial crisis. But the G20 has also shown that it is capable of much more than rescue. It has provide glimpses of its potential—rebalancing the composition and representation of major institutions and setting a global economic agenda. If it avoids the risks highlighted here, it can establish confidence in the new world order and help build a viable economic architecture for the twenty-first century.

*   *   *

International cooperation has a decidedly mixed record in furthering policy reform, and current multilateral disciplines cannot meet future challenges. There is, however, a glimmer of hope. The gains from international integration are becoming apparent and accepted, and the risks inherent in failure to coordinate increasingly recognized. The basis for a more international perspective on many of these challenges is emerging. And many of the most critical policies are being pursued independently, which will bolster support for common approaches. As the global population becomes richer, and thus has more to lose, and grows more sophisticated, thus better informed about the nature of current challenges, and more engaged in democratic processes, the beginnings of a global conscience could develop.

Note
1.   Patrick 2010.

References

Patrick, Stewart. "Irresponsible Stakeholders? The Difficulty of Integrating Rising Powers." *Foreign Affairs,* November/December 2010: 44–53.

ANNEX

THE MODEL UNDERPINNING THE LONG-TERM PROJECTIONS

The model underpinning the long-term projections is based on the Cobb-Douglas function:

$$Y = AK^{\alpha}L^{1-\alpha}$$

where GDP (Y) is a function of total factor productivity (A), physical capital stock (K), and labor force (L). Based on historical evidence, α represents the income share of capital and is assumed to be $\frac{1}{3}$. Annual real GDP growth is calculated from the following derivation of the previous equation:

$$y = a + (\alpha)k + (1 - \alpha)l$$

where y, a, k, and l all represent the change in Y, A, K, and L. Local currency GDP is transformed into U.S. dollar GDP using a real exchange rate model.

Projections for 2009–14 come from the IMF. For each of the next 10 years until 2025, the yearly growth rate calculated by the model is equally weighted by the average real growth rate during 1997–2007. After 2025 projections come exclusively from the model (table A1).

Labor

Projections for the working-age population (aged 15–59) are taken from the U.S. Census International Data Base.[1] The change in each country's labor force is calculated using these projections.

TABLE A1 PROJECTED GROWTH UNDER THE LOW-GROWTH SCENARIO

	AVERAGE ANNUAL GROWTH RATE 2009–50 (PERCENT)	REAL GDP (MILLIONS OF 2005 $)		
		2009	2030	2050
ARGENTINA	3.5	223	466	945
AUSTRALIA	2.4	787	1,331	1,703
BRAZIL	3.6	1,011	2,160	4,481
CANADA	2.1	1,171	1,846	2,378
CHINA	4.4	3,335	15,900	23,806
FRANCE	1.8	2,203	3,083	3,754
GERMANY	1.1	2,833	3,333	3,757
INDIA	4.9	1,065	4,103	8,381
INDONESIA	4.3	354	950	2,214
ITALY	1.0	1,732	2,063	2,207
JAPAN	0.8	4,467	5,433	5,319
KOREA, REP.	2.2	945	1,988	2,362
MEXICO	3.8	866	2,124	4,282
RUSSIAN FEDERATION	2.8	869	2,202	3,211
SAUDI ARABIA	4.0	348	752	1,622
SOUTH AFRICA	3.8	271	701	1,442
TURKEY	3.9	509	1,274	2,650
UNITED KINGDOM	1.6	2,320	3,174	3,649
UNITED STATES	2.2	12,949	20,423	31,111
ETHIOPIA	6.5	28	109	366
GHANA	6.7	17	91	337
KENYA	5.4	30	98	287
NIGERIA	5.0	213	733	1,636

Capital stock

Capital stock growth is calculated using the following formulation:

$$K_t = K_{t-1}(1 - \delta) + I(Y_{t-1})$$

where t denotes the time period, δ represents the depreciation rate of the capital stock, and I represents the investment rate as a percentage of GDP (Y). Based on historical evidence, δ is estimated to be 4.5 percent for all countries.

An initial capital stock is estimated using the capital stock to GDP ratios from King and Levine (1994).[2] The growth rate of the capital stock is calculated each year using the equation above, where each country's investment rate is assumed to follow its trend over the past decade until 2020. After 2020 the investment rate is expected to gradually converge toward 20 percent, the average investment rate in advanced economies.

Total factor productivity

Annual total factor productivity (TFP) growth in highly developed countries—France, Germany, Italy, Japan, the United Kingdom, and the United States—is assumed to stay constant at 1.3 percent, in line with previous forecasts and academic research.[3] For the remaining countries, TFP is a function of two inputs: per capita income and technological convergence conditions, as determined by education, infrastructure, governance, and the business environment. TFP growth (a) is calculated each year for country i, using the following expression:

$$a_t = 0.013 - \beta \left(\ln\left(\frac{IPCi_{t-1}}{IPCUS_{t-1}} \right) \right)$$

where t denotes the time period, $IPCi$ represents the income per capita in country i, and $IPCUS$ represents income per capita in the United States, both in U.S. dollars. Thus, as domestic income per capita increases, TFP growth slows, converging to the highly developed rate of 1.3 percent. The convergence factor, β, determines the speed at which TFP converges.

The convergence factor varies for each country, and is derived from the convergence conditions index (CCI, table A2). The CCI is the aggregate of three components: education and infrastructure, business climate, and governance. Data are from the World Bank's *World Development Indicators 2009, Doing Business 2010*, and Worldwide Governance Indicators.[4] For each component, an index is calculated using World Bank data. These indices are then standardized with the G20 average as the mean. The CCI is the sum of these three standardized components; thus, the average G20 CCI is 0.

For countries with a CCI greater than 0, β is assumed to be 0.015, as suggested by previous projection exercises.[5] For countries with a CCI below 0, β is calculated using the following equation:

$$\beta = \frac{(-CCI)^{\frac{1}{2}}}{-800} + 0.015.$$

TABLE A2 CONVERGENCE CONDITIONS

G20	PAVED ROADS (PERCENT)	INTERNET USERS (PERCENT)	ENROLLMENT IN SECONDARY EDUCATION (PERCENT)	EDUCATION AND INFRA-STRUCTURE INDEX	BUSINESS CLIMATE INDEX	GOVERNANCE INDEX	TOTAL CONVERGENCE CONDITIONS INDEX[a]
ARGENTINA	30.0	25.9	78	−0.81	−1.19	−0.91	−2.90
AUSTRALIA	40.0	68.1	87	0.17	1.19	1.41	2.76
BRAZIL	5.5	35.2	79	−1.03	−1.37	−0.54	−2.94
CANADA	39.9	72.8	96	0.38	1.25	1.40	3.03
CHINA	70.7	16.1	70	−0.44	−0.71	−1.14	−2.30
FRANCE	100.0	51.2	96	1.00	0.21	0.91	2.12
GERMANY	100.0	72.3	98	1.37	0.35	1.23	2.94
INDIA	47.4	7.2	55	−1.20	−1.53	−0.79	−3.52
INDONESIA	55.4	5.8	60	−1.01	−1.19	−1.19	−3.39
ITALY	100.0	53.9	89	0.93	−0.58	0.07	0.42
JAPAN	79.3	69.0	99	1.00	0.73	0.87	2.60
KOREA, REP.	88.6	75.9	96	1.21	0.62	0.27	2.10
MEXICO	50.0	22.7	70	−0.67	−0.23	−0.75	−1.64
RUSSIAN FEDERATION	80.9	21.1	75	−0.12	−0.96	−1.46	−2.54
SAUDI ARABIA	21.5	26.4	73	−1.02	0.72	−0.89	−1.19
SOUTH AFRICA	17.3	8.3	72	−1.39	0.05	−0.09	−1.43
TURKEY	45.0[b]	16.5	69	−0.86	−0.34	−0.65	−1.85
UNITED KINGDOM	100.0	71.7	92	1.26	1.48	1.20	3.94
UNITED STATES	100.0	73.5	88	1.23	1.51	1.05	3.78
AFRICA							
ETHIOPIA	12.7	0.4	24	−2.35	−0.79	−1.72	−4.86
GHANA	14.9	3.8	45	−1.93	−0.74	−0.51	−3.17
KENYA	14.1	8.0	43	−1.91	−0.89	−1.40	−4.19
NIGERIA	15.0	6.8	32	−2.09	−1.24	−1.84	−5.16

a. Composite index of the three previous indicators.
b. Unavailable in the World Development Indicators; estimated from 2008 Library of Congress Country Profile.

The following graph illustrates the relationship between the CCI and the convergence factor β:

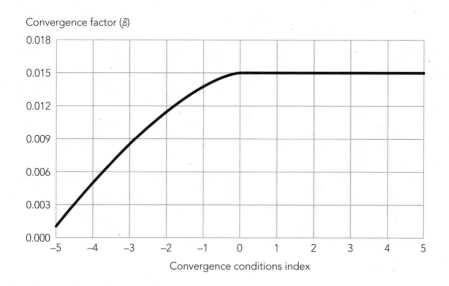

The convergence factor is assumed to remain constant over time for any given country.

Exchange rates
As in most models, the real exchange rate, expressed in local currency per U.S. dollar, is calculated as a function of labor productivity. These models typically assume that exchange rates appreciate (or depreciate) by 1 percent for every percentage point increase in labor productivity above (or below) 2 percent, the long-term advanced country average. For example, an increase in productivity of 3.5 percent would yield an exchange rate appreciation of 1.5 percent.

Empirical evidence suggests, however, that exchange rate appreciation requires a somewhat faster increase in labor productivity. We therefore assume that the threshold for exchange rate appreciation is a 3 percent increase in labor productivity. Nonetheless, the projections are not particularly sensitive to this threshold. If it were lowered to 2 percent, all countries, except the United States, would see a roughly equal total increase in U.S. dollar GDP of 10 percent in 2050 relative to the baseline, and would thus retain their relative sizes. (The U.S. share of G20 GDP would drop slightly from 24 percent to 22 percent.) All other results, including projections of real growth rates and PPP GDP, would be nearly unchanged.

Poverty rates

Poverty rates are projected through 2050 using poverty headcount, income distribution, and initial mean income data from the World Bank's PovcalNet. Each year, mean incomes are assumed to increase by 70 percent of the relative increase in per capita GDP (for India, the adjustment is 60 percent to reflect its historically lower translation) in line with academic estimates. Mean incomes for each decile are then calculated; the headcount index is estimated under the assumption that incomes are distributed uniformly within deciles. This method is similar to that put forth by Ahluwalia, Carter, and Chenery and expanded by Anand and Kanbur.[6]

Global middle and rich class

The size of the global middle and rich class is projected using a similar method to the one described above. After calculating the mean income of each decile, the percentage of the population earning more than $4,000 in PPP terms is estimated under the assumption that incomes are distributed uniformly within deciles.

Trade flows

To project trade flows, we assumed that imports into a given country will grow at the rate of GDP times an elasticity of 1.3 and exports will grow proportionally to the GDP of the exporting country. For simplicity, trade deficits and surpluses as a share of GDP are assumed to stay constant, at the rate of the base period.

Carbon emissions

Using emissions data from the World Bank, the ratio of PPP GDP[7] to carbon and carbon equivalent (CO_2e) emissions is calculated for 1990 and 2005 for each country in the G20.[8] To account for the expected gradual improvements in efficiency, from 2010 to 2030, each country's ratio is estimated to improve by 10.7 percent, or two-thirds of the G20 average total improvement from 1990 to 2005. From 2030 to 2050 each country's ratio is estimated to improve by 5.3 percent, or one-third of the current average.

Applying GDP projections to these assumptions yields yearly G20 emission data. Global emissions are calculated under the simple assumption that the ratio of G20 emissions to world emissions stays constant at 75 percent.[9] Yearly emission data are summed with the current stock of carbon—with both figures adjusted to account for the expected life span of carbon in the atmosphere[10]—to estimate the total carbon level. Carbon concentrations are then estimated;[11] the Stern Report estimates the effects of these concentrations.[12]

The model of proposals from Copenhagen assumes that the 13 countries in the G20 that proposed action at the summit achieve their goals in 2020, following gradual improvements from 2010 to 2020 (table A3). After 2020 the emissions in these countries are held constant. Countries that did not offer proposals at Copenhagen are assumed to follow the previous model outlined above.

TABLE A3 2009 CONFERENCE OF THE PARTIES PROPOSALS FOR EMISSION REDUCTIONS
PROPOSED EMISSIONS CUTS

	BY 2020 REDUCE:
AUSTRALIA	Total emissions by 25 percent relative to 2000 levels
BRAZIL	Total emissions by 40 percent relative to projected 2020 levels
CANADA	Total emissions by 20 percent relative to 2006 levels
CHINA	Emissions-to-output ratio by 40–45 percent relative to 2005 ratio
EUROPEAN UNION	Total emissions by 20 percent relative to 1990 levels
INDIA	Emissions-to-output ratio by 20–25 percent relative to 2005 ratio
JAPAN	Total emissions by 25 percent relative to 1990 levels
RUSSIAN FEDERATION	Total emissions by 10–15 percent relative to 1990 levels
SOUTH AFRICA	Total emissions by 34 percent relative to current levels
UNITED STATES	Total emissions by 17 percent relative to 2005 levels

Notes

1. U.S. Census Bureau 2009.
2. King and Levine 1994. The initial capital stock ratio is derived for Oil countries, using the estimates for "All" countries and for "Non-Oil" countries. The estimate for Oil countries is approximately 2.1.
3. Wilson and Purushothaman 2003; Hawksworth 2006; Baier, Dwyer, and Tamura 2006.
4. World Bank 2009a,b,c. Although these indicators, like all of their kind, have limitations (see, for example, IEG 2008 and Arndt and Oman 2006 for criticisms), they are generally regarded as the most comprehensive sources available.
5. Wilson and Purushothaman 2003.
6. Ahluwalia, Carter, and Chenery 1978; Anand and Kanbur 1991.

7. For a discussion of using market exchange rates or purchasing power parities in emissions projections, see Stern 2006.
8. World Bank 2010, table A1.
9. Given the expected growth of emerging economies outside of the G20, it is likely that carbon emissions in these economies will increase faster than in the G20, and this ratio will shift away from the G20.
10. See Stern 2006, p. 198. Of the initial carbon concentration of 385 ppm, 70 percent, or 270 ppm, are assumed to remain in 2050, in line with other projections, such as those by the IPCC and Climate Interactive.
11. The conversion factor is 1 ppm of carbon dioxide = 2.1 billion tons of carbon; there is 1 ton of carbon in 3.7 tons of carbon dioxide (Lam 2007).
12. Stern 2006.

References

Ahluwalia, Montek S., Nicholas G. Carter, and Hollis B. Chenery. "Growth and Poverty in Developing Countries." *Journal of Development Economics*, 6 (1978): 299–341.

Anand, Sudhir, and Ravi Kanbur, "International Poverty Projections." Policy Research Working Paper 617. World Bank, Washington, DC, 1991.

Arndt, Christiane, and Charles Oman. "Uses and Abuses of Governance Indicators." Paris, OECD Development Center Study, 2006.

Baier, Scott L., Gerald P. Dwyer Jr., and Robert Tamura, "How Important Are Capital and Total Factor Productivity Growth for Economic Growth." *Economic Inquiry*, 44 (2006): 23–49.

Hawksworth, John. "The World in 2050." PricewaterhouseCoopers, London, 2006.

IEG (Independent Evaluation Group). "Doing Business: An Independent Evaluation. Taking the Measure of the World Bank-IFC Doing Business Indicators." World Bank, Washington, DC, 2008.

King, Robert, and Ross Levine. "Capital Fundamentalism, Economic Development and Economic Growth." *Carnegie-Rochester Conference Series on Public Policy*, 41 (1994): 157–219, http://ideas.repec.org/p/wbk/wbrwps/1285.html.

Lam, S. H. "More Inconvenient Truths." Princeton University, Princeton, NJ, 2007, www.princeton.edu/~lam/documents/MoreTruth.pdf.

Stern, Nicholas. *The Stern Review: The Economics of Climate Change*. Cambridge, UK: Cambridge University Press, 2006, www.hm-treasury.gov.uk/sternreview_index.htm.

U.S. Census Bureau. "International Data Base." Washington, DC, 2009, www.census.gov/ipc/www/idb/index.php (September 2009).

Wilson, Dominic, and Roopa Purushothaman. "Dreaming with BRICs: The Path to 2050." Global Economics Paper 99. Goldman Sachs, New York, 2003.

World Bank. *Doing Business 2010: Reforming through difficult times*. Washington, DC, 2009a, www.doingbusiness.org.

World Bank. *2009 World Development Indicators*. Washington, DC, 2009b.

World Bank. *Worldwide Governance Indicators*. Washington, DC, 2009c, http://info.worldbank.org/governance/wgi/index.asp (October 2009).

World Bank. *World Development Report: Development and Climate Change*. Washington, DC, 2010, http://siteresources.worldbank.org/INTWDR2010/Resources/5287678-1226014527953/WDR10-Full-Text.pdf.

INDEX

Brazil
   among world's 10 largest economies, 3
   average annual GDP growth, 47
   college graduates at home, 136
   convergence conditions, 210
   expansion of, 47
   forest cover, 160
   GDP in, 49
   GDP projections, 50
   GMR class' share of population, 78
   illegal immigration in population, 128
   index of technological catch-up conditions, 46
   less equitable land distribution and lower self-sufficiency, 24
   poverty rates decreasing, 54
   projected growth under low growth scenario, 208
   proposal for emission reduction, 213
   size of global middle and rich (GMR) class, 55
   sustained, high growth, 28
BRIC acronym, 42
Britain. *See* Great Britain
burden sharing, agreements on, 113
Burundi, 27
business climate, in Africa, 188

C
Canada
   average annual GDP growth, 47
   convergence conditions, 210
   GDP projections, 50
   illegal immigration in population, 128
   index of technological catch-up conditions, 46
   limiting immigration to persons of European descent until 1960s, 127
   projected growth under low growth scenario, 208
   proposal for emission reduction, 213
   reproducing home country, 21
capital
   account openness, 116
   exports, 106
   flows, 9

demographic transition, 192–93, 194

dengue fever, 157

densely populated colonies, with established cultures and institutions, 22

derivatives, 111, 117

derivatives markets, 102

destination countries

    burden for improving migration policies, 143

    embracing immigrants rather than penalizing, 11

    enjoying increased supply of nontraded services, 122

    guarding prerogatives in immigration policy, 10

    policies formed by domestic social and economic concerns, 201

developed (North) countries, regional agreements, 74

developing countries

    accelerating out of recession, 41

    accumulating foreign assets, 99–102

    advance of several, 1

    among world's 10 largest economies, 3

    attracting émigrés to return home, 136

    authoritarian and unaccountable governments in, 166

    becoming an important destination for migrants, 11

    becoming more important export markets for one another, 79

    benefits of financial integration limited for, 105–8

    bettering the migration experience, 11

    cautious about free flow of capital, 92

    consumers in, 156

    contradictory influence on global financial sector policies, 111

    different levels of obligations applying, 198

    diversification of exports, 6, 70

    dominant force in world trade by 2050, 7

    dominating trade in manufactures, 75

    drivers of growth favoring, 43–45

    emissions remaining much lower per capita, 12

    establishment of globally recognized brands in, 78

    exporting bulk commodities in the nineteenth century, 68

    exporting labor-intensive manufactured goods, 68

    farther behind advanced countries, 4, 29

    financial development in, 98

    financial flows to, 98

    firms tending to use older technology, 156

projected growth under low growth scenario, 208

size of global middle and rich (GMR) class, 55

euro, second largest share of international reserves, 101

Europe

Industrial Revolution spreading to, 22

overrepresentation in G20, 204

passport system breaking down, 126

European countries, less success with integration of immigrants, 124

European financial markets, not as deep as United States markets, 101

European Monetary Union, home bias in equities declining, 103

European nations, conducting foreign policy under EU banner, 50

European Union (EU)

exception to irrelevance of international agreements on migration, 140

exports to China 1996 to 2006, 69

marketplace for trading emissions, 171

percent of world merchandise exports, 70

proposal for emission reduction, 213

exchange rates

appreciating in real terms in developing countries, 5

calculating as a function of labor productivity, 211

threshold for appreciation, 211

exploitative institutions, in colonies, 24

export performance, disappointing, 191

exports, to other developing countries, 191

"extensive" economic growth, 19

external assets, of developing countries' private sector, 100–101

external capital flows, developing countries opening to, 97–98

external capital transactions, crises related to, 107

external debt, Africa's, 186–87

externalities, effect on global welfare, 155

F

factor productivity, advancing faster in developing countries, 5

factory ships, threatening traditional fishing areas, 165

failed experiments, 30–31

finance

constraints on, 96

natural driver and complement to development, 8

progress in, 200–201

G

growth
    spreading across the world, 28
    still increasing migration, 134–36
growth benefits, of FDI, 108

H

Haiti, as an outlier, 51
Heavily Indebted Poor Countries (HIPC) initiative, 187
hedge funds, 96
high-income countries, less severe impact of crises on, 108
high-skilled migrants, immigration restrictions reducing inflow of, 130
high-skilled migration, dynamic gains from, 123
high-skilled workers, returning, 136
high-tech services, developing countries' rising demand for, 162
home bias, in portfolio allocation, 102
Hong Kong, sustained, high growth, 28
human traffickers, protecting migrants from, 11

I

ICT (information and communication technology), advances in, 76
illegal immigrants
    global stock of, 127, 128
    huge social problem, 122
    lower wages than legal immigrants, 127
illegal immigration
    enormous social problem, 11
    limiting, 127
illicit financial flows, from developing countries, 102
IMF
    COFER database, 115
    coordinating role of, 200
    increasing resources, 113
    projections for 2009–14 from, 207
    shareholding and board rebalanced, 203
    support to emerging market governments in crisis, 112
immigrant gangs, role of, 138
immigrant workers, supporting failing social security systems, 145
immigrants
    contributing twice as many patents as native graduates, 123

Mexican peso crisis, of 1995, 107
Mexico
    average annual GDP growth, 47
    college graduates at home, 136
    convergence conditions, 210
    expansion of, 47
    forest cover, 160
    GDP in, 49
    GDP projections, 50
    index of technological catch-up conditions, 46
    less equitable land distribution and lower self-sufficiency, 24
    poverty rates decreasing, 54
    prepared for adoption of foreign technologies, 45
    projected growth under low growth scenario, 208
    size of global middle and rich (GMR) class, 55
middle class, growing in developing countries, 7
Middle East, corruption obstructing progress, 25
Middle East and North Africa (MENA), 70, 183
middle-class consumers, emergence of in Africa and elsewhere, 192
migrants
    demand for, and supply of rising, 11
    standards for treatment of, 142
migration
    agreements, 139
    benefits and costs of, 143
    channel of global integration, 10–11
    differing from trade and financial integration, 137–39
    economic and social costs of, 123
    estimates of gains from, 123
    growth increasing, 134–36
    increasing, 58
    international agreements not allowing unrestricted, 140–43
    international cooperation limited, 137–43
    neglected pillar of globalization, 121–43
    networks helping future migrants, 132
    pressures for rising, 130–32
    reducing cost of, 122
    remaining a missed opportunity, 201
    rise of developing countries affecting, 136–37

New Zealand, reproducing home country, 21
Nigeria
    applying projection methodology to, 51–53
    convergence conditions, 210
    decline in manufacturing, 186
    GMR class in by 2050, 78
    incomes less than those in eighteenth England, 27
    index of technological catch-up conditions, 46
    low scores for governance, education, and infrastructure, 190
    projected growth under low growth scenario, 208
    reducing inflation rates, 186
    size of global middle and rich (GMR) class, 55
non-European countries, exploited, 23–25
non-resource-rich economies, 185–86

O
OECD economies, direct subsidies to farmers in, 72
oil, exception to downward trend in commodity prices, 58
oil exporters, increases in shares of world exports, 69
oil-exporting economies
    benefitting from rise in oil prices, 184
    large fiscal surpluses in, 186
old-age dependency ratio, in industrial countries, 131
Oman, sustained, high growth, 28
open financial system, likely to be more efficient over long run, 110
open immigration, before World War I, 125
open Internet, advocates of, 167
open trade policies, catalyzing growth, 30
Organization for Economic Co-operation and Development (OECD), 57
origin countries, 122, 138–39
outmigration, from main destination countries, 138
overfishing, record of international agreements in limiting, 169
ozone layer, 160, 167

P
Pakistan, incomes less than those in eighteenth England, 27
pandemics, addressing, 172
Panic of 1792, 114
passport requirements, at beginning of World War I, 127

pressures, for migration, 130–32
PricewaterhouseCoopers, developing projections, 42
primary products, African countries as exporters of, 191
private capital inflows, to developing countries, 9
private capital outflows, from developing countries, 102
private property rights, in less populated colonies, 23
private-sector risk assessments, as a basis for supervision, 96
productivity gains, inadequate in Africa, 190–91
productivity levels, rising, 19
project finance, 108
projections, after 2015, 207, 208
protectionism
    of creeping variety, 80
    relapse into, 60–61
protectionist measures, exacerbating, 59
public administration, weaknesses in, 165
public goods, insufficient supply of, 106
public sector debt, in advanced countries, 41
purchasing power parity (PPP), dramatic shift, 48
purchasing-power-parity (PPP) GDP per capita, growth of, 26

Q

Qatar, percentage of immigrants, 125

R

radar frequencies, developing countries claiming share of, 165
radio spectrum
    burden on scarce, 162
    division of, 173
    growing scarcity of, 161
rapid growth
    in developing countries, 42
    reducing incentives for some workers to migrate, 133
recruitment agencies, market power of, 137
regional agreements, 8, 83, 197
regional approaches, strengthened interest in, 74
regional migration agreements, 142
regional trade agreements (RTAs), expanding since 1990s, 74
regulatory arbitrage, 109, 200

AUTHORS

URI DADUSH is a senior associate at the Carnegie Endowment for International Peace. He previously served as the director of global prospects, director of international trade, and director of economic policy at the World Bank. He was also president of the Economist Intelligence Unit and a consultant at McKinsey and Company.

WILLIAM SHAW is a visiting scholar at the Carnegie Endowment. He previously served as lead economist in the World Bank research department and was the main author or co-author of several of the institution's flagship reports. He is a consultant to the World Bank, the African Development Bank, and other organizations.

Carnegie Endowment for International Peace

The Carnegie Endowment for International Peace is a private, nonprofit organization dedicated to advancing cooperation between nations and promoting active international engagement by the United States. Founded in 1910, its work is nonpartisan and dedicated to achieving practical results.

As it celebrates its Centennial, the Carnegie Endowment is pioneering the first global think tank, with flourishing offices now in Washington, Moscow, Beijing, Beirut, and Brussels. These five locations include the centers of world governance and the places whose political evolution and international policies will most determine the near-term possibilities for international peace and economic advance.

Officers

Jessica T. Mathews, *President*
Paul Balaran, *Executive Vice President and Secretary*
Tom Carver, *Vice President for Communications and Strategy*
Thomas Carothers, *Vice President for Studies*
Marwan Muasher, *Vice President for Studies*
Douglas H. Paal, *Vice President for Studies*
George Perkovich, *Vice President for Studies*

Board of Trustees

Richard Giordano, Chairman
Stephen R. Lewis, Jr., Vice Chairman
Kofi A. Annan
Bill Bradley
Gregory Craig
William H. Donaldson
Mohamed A. El-Erian
Harvey V. Fineberg
Donald V. Fites
Chas W. Freeman, Jr.
James C. Gaither
William W. George
Patricia House
Linda Mason
Jessica T. Mathews
Raymond McGuire
Zanny Minton Beddoes
Sunil Bharti Mittal
Catherine James Paglia
W. Taylor Reveley III
J. Stapleton Roy
Vanessa Ruiz
Aso O. Tavitian
Shirley M. Tilghman
Rohan Weerasinghe